ALLIED ARTILLERY
OF WORLD WAR ONE

ALLIED ARTILLERY OF WORLD WAR ONE

Ian V. Hogg

The Crowood Press

First published in 1998 by
The Crowood Press Ltd
Ramsbury, Marlborough
Wiltshire SN8 2HR

www.crowood.com

Paperback edition 2004

British Library Cataloguing-in-Publication Data
A catalogue record for this book is available from the British Library.

ISBN 1 86126 712 6

Photograph previous page: a 13-pounder anti-aircraft gun in use in France.

Typeface used: Times

Typeset and designed by D&N Publishing, Hungerford, Berkshire

Printed and bound by CPI Bath

Contents

1   An Introduction to Artillery

It is a well-worn observation that armies are always trained, equipped and organized to fight the previous war rather than the next one. In 1939 it was generally expected that the trenches of 1918 would be re-excavated and that the war would be a continuation of the previous affair; it turned out entirely differently, becoming a war of movement. In 1914 the reverse had been the case: it had been anticipated that the war would be similar to the earlier Franco-Prussian and Russo-Japanese wars, affairs of manoeuvre interspersed with set-piece battles. Armies, and their artillery, were organized for this; as a result the artillery arm went through some considerable changes in the ensuing years, as it adjusted to static warfare and to what was, in effect, an enormous siege.

In the armies of all the belligerents, artillery was divided into five groups: foot artillery (or field artillery), which accompanied the infantry and supported it; horse artillery, which accompanied and supported the cavalry; mountain artillery, specially trained and equipped for operations in mountainous country; siege artillery, which was laboriously trundled into position to reduce an obstinate fortress; and fortress or garrison artillery which defended fortified areas and, in the British and American armies, manned coast defences. (In continental Europe, coast defence was usually the responsibility of the navy.)

THE QUICK-FIRING GUNS

It should be borne in mind that the first decade of the century had seen a revolution in gun design and a mass re-equipping of almost every army in the world as a consequence of the introduction of the quick-firing gun, a term which had a specific meaning at that time. The quick-firing (QF) gun was inaugurated by the French with their 75mm Mle 1897, and the salient features of the class were as follows:

1. It used fixed ammunition, in which the cartridge and shell were a single unit, sealing the breech with a brass cartridge case.
2. It had a quick-acting breech mechanism which in conjunction with (1) allowed a high rate of fire.
3. It had an on-carriage recoil system which allowed the gun to remain in the same place when it fired, the recoil shock being absorbed solely by the movement of the barrel against an hydraulic buffer, after which it was returned by springs or compressed gas. This meant that the gunlayer was able to bring his sights back on to the target quickly, ready for the next shot.
4. In consequence of (3) it could have a shield, behind which the gunners were protected against small-arms fire and shrapnel bullets. With the gunners tightly clustered around a steady gun, ammunition supply and loading became faster.

The brass case, fixed ammunition, hydraulic buffer and recuperator were all separately known and in employment prior to 1897 on various guns, but the French brought all these things together on a field gun, added a shield and still had a weapon they could bring into action behind six horses and which had a rate of fire approaching twenty aimed rounds a minute. That was the significance of the 75mm Mle 1897. And since the accepted artillery tactics of

The French 75mm Mle 1897 at practice in pre-war days; an unusually accurate artist's depiction which shows the long recoil stroke and the steadiness of the gun; on the right, loading the fixed round of ammunition.

the period still called for the artillery to go into action in the open and pound the opposing artillery into silence before bombarding their infantry with shrapnel, they had a formidable weapon for this role. The result was that every nation had to re-equip with QF guns or be entirely outgunned. This re-equipment took place between 1898 and 1914, and in many countries had not been completed when war broke out.

FIELD ARTILLERY

Field artillery was primarily armed with a gun of about 3in (76mm) calibre, drawn by a six-horse team. Only the drivers of the team horses rode; the remainder of the gun detachments either marched alongside or rode in the ammunition and store wagons. The design of the gun was governed by the requirement that the load behind the six horses had to weigh no more than about 3,300lb (1,500kg) otherwise the team would rapidly become exhausted. This led to a somewhat minimal gun design of pole trail, axle-tree, shield, recoil system and gun which had the further result that, due to the pole trail, the maximum elevation of the gun was generally restricted to about 15 degrees and hence the maximum range was about 7,000yd (6,400m).

This was acceptable, since the fire control system of the time was also minimal. The guns went into action in line, in some convenient place from which the enemy were visible; the battery commander stood behind the guns with a telescope or field glasses, watched the fall of shot, called out corrections, and conducted the engagement in person from the gun line. So having a gun with a range in excess of 7,500yd (6,800m) was no real advantage, since it was rare that a field of vision of such a distance could be obtained, and even if it was, observation and correction at that sort of range was a difficult business.

It was, though, recognised that guns with limited elevation were at a disadvantage when attacking entrenched or fortified positions, since they were unable to lob the projectile high into the air in order to drop in steeply behind the defences to get at the defenders. For this task a howitzer was usually provided; some armies kept them in separate units, others provided a howitzer battery as part of a field regiment, supplementing the other battery or batteries (depending upon organization) which used the gun.

HORSE ARTILLERY

The horse artillery elements of the European armies were largely organized in a similar manner to the field artillery, except for one significant difference; in a horse artillery battery every man rode, so that the battery could keep up with the mounted cavalry and give them immediate support. And since they were liable to have to ride at a faster rate than the field artillery, their guns had to be lighter – an acceptable limitation because the tactical employment of the horse artillery was restricted to fairly short-range fire to support a cavalry action. It was not expected to have to do any longer-range shelling of an enemy position or bombardment of a supply route.

As a result, horse artillery guns tended to resemble those of the field artillery but of lighter build or smaller calibre. Thus the British used the 13-pounder gun, which generally resembled the 18-pounder field gun but was of 3in (76mm) calibre instead of 3.3in (84mm) and fired a lighter shell. The French used the 75mm Mle 1912, firing the same ammunition as the standard 75mm Mle 1897 field gun but using a shorter barrel, the whole equipment being some 195kg (429lb) lighter.

MOUNTAIN ARTILLERY

Mountain artillery required special equipment. The basic demand was the ability to take their guns (or howitzers) anywhere up a mountain that they might be required, and this was achieved by designing the gun so that it could be dismantled into loads which could be transported by mule or, in some cases and *in extremis*, man-carried into position. Not only did this call for some clever designing, it also meant making the weapon as light as possible and giving the assembled equipment a fairly generous amount of elevation and variable charges so as to provide a variety of trajectories for lobbing shells across mountain peaks. High velocity was not desirable,

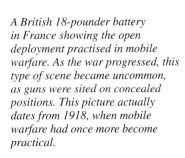

A British 18-pounder battery in France showing the open deployment practised in mobile warfare. As the war progressed, this type of scene became uncommon, as guns were sited on concealed positions. This picture actually dates from 1918, when mobile warfare had once more become practical.

A British 3.7in mountain howitzer in action in Salonika.

but the shell needed to be as effective as possible so as to get the best value out of the ammunition – since it, too, had to be mule- or man-carried, it would not be available on a lavish scale.

Britain was unique in this field for using jointed guns, or, as Kipling called them, 'screw-guns'. In these, the gun barrel was divided into two sections, the breech end with breech mechanism and the 'chase', that part of the gun in front of the trunnions. These two parts were joined together by a 'junction nut', a collar around the rear end of the chase section which could be rotated by a screw and crank mechanism. To assemble the gun, the breech section, which ended in interrupted lugs, was thrust into the junction nut and the crank revolved; this turned the junction nut so as to engaged the interrupted lugs and draw the breech and chase sections tightly against each other. Needless to say, means were provided to ensure that the rifling grooves aligned correctly. But nobody ever worked out a practical method of ensuring that the gun could not be fired if the junction nut was not properly screwed up, with the result that, very occasionally, the chase took off after the shell and landed about half-way to the target. I have to admit, though, that the only instances of this of which I have heard all took place in training; I don't

think a service battery with trained gunners ever made such a fundamental mistake. (If they did, they certainly wouldn't admit it.)

The French also had their idiosyncrasies in this department. They adopted the 'differential recoil' system in an endeavour to save weight. Briefly, the principle is that the gun barrel is pulled back to the fully-recoiled position and locked there against the pressure of the recuperator. It is then loaded and laid. When the firing lever is pulled, the barrel is released, to run forward into the firing position, but a fraction of a second before it reaches the end of its travel it fires. The recoil thus has firstly to arrest the forward-moving mass, then reverse it and complete the usual recoil stroke, at the end of which it is caught and locked, ready for the next round. This initial absorbing of the forward movement takes up quite a large proportion of the recoil shock, so the recoil system itself can be a good deal lighter than if it had to withstand the full recoil force in the normal way. The principal drawback to this system is what happens if the gun misfires, or, worse, hangs fire. In a misfire it is liable to come to the end of its forward run rather violently and tip the gun forward on to its barrel. If the misfire then turns into a hangfire, the result can be imagined.

The differential recoil idea didn't gain many followers in 1906, when the French adopted it, and it lay dormant until the late 1970s, when the US Army rediscovered it, calling it 'soft recoil'. It didn't gain many followers on its second appearance either.

SIEGE ARTILLERY

Siege artillery was still referred to, in many circles in 1914, as 'the siege train' or merely ' the train'. The term conjures up a medieval ponderousness which, in many respects, still showed. The siege train meant

A variety of heavy artillery at Aberdeen Proving Ground, USA, in 1918, all having been brought back from France.

heavy guns, sometimes moved in pieces on special carts, pulled by teams of up to twenty horses or, in some armies, oxen – and by the British in India, elephants. They trailed along in the rear of the army until a fortress or some other massive obstacle appeared, whereupon they were brought up, assembled on special ground platforms, and began a slow and relentless bombardment. But the steam traction engine and the internal combustion engine had begun to change that image by 1914. Hitherto, like every other piece of artillery, the weight and size of siege guns had been governed by the size and pulling power of a manageable horse team, but mechanical traction was pointing the way to larger weapons, as we shall see. In 1914, though, the general armament of the train was something in the order of a 6in (150mm) or a 24cm (9.5in) howitzer , moved in three or four loads. This also had its effect on fortification; if the largest gun that could be moved into the field was 24cm calibre, then the fortress engineer knew just what he had to defend against and built his fort accordingly and, more to the point, armed it similarly.

GARRISON ARTILLERY

This bring us to the final category, that of garrison and coast defence artillery. If the armament of a land fortress was governed by the artillery which could be brought against it, then 9.5in (24cm), or possibly 11in (28cm) became the upper limit. And, by analogy, the armament of a coast fortress was also governed by the force which could be arrayed against it, which meant the warships of a potential enemy. The coast gun had to be of sufficient power to inflict damage on a warship at a range at which the warship was unable to do likewise to the coast gun. However, the equation was rather one-sided; the coast gun, securely anchored in the ground on a firm platform, could fire more accurately than a ship's gun of equal power bobbing up and down on the sea; and the battleship was a very much bigger target than the coast gun. So the odds on hitting the target were far better for the coast gun than they were for the ship's gun. As Admiral 'Jacky' Fisher once observed, 'No sailor but a fool attacks a

A British 6in (150mm) Mark VII coast gun, one of several hundred scattered across the Empire in 1914.

fortress', a truism which was to be proved right in the course of the war.

Coast guns fell into three categories: first the light quick-firing gun designed to pour a stream of fire into fast and fragile torpedo-boats attempting to raid a harbour. Secondly, medium guns of about 6in (152mm) calibre to deal with light cruisers, boom-smashers and blockships; and lastly the heavy 'counter-bombardment' gun to deal with the well–armoured warship at long ranges. So the choice of calibre ran from 6-pounders of 2.2in (57mm) at the bottom end, to 12, 14 and 16in (300mm, 350mm and 400mm) monsters at the top. Another feature of coast defence was the antiquity of some guns; once a coast defence gun was emplaced, it was likely to stay in position for many years; there was no haste to replace it if some new design came along, provided the old gun could still deliver the type of fire it had originally been tasked to do. In 1914 Britain still had a handful of heavy rifled muzzle-loading guns in the coast defences, still capable of firing massive charges of case shot which could shred any torpedo boat that came within range.

The principal problem with coast gunnery was fire control. Most coast guns were direct-fire weapons; in other words they had to see their target to shoot at it. But a gun mounted 10ft above sea-level has a maximum sight line of about 4 miles (6.25km) to the horizon; this is satisfactory for close defence guns, but insufficient for counter-bombardment guns. It was better if the guns could be mounted well above the sea; a gun at 200ft above sea-level has a horizon some 16¾ miles (27km) away. But a gun at that height was of little use if the enemy got in close, since it would need a considerable amount of depression to bring it to bear. The compromise solution, therefore, was to place observing stations as high as possible and put them in communication with the low-set guns, ordering line and elevation. The guns would not actually see their long-range targets, and fired entirely on given data. The observers were given telescopes and rangefinders and, with two or three stations linked, could triangulate to obtain a precise position for the target. Various forms of mechanical

plotter allowed the future position of the target (its position by the time the shell had arrived) to be plotted and data deduced for the guns.

The exceptions to the direct fire rule were the high-angle guns or mortars, which were sited away from the sea and behind any convenient rise in the ground. They were sited so as to cover areas of sea from which a warship could bombard some vital target, such as a dockyard, but which was, for various reasons, not possible to cover by direct-fire guns. Moreover, attack by a high-angle gun meant that the shell struck the ship's deck, which was a lot thinner and less difficult to penetrate than the side armour. This, in turn, meant that a less powerful (and cheaper) weapon could be used and yet still have enough punch to defeat the largest warship. A similar system of observation and data transmission was used for these weapons, but the steep angle of descent of the shell made accurate fire very difficult. The width of a warship was a good deal less than the theoretical spread of the shells due to the normal laws of chance, and some countries grouped their mortars and fired them in salvos, hoping that one of the four or eight shells would land on the target.

FIRE CONTROL

Indeed, the question of fire control was demanding attention from every branch of gunnery; the South African and Russo-Japanese wars had brought home to gunners what had been obvious since the Franco-Prussian war, had they bothered to consider it: the fact that small arms fire from small-calibre high-velocity rifles could range very nearly as far as some field artillery, and the days when the artillery drew up in a line, in the open, alongside or slightly behind the infantry and in full view of the enemy were over. People who failed to see that, or ignored it, in 1914 and deployed their guns in the traditional manner seldom lived to boast about it.

But the age-old method of laying a gun was by direct sighting 'over the metal', and if the guns were to be concealed from enemy rifle fire they would be unable to see the target. The first years of

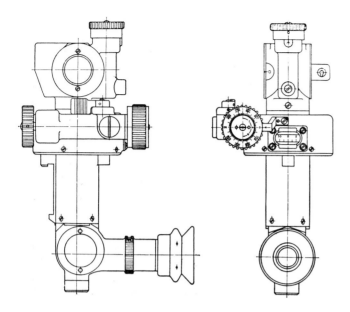

A typical panoramic or dial sight. The top section can be rotated, controlled by the knurled wheels, and the angular movement can be read off from an inner scale and from the scale on the wheels. This particular model is American and is graduated in mils.

the century, therefore, had been devoted to developing a method of directing fire at targets invisible to the gunners. The solution was variously known as a 'goniometer', 'panoramic sight' or 'dial sight'. In its refined form, which was generally going into service with most armies between 1912 and 1914, it was an optical periscope with a rotating head, so that the gunlayer, sitting in his seat or standing behind the sight, could direct his line of sight in any direction. The moveable head was graduated in whatever was the national form of dividing a circle – degrees, mils, grads – and provided with a second graduated scale which could be positioned and clamped in any position.

The theory was simple. From the map, the azimuth of the target was measured; suppose it to be 345 degrees. On the ground, a suitable 'aiming point' was selected, such as a church spire, a monument, a windmill or some other object which could be identified and located on the map. The azimuth to this object was measured; suppose it to be 50 degrees. The angle between these two lines was therefore 65 degrees. If the head of the sight was now set at 65 degrees and the gun rotated bodily around its centre until the line of sight was on

the aiming point, then the muzzle of the gun, which was parallel to the axis of the sight, would be pointing at the target.

In practice, of course, it was impractical to go through this performance for every target; what was done, therefore, was to set out, on the map, a line through the centre of the gun's intended arc of fire. The angle from this 'zero line' to the aiming point was deduced, set on the sight and the gun laid on the zero line. The slipping scale on the sight was now set at zero and clamped. From now on, targets were simply measured from the zero line and the necessary deviation ordered to the gun, set on the sight as so many degrees from zero, and the sight realigned with the aiming point.

Range was determined from the map and then, by consulting a table of ranges, the correct elevation of the gun barrel was read off and applied by a graduated spirit level on the gun. A minor correction could be set into this to compensate for any difference in height between the gun and its target, again read off the map.

So the gun could now fire at an unseen target. But it was, in obedience to the laws of chance, unlikely to hit it, although the shell would certainly land somewhere in the area of the target. What was now required was somebody to see where the shell landed, to measure or estimate its deviation from the target, calculate the necessary correction to the gun data, and order a second shot to be fired. And in the pre-1914 battery this generally devolved upon the battery commander himself. With all armies this demanded some skill, and with some it demanded mathematical ability of no mean degree: the French, for example, ranged by firing four guns at once, each with a different range and fuze setting, and the battery commander had to keep all eight bits of data in his head and mentally deduce eight fresh sets after he had observed the bursts. Whichever way it was done, once a ranging shot struck the target, the data were then given to the remainder of the guns and they then 'fired for effect'.

In the days when the guns fought in view of their targets, the battery commander simply stood behind the battery centre with a telescope and conducted his shoot from there. Occasionally the guns might be situated behind a slight crest, to give the gunners some cover, and the battery commander went forward to the crest to observe, or, especially in the German and Russian armies, he was provided with a light cart upon which was mounted a ladder, up which he clambered to a seat at the top so as to obtain an elevated view across the crest while remaining with his guns. But these systems were no good once the guns took up 'indirect fire' positions; the battery commander had to go forward to the infantry line in order to see the fall of shot, which immediately presented him with the problem of how to communicate the information to the guns. Flags and heliographs were the immediate answer, telephones came along later. But the fundamental problem lay in the fact that if the battery commander was in front, he was no longer looking after his battery. And so the 'forward observer' emerged. This was an officer sent in place of the battery commander to observe the fall of shot; note the verb – 'observe'. His was not the task of making corrections; that still lay with the battery commander at the guns; the forward observer merely said where the shots had landed with reference to the target, and left the deduction of corrections to the battery commander.

This, broadly speaking, was the position at which most armies had arrived in 1914, and had the war taken on the traditional form of manoeuvre, battle, manoeuvre it might have sufficed. But once the war settled down into a static form the limitations of this system became obvious. In the first place artillery became a 24-hour business, and no man could be expected to stay in charge day and night

An 18-pounder position in France; although apparently open, it is concealed from direct observation by the crest in front.

indefinitely. In the second place, it became essential that the artillery and infantry co-ordinate their actions to a much greater degree than hitherto, and therefore it was vital that the battery commander should be somewhere close to the infantry battalion commander. But the guns had to be well away from the infantry position, concealed behind some natural feature if possible, so the battery commander had to give up his immediate command of the guns, which now devolved upon a 'gun position officer'. (I use the British terms here, but other armies had comparable posts.) Indeed, there would be more than one gun position officer because of the 24-hour demand; they, and the gun detachments, would work in shifts around the clock, which made nonsense of pre-war establishments which had never contemplated such a thing, and led to an increase in officers and men in order to permit shift working.

The forward observer was still there, but now it was seen that the delay while he reported his observation, had the correction worked out somewhere else and saw the result, was too slow. So the observer was now given the authority to decide upon his own target and indicate it to the Gun Position Officer, who would then deduce the initial firing data and fire the first ranging shot. After that the observer deduced the position of the shot, calculated a correction to bring the next round on to the target, and ordered the fresh data. He continued doing this until he had a target round – or a 'bracket', which was one shot plus and one minus of the target by one probable error, usually taken as being 25yd – and then ordered fire for effect. Here again he was given a reasonable degree of freedom in how many guns and shells he used, the assumption being that as the man on the spot he could best determine what was needed.

This was the British system; it differed from the French (and later the American) system in one vital respect: the observer gave fire *orders*. The French observer made fire *requests;* he described the target and the gun position officer (or sometimes an even higher post – a regimental commander or adjutant) would assess the priority and worth of the target and allot the number of guns and number of shells permitted in accordance with his interpretation of the observer's information. Both systems worked, but they could lead to misunderstandings and friction when British troops were supported by French or American artillery, or vice versa.

From this relatively simple beginning, artillery began to extend itself technically. Until 1914 there had only ever been one sort of artillery fire, the bombardment of targets of opportunity. Occasionally there would be cases where a number of batteries would be grouped together under a single senior commander, for a specific task, but this was rare and no special regulations or forms of engagement were provided for such cases. It was simply a matter of each battery commander carrying on as he had always done, but having his targets pointed out to him by his senior commander, in order to conform with the general plan.

But now it became necessary to develop special forms of gunnery. Bombardment of trench lines; cutting of barbed wire entanglements; the engagement of dumps and forming-up points behind the enemy lines; the conduct of fire when corrections were provided by messages dropped from an aeroplane (a slow and tedious business); the use of observers in tethered balloons, so obtaining a higher viewpoint and allowing observation well behind the enemy's immediate front. The need to protect the infantry as they advanced led to the development of the barrage in various forms: the `standing barrage', a simple line of shells constantly being exploded so as to deter enemy reinforcements from approaching; the 'lifting barrage' where a line of shells was put down ahead of the infantry as they advanced, firing stopped and the line was 'lifted' a further 100yd (90m) or so, continuing in this way until the enemy trenches were reached; the 'rolling barrage' in which instead of one line of shells in front of the infantry there were two, and the line nearest the infantry would stop and leapfrog the other line as the walking troops got closer, so providing a continuous line of protection.

Before a major attack there would be a furious and prolonged bombardment in order to wreck the enemy's defences and kill as many of his front-line troops as possible. This worked the first time, but thereafter got bigger and bigger until it expired under its own weight. Before the Battle of the Somme in July 1916 the artillery preparation lasted eight days and consumed 1,732,873 shells; at Messines in July 1917 it again lasted eight days but this time managed to get rid of 3,258,000 shells. The drawback to all this was that this drumfire thoroughly wrecked the entire landscape, ruined the natural drainage and turned the battlefield into a moonscape of mud and craters over which the assaulting infantry had to walk as best they could (and through which, as events proved, the supporting artillery could not advance to keep with the infantry).

A better solution which was gradually appreciated and developed was to select the enemy artillery, strongpoints, forming-up points, communications trenches and similar vital installations, and subject them to a hurricane bombardment just as the attack began. This would, it was hoped, paralyse the enemy command and virtually reduce their defence to a matter of individual posts fighting individual battles, with no higher direction or reinforcements. This was perfectly correct, but tended to be compromised by the need to range the guns onto their individual targets before the battle commenced.

Ranging was always necessary, because the raw information of range and azimuth taken from the

Sinews of war; the howitzer barrel shop in Woolwich Arsenal, 1917.

Technical innovation; an early American experiment in self-propulsion was this 3in M1916 gun mounted on a Holt tractor in 1918.

map and converted into gun elevation and azimuth rarely produced a shell on the target. Such things as wind, air temperature and density, the temperature of the propelling charge, the actual (as opposed to the nominal) weight of the shell and even the rotation of the earth could all have an effect on the flight of the shell and cause it to deviate from its theoretical trajectory. Only actually firing a shell could show what this deviation was, and allow the observer to make the necessary corrections to make the shell go to the right place – until somebody took the trouble to fire several thousand shells in various conditions of weather and temperature, analyse the results, and produce a table of corrections, when it became possible to use 'predicted fire' in which the raw data were corrected, using information obtained by a special meteorological section which, every few hours, sent out a general message to all artillery units specifying the wind direction and speed at various altitudes, the air density and the air temperature. Using this, each unit could then correct its map data into predicted gun data which stood a very good chance of putting the shell on or very close to the target with the first shot. Now ranging was no longer necessary and the enemy would be unaware of the artillery's interest until the storm broke over their heads.

The distribution of meteorological information began in mid-1917, but perfecting the technique of predicted fire took somewhat longer; it was 1918 by the time it was generally mastered, and the German

Spring Offensive, followed by the Allied counter-offensive, broke the impasse, opened up the front to fluid warfare and, at the same time, brought back the simpler form of shooting at opportunity targets and tended to put predicted fire into a back seat. Nevertheless, once the idea had taken hold it was developed. Until the 1970s it remained very much the same as it was in 1917, a case of tables and graphical solutions; it was the invention of the computer and its application to artillery fire control that finally solved the prediction problem.

The First World War was, for all artillery of every nation, a watershed. Up until 1914 there was little about artillery that would have baffled a gunner from the Napoleonic Wars. After 1918 there was little about artillery that would not have baffled him. Mechanical traction, self-propelled guns, radio communication, aircraft spotting, prediction, sound-ranging, survey, artillery intelligence and much more were born in the 1914–18 period, struggled through their adolescence in the lean years of the 1920s and 1930s, and came into their estate during the 1939–45 conflict, years which saw the zenith of conventional artillery. The guns, too, took a leap into the future; at the outbreak of war muzzle-loading was still in use; by 1918 semi-automatic breech mechanisms, clockwork time fuzes, complex hydro-pneumatic recoil systems and sophisticated sights were commonplace. The rest of this book will attempt to chart a path through that development.

2   Field Artillery

In 1914 the expression 'field artillery' encompassed virtually all the mobile artillery available to an army other than the siege train. Horse and mountain artillery might hold themselves aloof, but in spite of their dedication to particular aspects of warfare, they were, nevertheless, part of the artillery in the field and hence of the field artillery. It was the massive expansion and specialization of artillery in 1914–18, combined with the gradual reorganization of armies, that eventually led to the phrase 'field artillery' having a closer definition.

BRITAIN

The standard British field guns were based upon experience gained during the South African War; this affair began with the British using an elderly 12-pounder breech-loader with no on-carriage recoil control, confronted with the Boers using modern Krupp quick-firers. This situation was rapidly corrected by the action of the Director-General of Ordnance, General Sir Henry Brackenbury, purchasing 108 15-pounder QF guns from Erhardt of Dusseldorf and thereby introducing the QF principle into British field artillery. Immediately after the war the Royal Artillery set up a committee to draw up specifications for new guns, and the result was the adoption, in 1904, of the 13-pounder QF gun for the Royal Horse Artillery and the 18-pounder QF gun for the field artillery. Both were similar designs, an amalgam of Armstrong gun, Vickers recoil system and Royal Carriage Department carriage. The 13-pounder was of 3in (76mm) calibre and fired a 12.5lb (5.7kg) shrapnel shell at 1,675ft/sec to 5,900yd (5,400m) range. The 18-pounder was a 3.3in (84mm) gun firing an 18.5lb (8.4kg) shell at 1,615ft/sec to 6,525yd (5,960m). Both used a simple pole-trail carriage which, of course, restricted the gun's elevation but

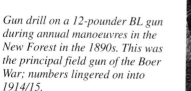

Gun drill on a 12-pounder BL gun during annual manoeuvres in the New Forest in the 1890s. This was the principal field gun of the Boer War; numbers lingered on into 1914/15.

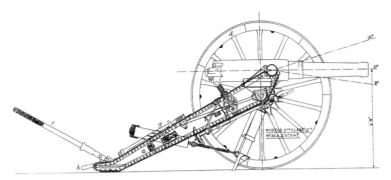

The 12-pounder BL, showing the spring spade recoil system. The spade hangs from the axle, and is connected by a cable to a powerful spring in the cylinder attached to the trail. On firing, the gun tries to roll backwards but the spade digs in and pulls on the spring, which also forces the trail end down.

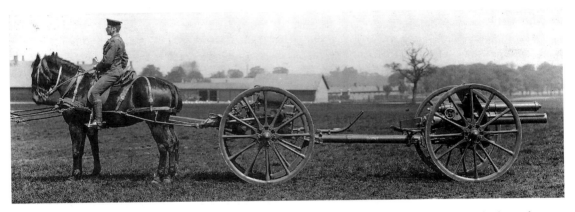

A 13-pounder Royal Horse Artillery gun with limber and two of the six-horse team. The driver's Brodrick cap dates this picture fairly closely to early 1905.

The 18-pounder Mark I, showing the stark simplicity of the carriage, Note also the provision of a direct sighting telescope, as well as the indirect-fire dial sight. The enormous slide rule strapped to the shield was for calculating shrapnel fuze lengths. This picture also makes obvious the restriction on elevation due to the pole trail; there is not a lot of distance between the trail and the breech, even before you make allowance for the recoil stroke.

this was acceptable in the light of contemporary methods of fire control and, indeed, the 18-pounder could outperform any field gun in Europe throughout most of the first ten years of its life.

By 1914, 1,126 18-pounders had been made in Britain and a further ninety-nine in India; of these some 280 had been supplied to Canada, Australia, New Zealand and South Africa. The war years saw another 8,393 made in Britain and 851 in the United States by the Bethlehem Steel Company. The 13-pounder had been produced in lesser numbers – 245 in Britain and twenty-one in India by 1914, and very few thereafter; for the first few months of the war confirmed that the 13-pounder, handy as it might be for cavalry support, simply did not have sufficient authority for modern warfare. 'In peace the call is for mobility, in war for weight of shell' said Lt-Col Alan Brooke, writing in the 1920s, and he was by no means the first person to have made this sort of observation. This, put simply, was the defect of the 13-pounder; mobility but no shell-power, or, at least, not sufficient for the conditions of 1914–18. It was the 18-pounder that was to arm the newly formed field batteries and which acted as the backbone of the Royal Artillery thereafter.

The Mark I carriage remained in service until 1916, by which time the one serious defect of the design had made itself plain under the stress of war-fare: the recuperator springs in the recoil system broke under the strain of continuous firing, something which had not been discovered in peacetime because nobody ever fired that much ammunition in peacetime. The defect was discovered early in 1915, and work began on designing a hydro-pneumatic recoil system which could be fitted into the existing recoil system casing so as to simplify construction and allow of modification in the field; with such a handicap as that it is remarkable that the design was completed, and successfully, in just over a year. Officially introduced in November 1916, and actually in service some time previous to that, the Mark II carriage also had a rather longer cradle, to give better support to the gun body during recoil.

But even as the Mark II carriage gun began to appear on the Western Front it was obvious that it would be even better if the gun had more range, and in 1917 work began on a completely new gun and carriage. The first attempt was the Mark III, but this, for various reasons, was considered unsuitable and abandoned, and the final design was the Mark IV gun on Mark III carriage. The gun was more or less the same as before but its operation was improved by fitting an Asbury pattern breech mechanism which had a vertical operating handle and was easier and quicker to open and close. The carriage was considerably different to its predecessors; it had a

An 18-pounder Mark I in action in France, 1915.

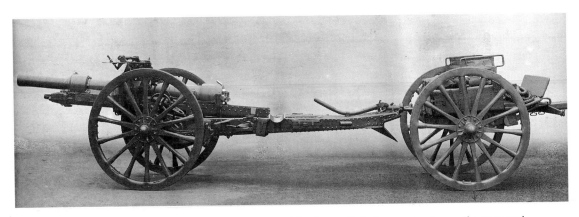

The 18-pounder Mark IV was a very different equipment, with a box trail, hydro-pneumatic recoil system and faster-acting breech mechanism. It also weighed more, but everything has its price.

Front view of the 18-pounder Mark IV, showing how the adoption of a box trail allowed a considerable increase in elevation and hence greater range.

box trail, allowing the gun to elevate between its sides to 30 degrees and thus reach out to a range of 9,000yd (8,200m). The recoil system was redesigned to fit into a simple rectangular cradle underneath the gun and given an automatic compensating system which varied the length of recoil according to the gun's elevation. With the gun horizontal the recoil was 48in (120cm), but as the gun elevated this was gradually reduced, because with elevation more of the recoil blow is directed down-

ward, into the ground, and less backward, tending to lift the gun wheels up off the ground. So at 30 degrees elevation the recoil stroke was reduced to 26in (66cm), but the gun remained perfectly steady. In the hands of a well-trained detachment a rate of fire of almost thirty rounds a minute could be reached. Unfortunately, all this perfection took time to design, test and put into production, and only a small number were completed and sent to France before the Armistice.

The 18-pounder Gun

Introduced in June 1904, the 18-pounder Gun Mark I was an amalgam of the best features of three designs: an Armstrong gun, with Vickers recoil system and Royal Gun Factory sights and elevating gear. The gun was wire-wound, with a screw breech mechanism and percussion firing, and was suspended in an underslung cradle by means of two ribs. The hydro-spring recoil system was above the cradle, attached to the gun by a piston rod. The trail was a simple tubular steel pole, restricting elevation to 16 degrees, and traverse was by moving the front end of the trail across the axle, allowing 4 degrees of movement to right or left of zero. Laying was by the independent line of sight method, using two layers; the man on the left laid for line, the man on the right for elevation.

The standard projectile was an 18.5lb (8.4kg) shrapnel shell filled with 375 balls weighing 41 to the pound and fitted with a Fuze, Time & Percussion No. 80, licensed from Krupp of Essen. High explosive, smoke, gas and star shell were provided during the course of the war. The muzzle velocity with shrapnel was 1,615ft/sec, giving a maximum range of 6,525yd (5,960m). At the time of its adoption the 18-pounder was the most powerful field artillery gun in the world.

The only serious defect which war brought out was the weakness of the recuperator springs, which broke under the constant firing. In 1915 a hydro-pneumatic recoil system was designed so as to fit into the existing casing of the hydro-spring system and thus reduce the amount of alteration required and allow modification to be done in the field. This then became the Mark II carriage, recognizable by having a front extension on the recoil cylinder, and was put into service in mid-1916.

18-pounder Mark IV on Mark IV carriage.

By 1916 the Army was asking for more range, and a fresh design was begun; this was to be the Mark III, but for various reasons it was turned down in favour of another design which became the Mark IV. The gun was ballistically the same as the Mark I but had an improved and faster-acting breech mechanism. The carriage used a box trail, allowing the gun to reach 30 degrees elevation, but retained the same cross-axle traverse as before. The recoil system was completely changed. There was now a trough cradle slung on trunnions, with the recoil system block inside the cradle and attached to the gun. On firing, the gun recoiled and took the cylinders with it, the piston rods being attached to the front end of the cradle. This was a hydro-pneumatic system in which the air and oil were kept apart by a 'floating piston', and the system automatically shortened the recoil stroke as the gun was elevated. The cradle was lengthened at the rear to give support to the gun during recoil, and the result was an exceptionally steady gun which could fire

The 18-pounder Gun Continued

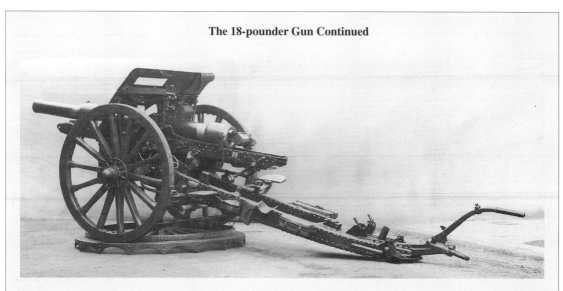

18-pounder Mark IV on Mark IV carriage with firing platform. This type of platform is more usually associated with the 25-pounder of World War Two, but as this 1918 photograph shows, the idea had been perfected by then, and was especially intended to assist in anti-tank firing.

thirty rounds a minute with a well-trained detachment. The ammunition remained the same, but the increased elevation gave a maximum range of 9,300yd (8,500m).

The 18-pounder was improved in the 1930s by the addition of pneumatic-tyred wheels, and remained in service until the early years of the Second World War, being officially declared obsolete in 1944.

DATA: Ordnance QF 18-pounder Gun Mk I on Carriage, Field, 18-pounder Mk I

Calibre	3.3in	Total weight	2,821lb
Weight of gun	1,004lb	Recoil	41in
Length of gun	96.96in	Elevation	$-5°$ to $+16°$
Length of bore	28 calibres	Traverse	4° right & left
Rifling grooves	18	Shell weight	18.5lb
Rifling twist	RH, 1/30	Muzzle velocity	1,615ft/sec
Breech	Screw, percussion	Max range	6,525yd

The third member of the field artillery family was the 4.5in (114mm) howitzer. This, too, had been produced by a committee, though in this case they simply set down the performance they desired and then sent this to the gunmakers and asked for their ideas. When the gunmakers produced their solutions, a few trials soon showed that none of them were worth considering, and they were all sent off to try again.

More extensive trials sorted the wheat from the chaff, and the result was the selection of a design produced by the Coventry Ordnance Works. This was a rather odd company which was put together by a consortium of shipbuilding and engineering companies led by William Beardmore & Co, their object being to try and break the duopoly of commercial gunmaking enjoyed by Vickers and Armstrong.

Their original intention was to break into the naval gun market, but they formed up just in time to reap the benefit of the post-Boer War armament programmes; firstly they were able to gain a useful contract for the manufacture of 18-pounder gun carriages, then they scored with their own design of 4.5in howitzer, then produced two other important designs and, during the war, expanded to manufacture a wide variety of weapons.

The 4.5in howitzer went into service in 1909 and it is a testimony to the soundness of the original design that it stayed in first-line service until 1944, with no serious modification other than changing the carriage to use pneumatic-tyred wheels in the 1930s. It was the first British field piece to use a sliding block breech mechanism, and in the course of the war it revealed the fundamental defect to which these mechanisms are prone: the block tends to set back under the force of the cartridge explosion, and if the corners of the mortice – the square slot in the breech ring through which the block slides – are cut sharply the set-back force tends to concentrate in these corners and may, eventually, cause the steel to shear, allowing the block and half the breech ring to fly backwards. The solution was to radius these corners very slightly so that the force, instead of being concentrated there, spreads out over the entire rear surface of the block in contact with the mortice. This modification resulted in the Mark II howitzer, introduced early in 1917.

By 1914 192 4.5in howitzers had been made; 108 of these equipped the Expeditionary Force, forty-five were in reserve, and the remainder had been sent to Canada, Australia and New Zealand. During the war a further 3,177 were built, of which 400 were given to the Russian Army in 1916. The howitzer fired a useful 35lb (15.9kg) shell at 1,010ft/sec to 7,300yd (6,670m) range. Its principal attraction, of course, was its ability to fire at angles of elevation up to 45 degrees and thus drop shells almost vertically on to targets which were protected from direct gun fire by field fortifications, buildings or simply the lie of the land.

A 4.5in howitzer emplaced in the mud.

Another 4.5in (114mm) howitzer, this time in a rather more comfortable gunpit.

It will be obvious from the figures quoted above that there were insufficient of these new guns and howitzers to equip the army, and a few Regular batteries, and all the Territorial Army batteries, were still equipped with older weapons. The most prominent of these were the 15-pounder QF gun, the model purchased from Erhardt in 1900, and the 15-pounder BLC gun, a totally different weapon.

The 15-pounder QF Mark I was a sound design, with an interrupted-screw breech mechanism, pole trail and hydro-spring recoil system, but the manufacture had involved a good deal of hand-fitting and thus the parts were not interchangeable, leading to problems in repair. The original wheels proved to be insufficiently strong and were replaced by British standard artillery wheels, and the gun was fitted with two axle-tree seats. Once the guns were replaced in Regular service by the 18-pounder, these seats were removed and a shield fitted in their place, turning the design into the

Mark I* carriage and producing a pattern which more closely resembled the 18-pounder.

The 15-pounder QF fired a 14lb shrapnel shell at 1,675 ft/sec to a range of 6,400yd (5,850m), which was quite a reasonable performance for its day. Three or four Territorial batteries went to France in 1914 armed with this gun, and some others to Egypt, but by the end of 1915 they had all been replaced by 13-pounder or 18-pounder weapons and the 15-pounder was then relegated to a training role, being declared obsolete as soon as the war was over.

The 15-pounder BLC (breech loading, converted) was an entirely different animal, one of several expedients adopted in an attempt to produce a weapon comparable with a modern QF gun but without actually going to the trouble and expense of developing such a gun. It was a conversion from an old 15-pounder breech-loading design which, itself, was a conversion from an even earlier

The 4.5in Howitzer

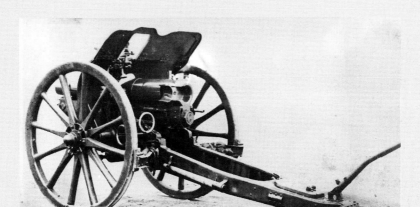

The 4.5in howitzer Mark I.

The South African War exposed the British army to the Boers firing a useful 4.7in (120mm) Krupp howitzer, and this made such an impression on the victims that even before a new field gun was agreed upon, a committee was exploring a new field howitzer. Four models, from different makers, were submitted in 1903, but none was satisfactory. Their accuracy was poor compared to that of a Krupp howitzer, and a long series of experiments with different types of rifling and shells was conducted. There was even talk of buying the Krupp design, but by 1905 enough confidence had been gained to lead to another four trials equipments, and from these the Coventry Ordnance Works design was selected in 1905. Six guns were ordered for trials, and it was not until 1908 that the 4.5in howitzer was finally approved for service. The long deliberation, however, was worthwhile; the 4.5in howitzer was to remain in service until 1944 without any significant modification apart from putting pneumatic tyres on to it in the 1930s.

It was a simple and robust design; a box trail which allowed 45 degrees elevation, 3 degrees of top-carriage traverse each side of zero, and a shield which was sloped back to such a degree that a hatch had to be cut for the dial sight. Recoil was controlled by a variable-length hydro-spring system which allowed 40in (985mm) of recoil at point-blank and to 20in (508mm) at full elevation. The only change came with the Mark II howitzer which, as noted in the text, had a modification to the breech ring to prevent stress cracking and changed the rifling from increasing to uniform twist, in the interest of quicker manufacture.

DATA: Ordnance QF, 4.5in Howitzer Mk I on Carriage, Field, QF 4.5in Howitzer Mk I

Calibre	4.5in	Total weight	3,010lb
Weight of gun	972lb	Recoil	40–20in
Length of gun	70in	Elevation	−5° to +45°
Length of bore	13.35 calibres	Traverse	3° right & left
Rifling grooves	32	Shell weight	35lb
Rifling twist	RH, Inc 0 to 1/41	Muzzle velocity	1,010ft/sec
Breech	Block, percussion	Max range	7,300yd

The 15-pounder QF gun purchased from Erhardt of Dusseldorf. A simple carriage, which proved to be a bit too simple under hard use, and with axle-tree seats for two of the gunners.

Side view of the 15-pounder Erhardt gun.

An early experiment in mechanization; the West Riding of Yorkshire Territorial Artillery borrowed some Sheffield-Simplex 30hp touring cars in July 1914 and covered 120 miles in the course of their summer exercises. Note that the axle-tree seats have gone, replaced by a shield.

The 15-pounder BLC gun was an attempt at modernizing an elderly design. It proved useless in modern warfare but served well as a training gun.

(1883) bag-charge gun. The BLC conversion consisted of plugging the vent in the gun body (it had been fired down a vertical vent by means of a friction tube), removing the old design of screw breech which demanded three distinct operations to open or close it and replacing it with a modern screw breech of the 'single-motion' type; fitting the carriage with a cradle and hydro-spring recoil system (above the barrel in a distinctive shroud), providing two seats for the gunlayers and improving the sights. It remained a bag-charge gun, firing the same 14lb (6.4kg) shrapnel shell as the 15-pounder QF at 1,590ft/sec and reaching a range of 5,750yd (5,250m).

The 4.7in naval gun on its original 'Scott carriage' in the South African railway yard which built it.

The 'regularized' design of 4.7in gun in action. The act of loading and the proximity of the horses makes one wonder …

These were issued to the Territorial Force in 1907, and proved sound enough weapons for training but when they went to France in 1914 their lack of range told against them and they were rapidly replaced by 18-pounder guns and, like the 15-pounder QF, were employed solely as training weapons thereafter, being declared obsolete in 1919.

One other Boer War veteran appeared in the field artillery armoury, the 4.7in QF field gun. The 4.7in QF gun had been introduced in 1888 for naval and coast defence purposes, and it would probably have stayed there but for the war in South Africa. There, with the Army faced with a shortage of heavy field artillery, Captain Percy Scott, the Royal Navy's foremost gunnery expert who was Commander Naval Forces in South Africa, removed some 4.7in guns from warships, had them mounted on to primitive field carriages built largely of wood, and sent them to the front. They proved to be highly effective, and to regularize the position the Royal Carriage Department designed a somewhat better-engineered carriage and brought the weapon into field service. It fired a 46lb (20.9kg) high explosive shell at 2,150ft/sec to 10,000yd (9,100m), which, it will be appreciated, was a welcome addition to the artillery in South Africa.

The new carriage was less cumbersome than the original 'Percy Scott Carriage' and it was unusual in employing two independent recoil-absorbing systems. The gun recoiled inside a ring cradle, controlled by two oil buffer cylinders above the cradle and a spring recuperator cylinder below it; in addition the carriage was provided with a 'spring spade', a device which was being tried on a number of gun carriages at about that time. It consisted of an arm, hinged to the axletree, and carrying a spade; this was linked by a steel cable to a spring cylinder on the trail. When the gun was brought into action the spring spade was dropped so that it extended rearwards from the axle and the point of the spade dug into the ground. When the gun fired, the cradle recoil system absorbed much of the force, but the carriage also recoiled. As soon as it moved the spring spade dug in even deeper as the gun tried to leap over it, and as the gun moved across the spade so the cable pulled on the powerful spring inside the trail cylinder, adding to the resistance to recoil. This Mark I carriage was followed by a cheaper model, the Mark I Converted, which was a conversion from the obsolete 40-pounder Armstrong gun carriage by adding the cradle, recoil system and spring spade. Apart from being heavier than the Mark I there was little difference between the two.

But when all was said and done, the 4.7in as a field gun was not popular with the gunners; it was awkward to manoeuvre and difficult to operate – for one thing, it had no on-carriage traverse – and barely stable when fired. They wanted to get rid of it, but fate was against them.

The 4.7in QF went to France in some numbers, but was gradually replaced by the heavier 6in weapon, which had better range and a more powerful shell. They continued in use in Salonika, Italy and Serbia throughout the war, however, and were not declared obsolete in their field role until 1922; they remained in coast defence for a further thirty-four years.

Mountain guns were employed by the British Army in India and in one or two other places in the Empire where their light weight and ease of dismantling for pack carriage were important. The original 'screw-gun', the 2.5in rifled muzzle loader, had been fielded in South Africa where its deficiencies soon became apparent and a new 10-pounder jointed gun had been developed and issued in 1903. It was an improvement on the 2.5in RML, insofar as it was a breech-loader, but that was about as much as could be said for it; the screw breech mechanism was an antiquated three-motion type and, worst of all, there was still no recoil system. After complaints from the mountain gunners, a fresh design was begun as the 2.75in (70mm) BL Mark I. This was more or less the 10-pounder gun with a faster breech mechanism, a hydro-spring recoil system and a shield. It fired a 12.5lb (5.7kg) shrapnel shell at 1,290 ft/sec to a range of 5,600yd (5,100m) and could be stripped down to six mule loads.

The 4.7in Gun

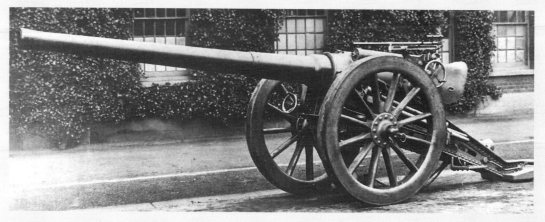

The 4.7in (119mm) gun on the Woolwich-designed carriage.

'The Gun the Army Didn't Want'. It has been explained in the text how the Army came to have 4.7in (119mm) field guns in South Africa, and once the war there was ended, work began on developing a new heavy gun, the 60-pounder. But while this was still in the early stages, Parliament passed a Bill to arm the Volunteer Artillery. The Bill specified that they would be provided with the 4.7in gun, with the fatal phrase, 're-armament of the Volunteers with the nature of the guns specified.' The vote passed and there was no way out of it; the Volunteers were to get 4.7s. Unfortunately the phrase 'four-point-seven' had struck some sort of popular chord – very much like the 'eighty-eight' of the Second World War, and with constant prodding in Parliament sixty batteries were provided in 1902/03. Having got them, they had to use them, which is why they appeared in France in 1914, but as soon as the 60-pounder was in production they were rapidly weeded out and sent elsewhere.

The gun had been designed for naval and fortress use, where weight was of little object, and once provided with a carriage strong enough to withstand the weight and the firing stress, the result was almost four tons in weight. The spring spade caused the trail to dig deeper into the ground with every shot, this problem eventually being remedied by the addition of a 'sole plate' under the trail end. The shell weighed 46lb (20.9kg) and contained just under 7lb (3kg) of Lyddite; it was not considered to be sufficiently effective for a gun of that weight. Later, of course, amatol-filled HE shell, gas and shrapnel were produced for the gun; of these, only the shrapnel was considered of any value, but by that time shrapnel was being outmoded by the changing tactics.

Although the gun remained in service with coast artillery until 1935, the field equipment was made obsolete in January 1922; few mourned its passing.

DATA: Ordnance QF, 4.7in Gun 'B' Mk I, on Carriage, Travelling, QF 4.7in Mk I

Calibre	4.724in	Total weight	8,419lb
Weight of gun	4,592lb	Recoil	12in
Length of gun	194.1in	Elevation	–6° to +20°
Length of bore	40 calibres	Traverse	Nil
Rifling grooves	22	Shell weight	46.5lb
Rifling twist	RH, Inc to 1/34	Muzzle velocity	2,150ft/sec
Breech	Screw, percussion	Max range	10,000yd

The 4.7in Gun Continued

The 4.7in gun was also mounted on the old 40-pounder BL gun carriage, complete with spring spade.

The breech-end half of the 10-pounder mountain gun on its mule.

And the carriage body of the 10-pounder; the wheels went on to another mule. The whole gun went together in about two minutes, with a skilled detachment.

The 10-pounder mountain gun assembled and ready for action.

The 2.75in mountain gun in action in Salonika – essentially a 10-pounder given a modern recoil system.

The first Indian Army mountain batteries which went to Europe in 1914 were armed with the 10-pounder gun but as soon as they reached Britain these were withdrawn and replaced by the 2.75in. They then went to France but there appeared to be little use for such a weapon there, and they were sent off to Egypt. Eventually 183 guns were built and all were employed in Egypt, Mesopotamia or India.

The Indian Army was still far from satisfied with this weapon and pressed for the development of something better. A design had been worked out before the war, but had been shelved in the face of more pressing demands. It was taken out again in late 1915 and work resumed, the first of these new 3.7in (94mm) QF howitzers appearing in late 1916 and formal introduction taking place in February 1917. It was another jointed gun, using a single-motion screw breech and a brass cartridge case, and the carriage was the first split-trail equipment

to see service with the British Army. It had a hydro-pneumatic recoil system which adjusted its length according to the elevation, and it fired a 20lb (9.1kg) shrapnel shell at 973 ft/sec to a range of 5,900yd (5,400m).

A total of seventy complete equipments had been made by the time the war ended, and some twenty-two were in action in the Middle East. It proved to be an excellent weapon with a good reputation for accuracy, and it was to remain in service until 1960, though few were seen west of India after 1945.

FRANCE

French field artillery was almost entirely built around the 75mm gun Mle 1897, the prototypical QF gun which set the artillery world on its ears

The 3.7in mountain howitzer, the first British gun to use a split trail.

The 3.7in Pack Howitzer

A rear view of the 3.7in mountain howitzer.

The 3.7in Pack Howitzer Continued

The use of a 'screw-gun', or jointed gun, in which the breech and and muzzle end were separate pieces connected by a junction nut, had long been in vogue in the Indian Mountain Artillery, and at the turn of the century a 10-pounder gun was in use. The Indian Army, requiring something more modern, asked for a suitable howitzer, feeling this would be more versatile than a gun, and designs were drawn up in about 1906, trial equipments made and tested, but then shortage of funds led to the design being shelved. Once the Indian troops arrived in France the shortcomings of their ancient 10-pounder were soon made obvious; an interim solution was the '2.75in gun', which was simply the same barrel mounted on a carriage with a recoil system, but this gave no ballistic improvement and in 1915 the funds were found to have the 3.7in (94mm) howitzer manufactured.

It was officially introduced in February 1917, though it must have gone into production and issue well before that, since it was in action in Mesopotamia in March and by the Armistice some 70 had been issued to the Mesopotamia and East Africa theatres.

The 3.7 was an ingenious and practical design. It was the first British gun to use a split trail, allowing ample elevation for work in mountainous regions, and the separate ammunition gave a variety of charge options to permit adjusting the trajectory to the terrain. It soon acquired a reputation for accuracy, a prime requirement in mountain guns which were called upon to shoot very close to their own troops.

A problem with split-trail guns is that they demand a reasonably flat piece of ground to support all four points of contact – trail ends and two wheels – at the same level, and this is something mountain equipments rarely find. So the 3.7 had an ingenious suspension system which allowed the four points to rest at different levels and still form a solid structure. A large shield was provided, with snipers on the North-West Frontier of India in mind, but outside that area it was rarely used.

For mule carriage the barrel split into two pieces, the chase weighing 212lb (96kg) and the breech portion 215lb (98kg), and the remainder of the weapon split into a further four mule loads. On roads it could have the trail folded, shafts fitted, and be drawn by two horses, or, later in its life, by a small truck.

DATA: Ordnance QF, 3.7in Mountain Howitzer Mk I, on Carriage, QF Mountain Howitzer Mk I.

Calibre	3.7in	Total weight	1,610lb
Weight of gun	427lb	Recoil	17–35in
Length of gun	46.8in	Elevation	–5° to +40°
Length of bore	11.8 calibres	Traverse	20° right and left
Rifling grooves	28	Shell weight	20lb
Rifling twist	RH, Inc to 1/22	Muzzle velocity	973ft/sec
Breech	Screw, percussion	Max range	5,900yd

when it was introduced. After its humiliating defeat by Germany in the war of 1870, the French Army set about cleaning house, rebuilding its morale and re-equipping with the best weapons they could design and manufacture. The development of the 75mm 'long recoil' gun must have begun in the late 1880s; 1894 is the date usually quoted in French texts, but it is hard to believe that such a revolutionary weapon could have been designed, tested and put into production in three years. It seems more probable that the design of the

hydro-pneumatic recoil system, which was the heart of the weapon, was arrived at in 1894 and the subsequent three years were spent in perfecting it, adapting it to the rest of the gun and carriage, and getting production started. Whatever the actual dates were, the fact remains that the gun appeared in service in 1897, the development having been propelled by General Deloye, often referred to as 'the father of the 75'.

An authoritative French text, *Les Canons de la Victoire,* (Alvin and Andre, Paris 1923), states that the superiority of the 75 was due to the combination of the recoil system, the trail spade, a quick-acting breech, fixed ammunition, the independent line of sight, abatage, and the use of an automatic fuze-setter (*débouchoir*). The recoil system is self-evident now, but it should be remembered that in 1897 such a mechanism had rarely been seen on a field carriage, and it was, to the French, the most important part of the whole assembly, and treated as a state secret. (In 1917, when the USA adopted the gun, there was considerable resistance by the French military mission to revealing the interior arrangements of the recoil system; so much so that one exasperated American officer recorded that 'The French would sooner lose the war than lose the secret of the 75'.) When the gun was issued to the army it was always kept locked away under guard, and during manoeuvres or firing practice police would be posted all round the area to keep the curious away.

The trail spade, another self-evident item today, was also a novelty; hitherto it had been impossible to imagine such a device, because the entire gun carriage had to be free to recoil across the ground when the gun fired. Putting a spade on a 'solid' carriage would simply have made the gun somersault.

The breech mechanism was the Nordenfelt Eccentric Screw, possibly the only part of the design which came from outside France. This type of breech uses a breech ring which is considerably larger in diameter than the gun body, and has the barrel opening from the upper part of the ring. Inside the ring is a large breech screw which has a U-shaped portion cut away. A handle allows the screw to be rotated about 120 degrees. In the loading position the U-shaped cut-out in the screw is uppermost and aligned with the chamber, allowing a fixed round of ammunition to be loaded. The handle is then moved across through 120 degrees and the screw turns, bringing the solid portion into place behind the head of the cartridge. A simple firing pin in the breech screw is now lined up with the cartridge cap, kept from contact by a spring. Hinged to the breech screw is a simple hammer and lanyard; pulling the lanyard causes the hammer to swing up and hit the firing pin, overcoming the spring and firing the cartridge. Throwing the lever back 120 degrees, to the open position, also drives an ejector which flings out the empty cartridge case ready for reloading.

Fixed ammunition meant that the cartridge case and shell were firmly attached to each other and

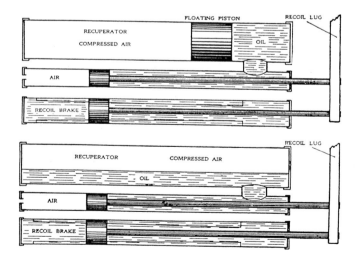

Schematic drawings of the French hydro-pneumatic recoil systems; in the upper picture the movement of the gun forces oil to push the floating piston forward against high-pressure air or nitrogen. In the lower picture the oil and air are in direct contact, a simpler method which appeared when the difficulties of making the floating piston a precise fit became apparent.

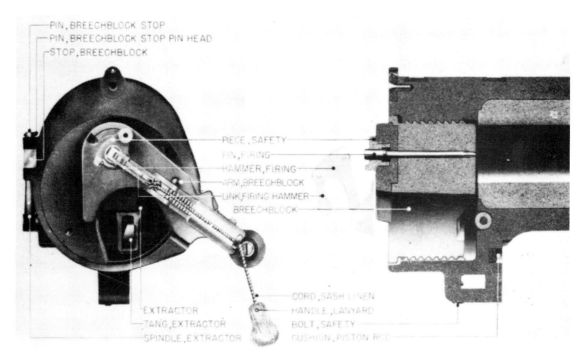

PIN, BREECHBLOCK STOP
PIN, BREECHBLOCK STOP PIN HEAD
STOP, BREECHBLOCK

PIECE, SAFETY
PIN, FIRING
HAMMER, FIRING
ARM, BREECHBLOCK
LINK, FIRING HAMMER
BREECHBLOCK

EXTRACTOR
TANG, EXTRACTOR
SPINDLE, EXTRACTOR

CORD, SASH LINEN
HANDLE, LANYARD
BOLT, SAFETY
CUSHION, PISTON ROD

The Nordenfelt breech mechanism of the 75mm Mle 1897.

the propelling charge was sealed away inside the cartridge case, and not capable of being adjusted in any way. This meant that loading was a one-man, one-movement task, simply flinging the round into the breech.

The independent line of sight meant that two gunlayers were used, one on the right side controlling elevation, one on the left controlling line. This speeded up gunlaying and helped the rate of fire. Moreover, since the gun carriage did not move during firing, the two layers could remain at their posts and commence relaying as soon as a shot had been fired. And the breech-worker and loader could also stay close to the gun ready to open the breech and reload. And since they were all clustered tightly around the gun it was sensible to add a bullet-proof shield to keep off infantry fire and shrapnel balls.

Abatage is a virtually untranslatable French term which covers the use of a form of metal shoe, attached to the trail by a rigid arm, which was laid underneath the wheel when the gun was brought into action. This improved the stability of the gun by translating any tendency of the carriage to recoil into a heavy downward thrust on the trail spade.

And finally, the automatic fuze-setter allowed very rapid setting of time fuzes. The French fired all their projectiles, explosive or shrapnel, with time fuzes and in consequence using a hand borer to set the fuze slowed up the service of the gun. So a mechanical setter was provided, which was kept set to the current range by one of the gun detachment. Two sockets and a lever on this machine allowed two shells to be dropped in, nose first, and the fuzes set correctly by simply pulling the lever down and releasing it, a matter of two seconds time. With two sockets a constant supply could be kept up, and fuzes could be set as rapidly as the gun could be fed.

It is worth remarking that the French could possibly have issued this gun earlier; but in fact they

The 'French 75'

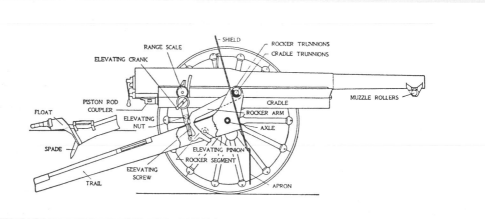

An American handbook drawing showing the salient features of the 75mm Mle 1897 gun.

A carefully preserved 75mm Mle 1897 on show at the French Army camp at Satory, near Versailles.

The French 75 has had more adulatory notices than any other gun before or since, most of it from people who know nothing else about artillery. True, it was the first fully integrated quick-firing gun; but once that has been said, the story of the 75 comes to an end. By 1914 it was outperformed by several contemporaries – the British 18-pounder, the German 77mm 96nA, the Austrian 76.5mm M1911 all fired heavier shell to a greater range, and the two latter weighed less. But, as we have seen, since the French had nothing else, and since the gun was tailored to their tactics of *attaque a l'outrance*, they were forced to make it work and made a virtue out of necessity. Its adoption by the Americans merely served to strengthen the legend, even though their 3in M1902 had a better performance.

Nevertheless, looked at in the light of 1897, the year of its introduction, it has to be said that it was an elegant and ingenious design and, taken together with its ammunition and fuze-setting machine, might almost be called a 'weapon system'. Looked at as a whole, the 75 seems quite conventional and simple, but examination of the details shows that considerable thought went into the design.

The 'French 75' Continued

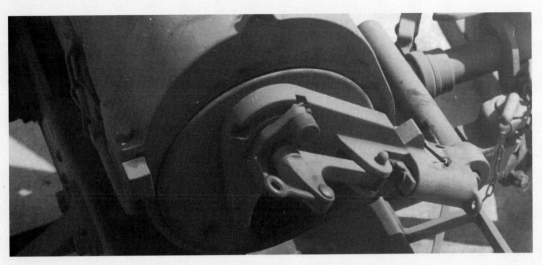

The breech of the 75mm Mle 1897, showing the firing hammer and, above it, the safety catch.

For example, the breech operating lever conceals a 'hangfire latch'. Once the gun is loaded and the breech closed, it cannot be opened by a casual movement of the lever. A concealed latch has to be released before the lever will move. This is so that if a hangfire occurs the gunner will not, in haste, be able to open the breech without some delay, during which time the hangfire might well explode safely inside the closed chamber. But once the gun has fired and recoiled, the lock is automatically released, so that the gunner merely has to fling the handle up, without worrying about latches, to open the breech for reloading.

Another feature which frequently puzzles observers is the two small rollers beneath the muzzle. Since the gun, weighing almost half a ton, recoils almost four feet, it can be appreciated that gravity will tend to pull it down and thus place an enormous strain on the recoil system piston rods and the small remaining bearing area of the cradle. The muzzle rollers, during recoil, slide into paths in the cradle and support the front end, taking much of the strain off the rest of the gun and promoting a smooth and steady recoil movement.

By the end of the war over 17,000 of these guns had been produced, and they had been liberally supplied to various allies. In later years they were provided with pneumatic tyres, and in 1933 a large number of guns were fitted to a new split-trail carriage. Improved ammunition eventually raised the maximum range to 12,300yd (11,300m), and it remained the principal armament of the French, Polish, American, Estonian, Greek, Lithuanian, Portuguese and Romanian armies until the 1940s

DATA: Canon de 75 modéle 1897

Calibre	75mm	Total weight	1,138kg
Weight of gun	460 kg	Recoil	1,093mm
Length of gun	2.721m	Elevation	–11° to +18°
Length of bore	36.6 calibres	Traverse	3° right and left
Rifling grooves	24	Shell weight	5.55kg
Rifling twist	RH, 1/25	Muzzle velocity	625m/sec
Breech	Screw, percussion	Max range	6,860m

deliberately delayed its introduction until the German Army had committed itself to the Krupp c/96 gun, a 77mm gun with rigid carriage and no other form of recoil control than a hinged and sprung trail spade. Once the German production was underway, the French went ahead and introduced the Mle 1897, a classic case of one-upmanship, since it made the c/96 obsolete overnight.

It made every other field gun in the world obsolete too, and we have already remarked upon the shifts and changes which ensued as the other armies of the world tried to catch up. The unfortunate result of this was that it made the French complacent; the 75 would do everything, it was superior to everything, it needed no improvement. As a result, they held on to it long after it was obsolete, and even went to war with it in 1939, by which time it was hopelessly outclassed. Another unfortunate result of their initial superiority was that the French government, being assured that the 75 would do anything and everything, looked askance when the army later asked for field howitzers. 'But you have just said the 75 will do everything …?' 'Ah, well, yes, but …' came the answer. The legislators were firm in their refusal, and an agile politician, Monsieur Malandrin, came up with the suggestion that flat discs could be clipped around the fuze, so as to spoil the ballistic shape and give the shell a steeper angle of descent, thus turning a 75mm gun into a 75mm near-howitzer. The army was not pleased, but had to live with it. The Malandrin Disc went into service and it, too, lasted until 1940.

The field gun strength of the French army was 1,011 four-gun batteries plus a reserve of 756 guns – a total of 4,800 guns held at the outbreak of war. This was considered sufficient to cover the needs of replacement during war, on the assumption that a modern war would be over before the 756 reserve guns had been used up; mobilization plans did not even contemplate the manufacture of artillery during the course of a war. The events of August/September 1914 soon showed the defects of this policy and contracts had to be hurriedly arranged for manufacture of replacement guns. A return of gun losses on 1 January 1916 reveals some interesting figures; up to that date, 1,000 guns had been destroyed due to faulty ammunition, 600 had been so damaged from the same cause as to demand rebuilding, 750 had been discarded as being worn out, and 400 had been captured or destroyed by the enemy. In the sixteen months since the declaration of war a total of 2,750 guns had been lost, more than half the number they had started with. The 1 January 1917 return was even worse: 1,100 blown up, 1,700 damaged, 2,250 worn out and 1,200 ineffective due to enemy action, total 6,250. But it was to be some time before production of 75mm guns reached a level sufficient to keep pace with the rate of attrition, and until then guns had to be found from somewhere.

The horse batteries of the French army were first issued with the standard 75mm Mle 1897, but this was replaced by a lighter weapon, the 75mm Schneider M1912. This fired the same ammunition as the Mle 1897 but had a shorter (31 calibres instead of 36) barrel and hence a maximum range of only 7,500m (8,175yd). The lack of range told against it once war put it to the test, and apart from throwing in the small stock of reserve guns, no more were manufactured after 1914. Instead, the St Chamond factory was put to manufacturing the Mle 1897, which eventually replaced the M1912 completely during the course of the war. St Chamond also had a stock of a longer-barrelled version of their M1912 which had apparently been developed for export sales, and the existing stock of these was taken into service as the 75mm Mle 1914.

The greatest addition to the field gun strength in 1914 was the reissue of a large number of older guns which had been retained in reserve stores. The principal weapon in the field group was the 90mm (3.5in) Mle 1877, an old screw-breech gun with no recoil system, the gun being trunnioned directly on to the carriage. But there were sufficient of these in store to outfit 100 batteries, and they were rapidly put back into commission to replace the first losses of 75mm guns. In their original form they fired an 8kg (17.6lb) shell to 7,000m

*The French handbook drawing of
the 75mm Mle 1912; as issued to
French horse artillery batteries.*

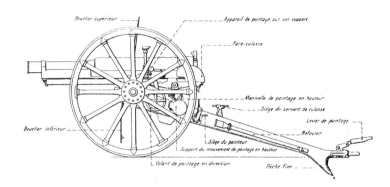

(7,600yd), but a more modern 8.3kg (18.3lb) shell was hastily designed and put into production and this, together with an improved smokeless powder cartridge, pushed the maximum range up to 9,700m (10,600yd).

A handful of field batteries were armed, in 1914, with the 120mm (4.7in) Mle 1890 howitzer (or 'short gun' as it was more usually called). This was an elderly design but nevertheless had an hydro-pneumatic recoil system which allowed the barrel to recoil through a ring cradle; this is all the more remarkable, when you remember that the 75mm with hydro-pneumatic system did not appear until 1897 and is often credited with being the first field piece to carry such a refinement. It was designed by a firm called Baquet, of whom little appears to be known, and fired an 18kg (40lb) shell to 5,800m (6,300yd), though this was later changed to a 20kg (44lb) shell with a loss of range to 5600m (6,100yd), the improvement in terminal effect being thought worth the odd 200 metres. The recoil system was a remarkably compact mechanism and quite unlike any other design which came after it. However it appears not to have been particularly successful; there was no refinement of control to brake the movement of recoil or recuperation, and hence the steadiness of the carriage tended to depend upon the nature of the ground. If the spade could be well dug in, then the gun stayed still; if not,

not. The 'Canon de 120 courte, mle 1890' was generally replaced in 1915 with an improved design.

The replacement was the 'Obusier de 120 Tir Rapide Schneider Mle 1915' and in most respects it was a scaled-down version of the Schneider 155mm (6.1in) howitzer Mle 1915, using a similar carriage and recuperator system and the same Schneider screw breech operated by a lever lying across the top of the breech carrier. It was a reasonable weapon; it fired an 18 or 19kg (40 or 42lb) shell to 8,300m (9,000yd) range, and at 1,475kg (1.45 tons) weight it was well within the power of a six-horse team. If you were fond of 120mm howitzers it could not fail to charm you; but the French were not charmed. It simply was not heavy enough to make its manufacture and presence on the battlefield worth while. So the number of these howitzers which went into service was limited, and as soon as they wore out they were scrapped, their place being taken by 155mm weapons.

In 1907 the Schneider company had built a 42-line (4.2in; 106.7mm) long-range gun for the Russians, who thereafter built it under licence at the Putilov factory. Feeling that this was a rather good design, the company approached the French Army and after some deliberation and slight changes it was adopted in 1913 as the 'Canon de 105 L, Modele 1913 TR' (Gun, 105mm Light, Model 1913, Rapid Fire). Although the calibre would suggest

The Schneider 105mm M1913

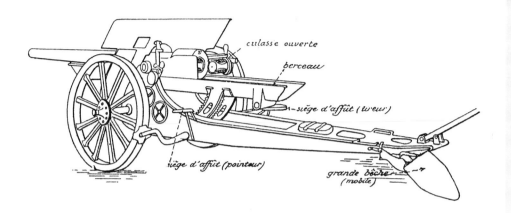

The Schneider Mle 1903TR gun.

One could, with some justification, call this gun Schneider's masterpiece, since it brought together a number of ideas the company had experimented with and welded them into a most effective whole. It began entering service just before the outbreak of war, and a total of 1,340 were built before the Armistice; there is room for thinking that more of these and fewer 75s might have been of more use to the French.

In 1907 Schneider were given a contract by Russia to produce a 105mm gun; the result was their Model 1910, subsequently made under licence in Russia. The company then submitted it to the French Ministry of War and after some minor changes received a contract in August 1913. As soon as war broke out the company was ordered to accelerate production, but at the same time they were swamped with orders for a whole host of other guns, hence the relatively restricted number which were produced.

Among the more innovative features of the M1910 were: a screw breech block with the side cut away so that it could be swung open without the need to withdraw the block axially from the breech ring; a shot guide built into the bottom of the breech ring which lifted as soon as the breech was opened so as to protect the screw threads from damage by the shell being carelessly loaded; a retaining catch which held the hand-loaded shell in place until the rammer could be placed behind it; an automatic hangfire latch; a quick-release latch which with one movement disconnected the gun from the recoil system and allowed it to be pulled back along the cradle so as to distribute the weight better for towing, or for longer moves completely removed to a transport wagon; and an entirely new hydro-pneumatic recoil system in which the recoil buffer and nitrogen-filled recuperator were completely independent of each other. All these added up to provide a gun which could be rapidly brought into action and which could easily fire eight rounds per minute.

The 105 TR survived the inter–wars years, and in 1939 some 1,030 of them formed the principal power of the French field artillery; numbers were also sold to Poland, where they were later modified to use a split-trail carriage. All were taken into German service after 1940.

The Schneider 105mm M1913 Continued

DATA: Canon de 105 Lourde, modéle 1913, Tir Rapide

Calibre	105mm	Total weight	2,300kg
Weight of gun	849kg	Recoil	1,310mm
Length of gun	2.987m	Elevation	0° to +37°
Length of bore	22.4 calibres	Traverse	3° right and left
Rifling grooves	40	Shell weight	16.0kg
Rifling twist	RH, 1/25	Muzzle velocity	550m/sec
Breech	Screw, percussion	Max range	12,700m

---

this to be a divisional gun, the long range of 12,600m (13,800yd) with a 15.9kg (35lb) explosive shell put it into the heavy support category. It became a maid-of-all-work, some 1,340 being built before the war ended, and it was sufficiently effective to stay in service long enough to see 1,029 of them in use in 1939.

Schneider had reason to be proud of the design, for it introduced a number of ingenious features, many of which became standard on later weapons. The breech mechanism was an interrupted screw carried on a swinging arm and so shaped that it could swing in and out of the breech ring without having to be withdrawn axially. There was a most unusual fitment inside the chamber: a hinged arm, controlled by the breech mechanism lever, which snapped out when the breech was opened so as to engage behind the driving band of the shell as it was loaded into the chamber and thus hold it from slipping back, if the gun was elevated, until the rammer could be positioned behind it and the shell rammed into the rifling. The lever was then retracted into the wall of the chamber as the breech was closed behind the cartridge. Opening the breech also lifted a shell-guide from the bottom of the breech ring, easing the path of the shell into the chamber, and a plethora of safety devices and interlocks ensured that the gun could not be fired unless the breech was closed and locked and the gun fully run-out in its cradle. The carriage was a conventional two-wheeled box-trail pattern with a new hydro-pneumatic recoil system of Schneider's own design, and with traverse obtained by moving the trail across the axle. The maximum elevation was 37 degrees, quite unusual for a gun of that period.

Another source of armament was the mountain artillery; like its British counterpart, the French mountain artillery was primarily used for colonial campaigns, notably in the North African mountains, and since this was now relegated a long way down the priority list, the mountain guns were rapidly called in to the general pool. This added 120 guns to the general strength, but what was most astonishing was that the gun was put back into production and remained in service well into the 1920s. Astonishing, because on the face of it the Schneider-Ducrest 65mm (2.6in) Mle 1906 was an odd design which most armies would have been happy to see the back of.

The oddness of the design was due to the need to absorb as much of the recoil as possible and yet keep the gun carriage light in weight and capable of being dismantled and mule-packed; even allowing for this, however, one cannot help thinking that a little too much complication had crept in. In the first place, the trail was built with hinged sides resembling an A-frame, the cross-piece being a spring, so that when the gun fired, the trail could expand and absorb some of the shock.

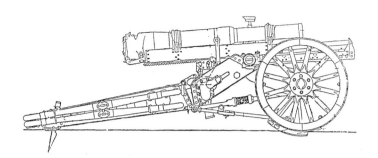

The 65mm Schneider-Ducrest mountain gun with the barrel pulled back ready for firing.

The Schneider-Ducrest gun with the barrel in the forward position.

The 65mm Schneider-Ducrest

The Scheider-Ducrest 65mm mountain gun, with the barrel drawn back against the pressure of the recoil system and ready to be fired.

The 65mm Schneider-Ducrest Continued

The Schneider-Ducrest mountain gun was an oddity because the designer – Colonel Ducrest – was prepared to put up with mechanical complications in order to save weight. He succeeded brilliantly, producing a gun which weighed far less than any other mountain equipment of comparable power before or since, and one of the lightest guns ever made. The secret lay in two places, the trail and the recoil system.

The trail – which was essentially a box trail – was split into three sections, hinged to each other and to the axletree in front. The two front sections were hinged together by the gun cradle trunnions and, viewed from the side, formed a flattened letter A, the cross-piece of which was a spring-loaded strut. The tip of the A carried the trunnions, the bottom of the right leg was pivoted on the axle, and the bottom of the left leg was pivoted to the remaining length of trail. This junction, between the trail and the A, could be set at two different angles by means of a wedge; by removing the wedge the trail came closer to the ground and thus allowed the gun a greater elevation without having to build an excessively large elevating arc into the design. Moreover, when the gun fired, and particularly when it fired at angles of elevation, much of the recoil force pressed down on the tip of the A and forced the legs apart, a movement which was resisted by the tension-sprung strut forming the crossbar of the A. This absorbed a certain amount of the recoil force. If necessary the rear section of the trail could be removed and the gun could still be fired,, which was a useful feature in confined spaces.

Much of the remaining recoil force was absorbed by the next oddity, the 'differential recoil system' or as the French manual calls it, the *principe du lancer*. There is a hydro-spring recoil system attaching the gun to the cradle, but it works in a unique manner. The gun is wound back manually to its fully recoiled position and there held by a catch connected to the firing lever. After loading and laying, pulling the firing lever releases the gun and the recuperator immediately pulls it forward into the 'in battery' position. A fraction of a second before it reaches the fully-forward point, the firing pin is struck and the gun fires. Again quoting the manual: 'The moving mass attains certain velocity v; on the departure of the shell the moving mass is projected to the rear with a free recoil velocity V; it follows that the true recoil velocity is V – v, the difference between these two velocities. The work of absorbtion done by the brake is thereby diminished by having a smaller recoil and smaller resistance.' Or, putting it another way, the recoil generated by firing has first to stop the forward-moving weight and then drive it in the opposite direction.

Odd or not, it worked well enough to survive the war; it then became a colonial infantry support gun, and some were given to Poland. Some survived long enough to be taken by the German Army after 1940 and assimilated into their mountain troops as the 'Gebirgskanone 221(f)'.

DATA: Canon de 65 de montagne modéle 1906

Calibre	65mm	Total weight	400kg
Weight of gun	105kg	Recoil	550mm
Length of gun	1,315mm	Elevation	–10° to +35°
Length of bore	16 calibres	Traverse	3° right and left
Rifling grooves	24	Shell weight	3.81kg
Rifling twist	RH, 1/25	Muzzle velocity	330m/sec
Breech	Screw, percussion	Max range	5,500m

Secondly, this is the gun with the 'differential recoil' system, in which the recoil had first to stop the moving barrel and then reverse it, another move to soak up much of the shock before it got to the trunnions.

And so, between the differential recoil and the sprung trail, the actual recoil force which eventually transferred to the ground was quite small; and the all-up weight of the gun was only 400kg (880lb). For a mountain gun there is a sound argument for the design; but as a field piece it was over-complicated. However, Schneider had the tooling and skill, so they continued to make it for some time in order to fill the gaps in the front line. Its performance was not inspiring; it fired a 4.1kg (9lb) shell to a maximum range of 5,500m (6,000yd). But it was small and handy, could be man-carried in four loads, and could thus be manoeuvred into places where an ordinary field gun could not go. It even spent some of its time playing trench mortar until 'proper' trench mortars came along.

USA

America opened the QF era via the same route as Britain; by purchasing an Erhardt design, much the same as the British 15-pounder but slightly modified to meet American preferences. This became the 3in Gun M1902, and Erhardt built fifty of them, after which production continued at Rock

Island Arsenal; these, together with a number of Vickers 2.95in mountain howitzers, were the sole armament of the US Field Artillery in the opening decade of the century. A 3.8in Gun M1907 was developed by Rock Island Arsenal, followed by a 4.7in gun M1908, but the 3.8in was a failure and only the 4.7in was put into production, and that in small numbers.

In 1912 work began on an entirely new American design of field gun to replace the M1902. This was scheduled to become the M1916, but the development was slow; it was to use a split trail, a device invented in France by Colonel Deport and first adopted by Italy in their 75mm M1911 gun. Its attraction was the wide range of traverse which could be achieved without having to 'run up' the gun and free its spades from the ground, and also the high elevation which could be achieved because of the clear space between the trail legs. So the M1916 gun was to have a split trail carriage, with a 'top carriage' allowing 45 degrees of traverse and

The American 3in M1916 gun; a split trail and high elevation were the worthy aims of the design, but the execution fell short.

53 degrees of elevation with a 28-calibre barrel giving a maximum range of about 9,000yd (8,200m). So far, so good.

1916 came and went, but the M1916 did not appear; it was still being tinkered with. One of the less appealing features of the US Army organization of the time was that the Field Artillery had no Chief; they were subsidiary to the infantry in the field and, being a relatively small arm of the service, did not rank a general officer to look after their interests in Washington. On the other hand the Ordnance Department was a powerful organization with an autocratic chief, General Crozier, who laid down that the design and testing of field guns (and pretty well everything else) would be 'conducted by the Ordnance Department, through the instrumentality of Ordnance officers, by the methods of the Ordnance Department, and at the Ordnance Department's place' and the artillery would take whatever they were given. As a result there was absolutely no gunner input to the M1916 design and numerous problems had arisen. Nevertheless, somebody had sufficient faith in the design to place an order for 300 carriages in 1916. After the US entered the war, in May 1917 a second order for 340 carriages was placed. June 1917 saw the New York Air Brake Company given an order for another 400 carriages. The gun to go on top of these carriages was not a particularly complex design and contracts for those were also issued, though this was confounded in June 1917 by the decision to adopt 75mm as the standard calibre; gun production had to be stopped while fresh drawings were prepared, after which it started up once more.

In March 1918 – two years after the first contract was issued – the first M1916 carriage left the production line. By the middle of the year, eighteen had appeared. By December – by which time the war was over – 249 had been delivered. And long before then the artillerymen had given up calling it the 'Model of 1916' and referred to it as the 'Crime of 1916'.

There were two reasons for this abysmal production performance. First, the desire to have the best, to improve and improve on the basic design, was such that scarcely a week went by without some design change being notified to the manufacturing companies, every one of which meant stopping production, making changes, modifying work which had already been done, and then starting up once more. There was nobody in overall charge of the project who was in a position to 'freeze' the design and give the manufacturers a chance.

Secondly, it was a basically bad design, variously described by experts as 'an abomination' and 'an impossibility as a practical manufacturing proposition.' One problem area was the recoil system; this had been designed as a hydro-spring system, using an oil buffer to brake the recoil and a bank of springs to return the gun into the firing position. But whilst this worked well at angles up to about 25 degrees, above that it refused to haul the gun uphill. So a hydro-pneumatic design was canvassed, and eventually the French officer who had designed recoil systems for Schneider was called in and, for a fee reputed to be not far from $60,000, designed a suitable system which became known as the 'St Chamond' recuperator. This led to an uproar from the French government, who accused the US government of stealing their military secrets.

The top carriage, which supported the gun and cradle and recuperator and which traversed on top of the basic carriage, was a casting of such extreme complexity that, eventually, every manufacturer gave up on it. It had to be redesigned so that it could be fabricated from smaller and simpler castings and steelwork. Eventually, in about April 1918, the first complete gun and carriage, less recuperator, was shipped off to France to be fitted with the St Chamond recuperator. It vanished, to turn up several weeks later lying on the dockside in Halifax, Nova Scotia, and nobody, to this day, ever found out how or why it got there. It finally reached France, had the recuperator fitted and was then shipped to (of course) an Ordnance Department test facility in France to be tried out. The recuperator came through with flying colours,

A post-war version of the M1916 (with pneumatic tyres), which shows the complex upper carriage and recoil system.

but in the course of cross-country mobility trials the rest of the carriage fell to pieces. And the amount of free play and backlash in the elevating and traversing gears meant that its accuracy was terrible, and the gun was quite unfitted to be fired over the heads of one's own troops.

All of which is a necessary explanation so that the eventual course of field artillery in the US Army can be understood. When the USA declared war in April, the Field Artillery had 544 M1902 3in guns, 113 2.95in mountain guns and sixty 4.7in guns in service, and it was obvious that this number had to be considerably increased to provide the artillery support for the enormous army which was

planned. The M1916 was an obvious non-starter, and the first solution was simply to ask the French and British to supply artillery for the first US troops as they arrived in France. This was agreed; the French would provide the 75mm Mle 1897 in quantity, while the British would provide heavier weapons. The next task was to organize production in the USA to provide the guns required for the remainder of the American Expeditionary Force.

As it happened, the British government had placed large orders with American companies for the manufacture of some artillery pieces, contracts which, in early 1917, were approaching the end of their run. This meant that manufacturing plant with the necessary tools and skills would be available to make guns, provided that the US Army was willing to accept the British designs. So far as heavy artillery went, this was acceptable, but in the case of field artillery, if the AEF began equipping with the 75mm Mle 1897 it made sense to continue to manufacture this weapon and, moreover, to adopt the French 75mm shell and cartridge as the standard throughout. This meant that the British 18-pounder, being made by the Bethlehem Steel Corporation, would have to be rebarrelled in 75mm calibre. It also meant yet another change to the 3in M1916, rebarrelling it too to the new calibre. So that eventually three 75mm guns, all firing the same cartridge, would be in production: the 75mm M1916, the 75mm M1917 (the Americanized British 18-pounder), and the 75mm Mle 1897, manufactured in the USA under licence from the French.

Once the change of calibre was approved and drawings prepared, the M1917 gave no trouble. Bethlehem Steel were given an order for 268 guns in May 1917, and this was followed by a further

contract for 1,000 complete equipments. By January 1918 the new weapons were coming off the production line and by the middle of 1918 there were 300 guns in use as training weapons.

Unfortunately it met with a good deal of resistance. In the first place it used a spring recuperator, and by 1917 everybody who was anybody simply knew that spring recuperators were old-fashioned, and only hydro-pneumatics were the thing. Tales of Flanders battlefields knee-deep in broken 18-pounder springs were assiduously spread around. Then again, it was a wire-wound gun, and wire-wound guns were no good at all, everybody knew that. They were crooked and couldn't shoot straight. And, of course, the USA was being flooded with French artillery 'advisers' who were primarily there to see that the US artillery learned how to do things the French way with French equipment so that they could be quietly assimilated into French formations just as soon as they got to France. And British guns were not made in France.

But when the soldiers got their hands on the M1917 it was a different story. After some

The 4.7in M1906 gun, which was eventually converted to 120mm calibre to standardize with the French.

The 3in M1917, the British 18-pounder Mark I rebarrelled to take the French 75mm ammunition which the USA adopted as their standard.

experience with the gun they were so pleased that additional contracts, bringing the total to 2,868 complete guns, were issued in October 1918, these being intended for Pershing's 1919 offensive. But the war ended a month later and after making 921 guns the contracts were cancelled.

The M1916 we have already examined; suffice it to say that contracts for 827 guns were issued during the war period and a total of 307 were actually produced by April 1919.

Which leaves us with the third choice, the French 75mm Mle 1897. The original intention was to have this as a stopgap until the M1916 was in volume production, but once it became apparent that the M1916 was never going to get into volume production the Mle 1897 became the prime choice. Drawings were requested from France, after which they had to be converted into US standard measurements and tolerances and redrawn. The gun carriage would be manufactured by the Willys-Overland company, and they received an order for 2,927 equipments in December 1917. The recoil system, however, was to be made elsewhere by companies considered to be better fitted for that type of work. The Singer Sewing Machine company contracted to make almost 3,000 recuperators,

and a further 1,000 were to be made by Rock Island Arsenal.

An Ordnance officer was sent off to the French arsenal at Puteaux to learn how the recuperator was manufactured, assembled and tested; he was heavily indoctrinated by the French in the matter of secrecy, returned to the USA, locked the drawings of the recuperator in his safe and took off for a month's leave. During his absence the fact that the drawings had arrived became known but it took some very high-powered orders before he could be induced to hand them over so that the manufacturers could start work.

By the time of the Armistice, Willys-Overland had made 291 gun carriages without recuperators. Rock Island Arsenal had made one recuperator. Singer didn't even get a recuperator to work until March 1919. In the same period two firms had manufactured 112 Mle 1897 gun barrels. Which explains why the AEF received 1,828 75mm guns from the French and 143 (almost all M1917s) from the USA by the time of the Armistice.

The 4.7in gun M1908 fared little better; there was no particular mechanical complication in the manufacture of this gun, but it appears to have been given very little priority. Which is strange, because on paper it was a useful weapon which could out-range the German 77mm gun and fired a heavier shell. But only forty-eight of them ever arrived in France; only 320 carriages and 149 guns had been manufactured by the time of the Armistice. One complication was the ammunition, which was peculiar to this gun and could not be obtained in Europe, every round having to be shipped across the Atlantic. In an attempt to improve matters the gun was redesigned in 120mm calibre so that it would accept French ammunition – which apparently ignored the fact that the French had more or less abandoned 120mm as a service calibre and had only a limited production capacity for this ammunition. In any event this stopped the manufacture of 4.7in gun barrels late in 1918 so that drawings and tooling could be changed and, once the war was over, the 120mm idea was abandoned and manufacture of the 4.7 ceased completely.

RUSSIA

Russia had two gun-making companies, Putilov and Obuchov, but their production capacity was low and their native designs not particularly inspiring, and therefore a good deal of their artillery was imported from major gunmakers such as Krupp, Schneider and Armstrong. This was because in the aftermath of the Russo-Japanese War, the Russian army was being given a thorough overhaul, a programme of reorganization and re-equipment being planned which would be completed by 1917. The war had shown serious deficiencies in Russian field artillery and after 1904 two new equipments were introduced, the 3in (76.2mm or, in Imperial Russian terms, '30-line') Model 1902 gun from Putilov and a 4.8in (122mm, or 48-line) M1904 howitzer which was a combined development by Putilov and Obuchov. The latter design failed to achieve the performance anticipated and it was rapidly supplemented by the 122mm M1909 howitzer from Krupp and, in order to get a quantity into service as quickly as possible, a similar M1910 howitzer from Schneider. In addition the

mountain artillery were equipped with a 76.2mm gun M1904 from Obuchov, a 76.2mm gun M1909 from Schneider, and a 105mm howitzer M1909, also from Schneider. It was this collection which formed the greater part of the Russian artillery strength throughout the war. All manufacture of guns, of course, came to a sudden stop in November 1917 with the Revolution, was gradually resumed but never reached any worthwhile figure until the 1920s. Moreover the purge which accompanied the Revolution got rid of most of the older gun designers and technicians and it was not until the end of the 1920s that anything resembling new equipment began to be manufactured.

The 76.2mm (3in) M1900 gun, although officially superseded by the M1902, had been put into reserve store and numbers of them appeared in the early part of the war to replace serious Russian losses on the Eastern Front until new M1902s were available. Like almost all Russian designs it was powerful for its weight; with a 30-calibre barrel it fired a 14.5lb (6.6kg) shell at 1,950ft/sec to a range of 7,000yd (6,400m) and in action it weighed exactly one ton. Originally it had no shield, but one was added during the Russo-Japanese War; this made the equipment somewhat heavier and less manoeuvrable. The most remarkable feature of this gun was the recuperator system. The barrel was mounted on a top carriage which could slide backwards on top of the trail, an oil buffer in the trail acting as a recoil brake. Two lugs on the top carriage rode on rods inside the trail upon each of which were 40 india-rubber 'doughnuts' which were compressed during the recoil stroke and then expanded again to return the gun into battery. (It is worth noting that the only other time a rubber-ring system was ever used was on the British 'Smith Gun', issued to the Home Guard in 1941. In that case the rings acted as the recoil buffer as well.)

The 1902 model was a much better weapon; essentially the gun was the same, but the carriage used a hydro-pneumatic recoil system – with a few oddities of its own – which worked very well. Again, there was no shield on the original model, axle-tree

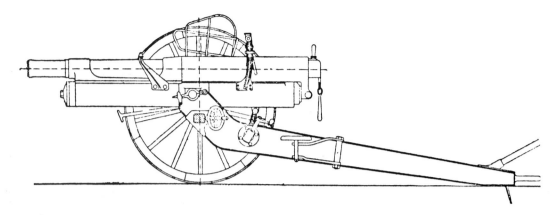

The Russian 76.2mm Model 1902 gun, their first attempt at a long-recoil design.

seats for two gunners being fitted. However, a three-part shield was later produced and some guns had the axle-tree seats removed in order to fit this shield. The ammunition was somewhat improved and the gun then fired a 16.4lb (7.4kg) shell at 1,950ft/sec to a range of 9,575yd (8,750m). Without the shield it weighed 2,292lb (1,041kg) in action.

The three 122mm howitzers were fairly similar and fairly representative of the class, which was pretty numerous in the first decade of the century; every gunmaker in Europe seemed to have a 120mm howitzer on his books. The Model 1904 had been developed by the Obuchov and Putilov arsenals in cooperation, and at this remove there is no way of telling who was responsible for what. The hydro-pneumatic recoil system appears to have been a strengthened version of that used on the M1902 field gun, so probably this was the Putilov input. There was a long box trail, no shield, and a short 12-calibre barrel. It fired a 46lb (20.9kg) shell at 960ft/sec to a range of 7,325yd (6,695m).

This performance of the M1904 howitzer was not considered sufficient, and without troubling either Putilov or Obuchov, the government went to Krupp and bought a stock of his Model 1909 120mm (4.7in) howitzer, bored up to 122mm (4.8in) for Russian ammunition. This had a 14-calibre barrel, a hydro-pneumatic recoil system, a shield, and fired a 50lb (22.7kg) shell at 1,100ft/sec to 8,400yd (7,680m), which was certainly an improvement on the M1904 weapon.

There were two schools of thought in the matter of howitzer recoil at that time; one school, originated by Erhardt and adopted by Schneider among others, was to automatically adjust the recoil stroke in accordance with the elevation, so that the breech never struck the ground. The other viewpoint, exemplified by Krupp, was to put the trunnions as close to the breech as possible and settle for a constant recoil stroke which, due to the breech height remaining constant, would never strike the ground at higher elevations. Whether the Russians were consciously buying into both systems so as to weigh one against the other, or whether they were merely buying from two suppliers in order to fill their batteries quicker, we cannot say. But in effect, they were comparing the two systems, because the other half of their order went to Schneider for their M1910 120mm (4.7in) howitzer, again bored-up to the peculiar Russian 122mm (4.8in) standard. This was very similar to the 120mm adopted by the French army, a short-barrel weapon using controlled recoil and with a large trough-like cradle extension behind the gun to support it during recoil. This weapon fired the same 50lb (22.7kg) shell as the Krupp design and provided exactly the same performance; moreover it was within 50lb of the same weight as the Krupp weapon.

A Russian Krupp 122mm howitzer M1909 in action.

Another view of a Russian 122mm M1909 howitzer battery.

The three mountain guns mirrored the howitzer experience; the initial weapon was the 76.2mm (3in) M1904, a design from Obuchov Arsenal with some unusual features. The gun was mounted very low in the carriage, passing through a large ring formed in the axle, with an oil buffer above the barrel and a spring recuperator below it. The sights were therefore carried high on a spindly framework so as to be at a convenient height for laying. The box trail allowed 25 degrees elevation, and the gun fired a 14lb (6.4kg) shell at 965ft/sec to a range of 4,550yd (4,160m). This performance was not particularly good, and in 1909 a longer barrel was fitted which raised the velocity to 1,250ft/sec and the range to 7,000yd (6,400m), but this placed too much stress on the mounting and the gun became very lively when fired.

As early as 1906 the hunt was on for a replacement, and the choice fell on the French 76.2mm (3in) Schneider-Danglis gun. Col. Danglis was a Greek artillery officer who designed a method of gun construction which allowed the gun barrel to be quickly removed from an enveloping jacket which carried the breech mechanism; Schneider were asked to incorporate this into a mountain gun they were developing for the Greeks in about 1905 and they then adopted it for one or two other designs, one of which was the gun bought by Russia. Another notable feature of this design, which may also have been due to Danglis, was that the wheels were mounted on cranked axle stubs which could be rotated so that the gun could be set either high or low, the high position being used when high elevation was required, thus allowing the breech sufficient room to recoil without striking the ground. A large S-shaped shield was fitted, making this model instantly recognizable, together with a hydro-pneumatic recoil system in a cradle beneath the gun. The box trail was hinged in the middle and could be folded back so as to allow shafts to be fitted for horse draught, or the entire equipment could be stripped down into six mule-loads, the heaviest of which

was the 245lb (11kg) cradle and recoil system. It fired a 13.7lb (6.2kg) shell at 1270ft/sec to a range of 9,450yd (8.640m). An unknown number of guns came from Schneider in France, but some 400 are believed to have been licence-built in Putilov Arsenal.

Russia had been at loggerheads with Turkey since time immemorial, and their mutual border in the Caucasus mountains was a likely battlefield, so mountain artillery was taken seriously. And whilst the 76.2mm guns were handy weapons, their 14lb (6.4kg) shells were not much use against the sort of field fortifications run up from convenient rocks which were liable to be encountered in the mountains. A heavier weapon was therefore sought; again, Schneider came up with the answer, in the form of the 105mm (4.1in) mountain howitzer M1909. This used the same loose-barrel-and-jacket design as the 76.2mm gun (though for some reason the Danglis name never attaches to this model) and, in most respects, was little more than a beefed-up version of the gun. It broke down into seven mule-loads or, like the gun, the trail could be folded back and shafts fitted to permit horse draught on roads. It fired a useful 26lb (11.8kg) shell at 985ft/sec to a range of 6,550yd (6,000m)

The Schneider-Danglis mountain gun adopted by Russia; the cranked axle has been turned so as to set the gun carriage high and allow the gun to recoil through the gap in the trail without striking the ground.

Demonstrating how the Schneider-Danglis mountain gun came to pieces; the barrel is being removed from the jacket which carries the breech mechanism.

and could elevate to 60 degrees, somewhat unusual for mountain artillery of that period. This also went into production in Russia and continued in service after the war, some even appearing in World War Two.

ITALY

In Italy at the turn of the century there were only two firms capable of manufacturing artillery: Oderno Terni Orlando (OTO) and Vickers-Terni.

The Krupp-designed 3in Model 1906 as used by the Italian army.

The 75mm Deport M1911

The Deport field gun, illustrating how the gun elevates but leaves the cradle horizontal.

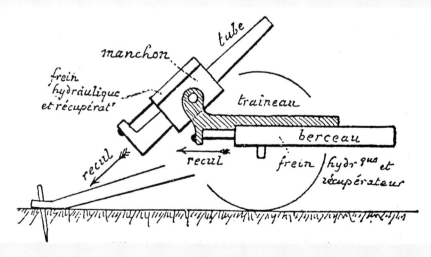

A French diagram which shows the salient features of the Deport recoil system.

Colonel Deport of the French Army had been part of the design team which produced the 75mm Mle 1897 gun; he later retired from the service to work as designer for the Forges de Chatillon, and his particular talent appears to have been in the matter of recoil systems. His first successful design used an arrangement of twin

The 75mm Deport M1911 Continued

An Italian detachment with their Deport field gun.

cylinders such that the gun forced a piston into the cylinder block at the same time as the cylinder block moved backwards over a second piston attached to the cradle. He then promoted a differential recoil gun which used a massive coil spring as buffer and recuperator, but had no luck with the idea. Finally he developed the unusual twin recoil system used on this 1911 gun which was adopted by Italy. He also pioneered the use of the split trail, and brought the two ideas together in this gun.

The split trail involved two trail legs which were closed together for transport and opened wide for emplacement. They allowed the gunners to stand inside the trail, close to the gun; more importantly they allowed the gun a hitherto unknown span of up to 52 degrees of traverse and 45 degrees of elevation, without interference from the trail. The only drawback was that the trail legs had to be longer than a simple box or pole trail would be, so as to provide the necessary stability when fully opened and when the gun was being fired at an extreme angle of traverse. If the legs were too short then the gun would tend to rear up in the air, driving the recoil force down one leg of the trail and lifting the other leg, and probably the wheel as well, off the ground at each shot.

The recoil system was divided into two components: there were two cradles, a lower cradle fixed solidly to the top carriage and capable only of being traversed, and an upper cradle, trunnioned to the rear end of the lower cradle, and carrying the gun. The upper cradle had a spring buffer/recuperator which allowed the gun to recoil about a foot and then spring back into battery. But the trunnions to which this upper cradle was attached were connected to the recoil pistons of a second, hydro-pneumatic, recoil system inside the lower cradle. When the gun was elevated only the upper cradle and gun moved; the lower cradle stayed horizontal. When the gun, at whatever angle of elevation, fired it would recoil 15in (381mm) against the spring in the upper cradle, and the upper cradle and gun assembly would recoil 40in (1,016mm) horizontally in the lower cradle. This separation of the major recoil assembly from the gun allowed it to stay cool, unaffected by the heat of a rapidly firing gun barrel. The Deport gun's 45 degrees elevation and 52 degrees traverse gave it much greater tactical flexibility and even tempted the Italians into thinking it might very well make a useful anti-aircraft gun. Six hundred of these Deport guns were manufactured under licence by OTO and Vickers-Terni between 1911 and 1914. A number remained in service well into the Second World War.

The 75mm Deport M1911 Continued			
DATA: Cannone da 75/27 modello 11			
Calibre	75mm	Total weight	1,076kg
Weight of gun	305kg	Recoil	Dual; see text
Length of gun	2,132mm	Elevation	−15° to +45°
Length of bore	27 calibres	Traverse	27° right and left
Rifling grooves	24	Shell weight	6.5kg
Rifling twist	RH	Muzzle velocity	510m/sec
Breech	Screw, percussion	Max range	7,600m

Neither had a design staff and both made foreign guns under licence for the Italian armed forces. The Italian army tried its hand at designing a gun in the early 1900s, but after they had produced a design for a non-recoil gun, and after the manufacturers had gently pointed out that the rest of Europe was furiously re-equipping with on-carriage recoil systems, the design was quietly scrapped and in 1906 a 75mm (2.95in) gun was bought from Krupp. A total of 642 guns were delivered by Krupp by February 1909, after which 230 more guns were supplied by Krupp and 272 were assembled by OTO in Italy from Krupp-supplied parts. The gun was a straight-forward design with no novelties, using a hydro-spring recuperator, and fired a 14lb (6.4kg) HE or shrapnel shell at 1,675ft/sec to a range of 7,450yd (6,800m). The adoption of better-designed projectiles during the war advanced this to 11,200yd (10,235m).

In 1911 the Italian government invaded Libya and precipitated the Italo-Turkish war, which led to an expansion of the army and a demand for more artillery. This was met by examining the various products on offer and then organizing a competitive trial of three 75mm guns; one from Krupp, one from Schneider, and one from the French company Forges de Chatillon. The test involved two guns from each maker formed into a six-gun battery which then proceeded to engage targets at various ranges and directions, firing continuously until 500 rounds had been expended by each gun. The

Krupp and Schneider guns failed the test, due to their recoil systems overheating and the Forges de Chatillon gun was selected as the Italian 75mm Gun Model 1911.

The M1911 had two unusual features, one of which is now so commonplace that it is hard to imagine what a revelation it was when introduced: the split trail, or, as it was then called, the 'scissors trail'. The other was a unique compound recoil system, which was the reason for its success in the competitive trial. It separated the principal parts of the recoil system from proximity to the hot gun barrel and thus survived the punishing 500-round test. Originally intended for use by horse artillery, it was then issued to field artillery as well; originally the maximum range was 7,600m (8,300yd), but this was improved during the war by better ammunition, and it could eventually reach 10,250m (11,170yd).

The Italians had joined with the Prussians during the six-week long Austro-Prussian War of 1866; their object had been to gain control of the Trentino, an area of Italian-speaking area which formed part of Austria, but all that they achieved was a military defeat at Custozza and a naval defeat at Lissa. They were therefore conscious of the possibility of renewed hostilities against Austria, which meant fighting in the Alps, which in turn meant mountain artillery. In 1902 the army arsenal at Turin developed a 70mm (2.76in) mountain gun which dismantled into four loads, fired a 10lb (4.5kg) shell to

7,250yd (6,630m) but had no recoil system, the gun being trunnioned directly on the trail. This was scarcely the most modern approach, and after issuing a number of these guns the designers went back to work and eventually produced a 65mm (2.56in) gun Model 1911 with a hydro-spring recoil system. This fired a 10lb (4.5kg) shell at 1,130ft/sec to reach a range of 7,450yd (6,810m) and was a much better piece of equipment; 400 were produced before Italy entered the war, and subsequent production exceeded 1,000 guns. Even so, the losses during their Alpine campaigns were such that they were forced to buy a quantity of 70mm (2.76in) M1908 Schneider guns from France. This design had originally been produced for the Spanish army; it dismantled into five parts for transport, fired a 12lb (5.4kg) shell to 5,450yd (5,000m) and used a cranked axle to obtain clearance for the breech when firing at higher elevations.

BELGIUM

In spite of there being two Belgium gunmakers, Cockerill and the Royal Cannon Foundry, the Belgian Army bought its guns elsewhere, a 75mm (3in) design from Krupp and a 120mm (4.7in) howitzer from St Chamond in France. The 75mm Model 1905 was first bought complete from Krupp, then in components for assembly by Cockerill and the Cannon Foundry, and finally all components except the barrel came from Krupp while the barrel was made in Belgium from material procured from Britain. It was a conventional enough design, using a hydro-spring recoil system, and fired a 14.3lb (6.5kg) shell to a range of 8,750yd (8,000m).

The 120mm howitzer was adopted in 1913, but relatively few had been supplied by St Chamond before war broke out. A box-trail carriage, it offered 40 degrees elevation for the howitzer, used a hydro-pneumatic recoil system, and fired a 44lb (20kg) shell to about 7,000yd (6,400m).

Almost all of both these equipments were lost to the Germans in the early stages of the war; subsequently the Belgian Army was equipped by

France with their standard weapons, the 75mm Mle 1897 gun and the 120mm Mle 1911 Schneider howitzer.

SERBIA

Serbia had no heavy engineering industry at all prior to 1914 and bought all its military equipment abroad. The principal supplier was France, and its artillery was therefore entirely of French origin. There were two 75mm (3in) field guns, the Model 1906 and the Model 1911, both made by Schneider; two 120mm (4.7in) howitzers, the Model 1897 and Model 1911, also by Schneider; and a 70mm (2.76in) mountain gun Model 1907, another Schneider design.

The Model 1906 gun was of conventional design, using a hydro-pneumatic recoil system, a rectangular steel pole trail and shield. The 31-calibre gun fired a 14lb (6.4kg) shell to a maximum range of 8,000yd (7,300m). This gun was more or less a stock Schneider design and very similar to guns supplied around the same time to Spain and Portugal.

The Model 1912 was actually the same gun which the French had adopted as their horse artillery gun. Having it in production for the French army at a fairly low rate, Schneider were doubtless able to offer a good price to Serbia and deliveries began in 1912, though the number supplied is not known.

The Schneider 120mm howitzer Model 1897 was an elderly design with no recoil control apart from a sprung spade. The gun was trunnioned directly to the carriage and, as with most Schneider designs, traverse was by moving the trail across the axle. Nevertheless, it allowed 45 degrees of elevation and could fire its 46lb (20.9kg) shell to a range of 7,275yd (6,650m), which was quite good performance by 1897 standards. Thirty-six of these howitzers were supplied in 1897, but with tension building up in the Balkans more were needed and this led to the purchase of a number of Model 1911 howitzers. These were similar to the equipments that had been adopted by Belgium; in its original

A 3in (75mm) Schneider M1906 field gun as used by the Serbian army.

form it fired a 47lb shell to a range of 7,325yd; later improvements in the ammunition stretched the range to 8,750yd, but it is doubtful if the Serbian Army ever got that far with it.

The 70mm mountain gun M1907 was more or less the same weapon as supplied to Italy and Spain as their M1908 model. It was of the usual dismantling type, coming into five mule-loads, and with the usual hinged trail which could be folded back for the fitting of shafts for horse draught. It fired a 11lb (21.3kg) shell to a maximum range of 5,500yd (5,000m).

The Serbian Army put up a remarkable performance in the opening phase of the war, repelling the Austrian army no less than three times before being finally invaded by a combined Austro-German force. But in November 1915 it was trapped in the Plain of Kossovo and torn to shreds, the survivors marching out through the Albanian mountains, leaving all their equipment behind them. When the army was re-formed in 1916 and sent to Salonika, it was entirely equipped with standard French or British guns, depending upon which army the regiments were attached to.

3   Heavy Artillery

As we have already said, in 1914 heavy artillery was still very much considered the 'siege train', a slow-moving tail to the field army, which was only called upon to perform if the enemy shut himself up inside a fortress. Bearing in mind that every European frontier was liberally provided with armed and garrisoned fortresses, there was still something to be said for this point of view, and the course of the war, particularly on the Eastern Front, certainly justified the retention of siege artillery. But the South African War and the Russo-Japanese War had also pointed to the need for a more mobile form of heavy support artillery and some tentative moves in that direction had been taken by the major European armies. The simple reason for not taking heavy artillery into the field had been the problem of moving such loads with horse traction; there is a limit to the number of these animals which will work in concert, and that automatically sets a limit to the size of gun, for even if the carriage could be transported in pieces, the gun could not. (Britain had tried jointed howitzers of up to 8in calibre in the 1880s, but these had proved to be impractical.) But by about 1910 motor vehicles capable of hauling considerable loads were in existence, and most armies had made some tentative experiments. Austria took two 9.45in howitzers on manoeuvres in 1912, and the French took a battery of 120mm siege guns, one of 22cm siege howitzers and one 28cm howitzer to their autumn manoeuvres in the same year. In 1913 it was reported that the Austrians had actually taken a 12in howitzer into the field behind motor tractors. And also in 1913 the *Journal of the Royal Artillery* reported that 'the Krupp 6in howitzer

supplied to Italy has a motor limber for use on the road, while horses are employed to take it into position.'

It is interesting to speculate how heavy artillery might have developed during the war years had the Russo-Japanese War not been fought; for it was this war in which the Japanese uprooted a dozen of their 28cm coast defence howitzers, transported them to the docks by means of wheeled trailers dragged by hundreds of men, shipped them to Korea (losing the first shipment to a Russian minefield) and then laboriously dragged them, again by hundreds of men, to positions on the hills around Port Arthur. There they opened a bombardment upon the forts and upon the Russian fleet lying at anchor in the harbour protected from attack (as they thought) by their coast defence guns. This led some people to wonder what might be achieved in less formidable country with motor traction, and led to the 42cm and 30.5cm howitzers which hammered Liège, Maubeuge and Brest-Litovsk into surrender in 1914. And with those monsters as their examples, designers realized that there was no longer such a rigid limit upon the size of ordnance; if you could dismantle it until the heaviest item was within the draught capabilities of a road tractor, it was capable of being taken to the battlefield. It also allowed ballisticians to speculate on what they might be able to achieve, given a big enough gun. By 1909 Professor Rausenberger of Krupp's was postulating a long-barrelled gun which would fire a shell across the Alps; not that he had any ill-will towards the Italians, it was simply an intriguing ballistic problem. And it undoubtedly played a part in his development of the 21cm Paris Gun in 1917.

A Japanese 28cm howitzer Model 1890 firing against the fortress of Port Arthur in 1904; the deployment of such enormous weapons with a field army opened the eyes of many people. Over 100 of these coast defence mortars were still in operational service in 1945.

Perhaps some designers on the Allied side also postulated enormous guns in the 1905–14 period, and there are certainly hints in various writings which suggest this, but nothing came of them. The general view of future warfare was one of mobility, and therefore ponderous weapons requiring special transportation and weeks of work held no attraction. Light howitzers for the field army, heavier guns for the siege train; that was the end of the argument.

But wars have a way of imposing their own conditions, and after the 'Race to the Sea' was run and the trench lines struck, the entire Western Front took on the aspect of a siege, from whichever side you looked at it. The siege trains were therefore brought forward, and it was immediately apparent that the siege train capable of encircling a fort was far from sufficient to spread across miles of front. More heavy guns were necessary. The French, with the highest proportion of troops and front line, resurrected long-forgotten cannons from every quarter of the country; the British, with a smaller force to support, were slightly less pressed and

therefore had no need to plunder the museums and scrap-yards, but put all the resources they could spare on to the job of building proven designs as fast as they could. The Russians, fighting a much more fluid war, initially had less call for heavy guns, but as the pace slowed down and as the Germans began putting heavier artillery into the field, they had to maintain a balance. Fortunately, by that time the factories of Britain and France were functioning and the Russians were supplied with heavy guns by both countries.

Italy had time to get things together, and, faced with the prospect of having to deal with a chain of Alpine fortresses if they were to make an impression on the Austrians, they had an adequate supply of heavy guns at the start of their war, although, like everyone else, what was adequate on Day One was less so by Day One Hundred and One, and the arsenals and factories were soon busy keeping up the numbers. And the Americans, of course, had no heavy artillery worth speaking of, ignored what was going on in France, and had their work cut out when the need arose in 1917.

BRITAIN

The British Expeditionary Force took three types of heavy gun to France. The Divisional heavy batteries were armed with 60-pounder guns, the Territorial Force had some obsolescent 5in howitzers, and the siege batteries of the Royal Garrison Artillery had the equally obsolescent 6in 30-cwt howitzers. The only other heavy weapons the army possessed were eight obsolete 9.45in Skoda howitzers which had been purchased during the Boer War, had never been used, and which were only fit for use as training weapons; a small number of 6in guns; and a single 9.2in howitzer which had been produced to the Army's specification by the Coventry Ordnance Works and which was, at the outbreak of war, still undergoing its acceptance trials.

The 60-pounder gun, of 5in (127mm) calibre, was a relatively modern weapon, having been introduced in 1904. Experience with the 4.7in (120mm) guns in the Boer War had shown the need for a heavy support gun, and a 5in calibre 60lb (27.3kg) shell had been chosen as being the right combination of lethality and ballistic performance. The gun was designed by the Elswick Ordnance Company (Armstrong's) and the result was a conventional box trail, two-wheeled equipment but with the ability to disconnect the top carriage, cradle and gun and pull the whole assembly back across the trail for travelling, so as to distribute the weight more evenly between the two gun wheels and the two wheels of a removable limber which supported the trail end. This 60-pounder Mark I fired its shell (either shrapnel or high explosive) at 2,080ft/sec to reach a maximum range of 10,300yd (9,400m). By 1914, forty-one of these had been made and issued, thirteen of which were in Canada or India, the rest with the BEF.

As soon as war broke out orders were given to produce more of these useful weapons; but this posed a problem. The original design had never been intended for rapid production in wartime, and some changes had to be made in the interests of faster manufacture. The construction of the actual

The 60-pounder gun with 'traction engine' wheels. This one is also fitted with an 'engine draught connector' on the end of the trail for hooking it up to a traction engine.

The 60-pounder on Mark III carriage, less cumbersome than its forerunner and with rubber-tyred wheels.

gun body was simplified, and the carriage was simplified by doing away with the running-back arrangement for transport. In place of this, and so as to support a greater weight, the gun wheels became 'traction engine' pattern, 5ft (1.5m) in diameter and 1ft (30.5cm) wide. This added another ton to the weight, which put it above the limit for horse draught, and so batteries which received this Mark II carriage were also provided with Holt caterpillar tractors to tow the guns.

But an all-up weight of over 5 tons was really excessive for a gun of this size, and complaints were soon heard about the frequency with which the wheels sank into the ground and had to be dug out. So in 1915 work began on a Mark III carriage. This reverted to the earlier idea of redistributing the weight for transport, but did it in a much simpler manner. The gun was simply disconnected from its recoil system piston rods and pulled back in the cradle to the fully-recoiled position. There it was clamped to a bracket on the trail, lessening the weight on the gun wheels and making it rather more manoeuvrable. Existing Mark II carriages were withdrawn, as opportunity offered, and converted to Mark III type.

The performance of the 60-pounder was gradually improved by the adoption of better ammunition, particularly shells with a more streamlined shape. This eventually raised the maximum range to 12,300yd (11,240m). But more range was still

desired, and so in 1916 work began on a completely new design with a longer barrel, greater elevation (35 degrees instead of 21.5 degrees) and a better-proportioned trail. The breech mechanism was also improved and the recoil mechanism was hydro-pneumatic and retained the ability to disconnect the gun and pull it back along the trail for travelling. This new Mark II gun on Mark IV carriage weighed slightly more than the original design but was capable of 15,500yd (14,160m) range. However, design, development and production were a slow business; although the carriage was approved in June 1917 the gun's approval did not come until mid-1918, and only four had been built before the Armistice.

The 5in howitzer, fielded by the Territorial heavy batteries, had first seen action in the Nile campaigns of 1897-98, and it acquired a reputation for accuracy and shell-power. The adoption of the 6in 30-cwt howitzer (below) relegated it to the reserve and the Territorial Force. It saw service in France in 1914-15, being replaced by the 4.5in QF howitzer, whereupon it was relegated once more, this time to become a training weapon. Some sixty were sent to Russia, and another fifteen to Italy, though the latter appear never to have been used.

The 6in 30-cwt howitzer which replaced the 5in in regular batteries introduces a peculiarity of British ordnance nomenclature which is of some importance: the addition to the title of the gun's

Laying a 60-pounder; the gunlayer looks through his dial sight while everybody else heaves on the left wheel, so as to slew the gun round until the layer can use his on-carriage traverse.

weight – not the weight of the entire equipment, just the weight of the barrel and breech mechanism. This system was adopted in order to distinguish guns of similar calibre but different performance and using different ammunition. In this case, '30-cwt'(3,360lb, or 1.5 tons) distinguished the gun from another 6in howitzer in British service – a 6in 25-cwt used by the Army in India. And, as will be seen, a third pattern was to appear in due course.

The 6in 30-cwt had been designed to fill two roles: that of a heavy field weapon and that of a heavy siege weapon. In the former role it was mounted on a conventional carriage, similar to but bigger than the 5in howitzer. The barrel moved in a ring cradle controlled by an hydro-spring recoil system, the springs appearing very prominently beneath the barrel. The carriage was a simple two-wheeled affair, with the cradle trunnioned directly into the trail side-pieces and with no provision for traverse other than physically shifting the trail. The maximum elevation reached on this carriage was 35 degrees, giving a range, with a 118.5lb (53.8kg) shell, of 5,200yd (4,750m).

For use in the siege role, where high angle plunging fire was desired in order to get behind fortified defences, an entirely different carriage was provided. Once the gun's position had been determined, the first step was to lay a 'Platform, Siege, Double-Decked, Mark II', which was simply a heavy platform, 12ft square, made of wooden planks in three layers, bolted together. A 'bed', a round steel casting with an upstanding pivot, was then bolted down to the platform.

A gyn, or simple wooden tripod hoist, was then erected over the platform and the howitzer pushed on to the platform. The barrel and cradle were removed by use of the gyn, then the trail was lifted up and the wheels and axles removed. The trail was then lowered until it rested on the steel bed, the pivot pin locating into a socket in the trail. The rear end of the trail was supported on blocks of wood. A 'carriage top' was then brought up and lifted on to the trail; this was a triangular structure with trunnion sockets, and it bolted rigidly to the trail. Now the howitzer and cradle were lifted again, swung over the carriage top and lowered

The 60-pounder Gun

The 60-pounder Mark I at full recoil.

The 60-pounder Mark III drawn back on the trail by disconnecting the recoil system, so distributing the weight between the gun and limber wheels.

The 60-pounder was developed as a result of the South African War. The 6.1in (155mm) 'Long Tom' guns of the Boers had outranged the British field artillery, and the naval 4.7in (120mm) had been brought in to redress the balance, while 6in naval guns were put on railway trucks, though they were too late to do much. This showed the need for a heavy field piece, and the RA Heavy Battery Committee sat down and drew up a specification. As already noted, Parliament decreed the 4.7in, which delayed the funding and introduction of the 60-pounder.

The 60-pounder Gun Continued

The 60-pounder Mark III in the firing position.

Three designs, from different makers, were tested in 1903; the guns were satisfactory but the carriages were not, and the Committee called for fresh designs. A series of severe travelling and rough-use trials followed, modifications were made, and eventually, in 1905, the 60-pounder was approved, though it was half a ton over the recommended 'four tons behind the team' weight limit. In order to equalize the weight on the gun and limber wheels when travelling, the gun, cradle and top carriage could be pulled along the trail and locked in place. This was a satisfactory system as far as operation of the gun went, but neither the carriage nor the gun were well adapted to wartime mass production, and as soon as wartime manufacture was needed, steps were taken to simplify things.

The gun, originally a wire-wound piece with a removable 'Inner A Tube' and breech bush was simplified by doing away with these and simply cutting the breech screw into the 'A' tube. The carriage was redesigned by doing away with the ability to shift the gun, and in order to support the weight on the gun wheels they were increased in size. The whole equipment gained one ton in weight and mechanical traction became a necessity.

Even with a Holt tractor doing the pulling, the weight caused the gun wheels to bog down more often than not, and a fresh design was begun in 1916. The gun shift was brought back, but this time it was done by simply uncoupling the gun from the recoil system rods and pulling it back in its cradle. This became the Mark III carriage, and the earlier Mark II versions were modified to this standard as and when opportunity offered.

An interesting point is that the Heavy Battery Committee had decided on the 60-pounder as a result of its 'superior shell power'. Yet, on examination, we find that the 4.7 shell actually held more Lyddite (6lb 13oz; 3.1kg) than

The 60-pounder Gun Continued

did the original 60-pounder shell (4lb). This was rapidly improved into a Mark II shell with 7½lb (3.4kg) of Lyddite, but one is still left wondering where the original claim of shell power came from.

During the war years the 60-pounder was provided with amatol-filled HE, shrapnel, smoke and gas shells in many varieties. It continued in service, using only the Mark III carriage, after the war and was finally made obsolete in June 1944, though a handful lingered on as training guns until early 1945.

DATA: Ordnance BL 60pr Gun Mk I on Carriage Field BL 60pr Gun Mk I

Calibre	5in	Total weight	9,856lb
Weight of gun	4,480lb	Recoil	55in
Length of gun	168.05 in	Elevation	−5° to +21½°
Length of bore	32 calibres	Traverse	4° right and left
Rifling grooves	24	Shell weight	60lb
Rifling twist	RH, 1/30	Muzzle velocity	2,080ft/sec
Breech	Screw, percussion	Max range	12,300yd

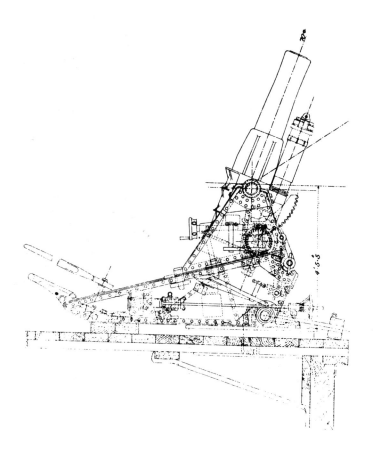

A handbook drawing of the 6in 30cwt howitzer on siege platform, allowing it a maximum elevation of 70 degrees in return for several hours of hard work.

until the trunnions entered their sockets and could be secured there by bolting down the capsquares. Finally, an 'anchorage buffer', a massive volute compression spring device, was bolted to the front of the trail and the front edge of the platform, so that any liability of the trail to move back was firmly resisted. The gyn was then removed and the siege howitzer was ready for action. In this configuration it could reach 70 degrees elevation, had virtually unlimited traverse by swinging the trail end from side to side around the bed pivot, and could reach to a maximum range of 7,000yd. Diligent study of the records has, however, failed to indicate whether this system was ever employed in France.

It probably was not, because the prime complaint about the 6in 30-cwt howitzer was its lack of range, suggesting that it was always fired off its field carriage. For this and other reasons a completely fresh design was begun in January 1915; trials were fired at the Eskmeals proof ground in July, and by December 1915 695 new howitzers had been built and delivered, the sort of production history which today sounds like a fairy-story. The new weapon became the 6in (152mm) 26-cwt howitzer, even though the barrel and breech weighed only 25.5cwt, so as to distinguish it from the other two members of the family.

The principal improvement lay in the ability to elevate to 45 degrees and thus launch its 100lb (45.4kg) shell to 9,500yd (8,680m) or a lighter 86lb (39kg) shell to 11,400yd (10,420m), a very good performance by the standards of 1915. The breech mechanism was improved, a new hydro-pneumatic recoil system fitted, and for all that the weight of the complete equipment only went up by 3cwt (153kg). It became the sturdy workhorse of the heavy batteries, and by the end of the war no fewer than 3,633 had been built and issued, and ammunition expenditure in France and Flanders amounted to over 22 million rounds.

The small number of 6in guns in existence were more or less trial pieces. During the South African War Captain (later Admiral Sir) Percy Scott RN

A battery of 6in 26-cwt howitzers in France, 1917.

71

6in 26cwt Howitzer

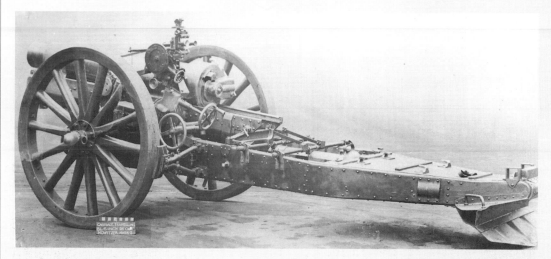

The 6in 26cwt howitzer, left rear.

The 6in 26cwt howitzer, right front.

6in 26cwt Howitzer Continued

Australian gunners about to load a 6in 26cwt howitzer.

The 6in 30-cwt howitzer in service in 1914 was an antiquated design with a slow breech mechanism and a hydro-spring recoil system which was largely exposed to the elements and which choked down the recoil far too violently. Without its siege carriage its range was poor, and as a result something better was soon in demand. The result was this 6in 26-cwt weapon.

Considering the amount of technical improvement in this model, its speed of production is astonishing. Design began in January 1915; the first prototype was proof fired on 30 July 1915, and by the end of the year 695 complete equipments had been built and were in service. By November 1918 3,633 had been built, and a further 713 had been relined, repaired and reissued, of which 1,246 were in action with British batteries, 212 had been supplied to various allies, and the rest were either in use as training guns or in reserve stocks. Total ammunition expenditure on the Western Front by the 6in 26-cwt howitzer, from its introduction to the end of the war, was no less than 22.4 million rounds, which gives some indication of the value and utility of the weapon.

6in 26cwt Howitzer Continued

Among the improvements was an 'Asbury' breech mechanism; this means a multi-step screw on a swinging carrier and a vertical breech lever, which when simply pulled down upon was sufficient to open the breech. This replaced the three-distinct-and-separate-movements type of breech on the earlier howitzers, and speeded up the rate of fire. The recoil system was a hydro-pneumatic one of such simplicity and efficiency that it was virtually copied as it stood for the 4.5in and 5.5in medium guns of the Second World War. It varied its stroke according to the elevation, and even at maximum elevation there was 2ft (610mm) of movement to soak up the recoil. The box trail allowed some traverse, which the earlier weapons were denied. The maximum range was lifted from 5,200yd (4,750m) to 9,500yd (8,700m), and during the war an 85lb (38.6kg) shell was developed which allowed the range to be increased to 11,400yd (10,400m). And yet all this improvement added only 784lb (356kg) to the all-up weight.

As with other wartime designs, the 6in 26-cwt stayed in service after 1919 and soldiered on to serve with distinction in North Africa in 1941-42 and in Burma in 1944, before being declared obsolete in October 1945.

DATA: Ordnance BL 6in 26cwt Howitzer Mk I on Carriage, Travelling, Mk I

Calibre	6in		Total weight	8,142lb
Weight of gun	2,856lb		Recoil	24–54in
Length of gun	87.55in		Elevation	0° to +45°
Length of bore	13.3 calibres		Traverse	4° right and left
Rifling grooves	36		Shell weight	100lb
Rifling twist	RH, 1/15		Muzzle velocity	1,235ft/sec
Breech	Screw, percussion		Max range	9,500yd

A 6in 26-cwt howitzer in Palestine, 1916, being towed by a Holt tractor. The two men behind the gun are operating the individual wheel brakes whenever the tractor stops, to prevent the gun's weight pulling it backwards.

commanded a Naval brigade in the field, the guns of which were removed from warships and mounted on extemporized field carriages largely made from timber. Among these were some 6in guns, which did good service, and after the war a few mountings were made up in Woolwich Arsenal from steel and issued in order to find out if there appeared to be any future in the design. These were, incorrectly, known as 'Percy Scott carriage guns' and were sent to France early in 1915, making their debut at Neuve Chapelle in March. They were cumbersome, and the limitations of the carriage restricted the maximum range, and in early 1916 the Director-General of Munitions Development asked for an improved design which would give at least 30 degrees of elevation and thus more range. The gun was the standard 6-in (152mm) Mark VII, widely used in coast defence, and the new 'Travelling Carriage Mark II' which appeared early in 1917 was simply an improved version of the Scott design. It gave the desired elevation and reached a maximum range of 13,700yd (12,520m) with a 100lb (45.4kg) shell. A distinct drawback was that the recoil system was the hydro-spring pattern designed for use on coast mountings, which were anchored solidly into concrete. On a field mounting they absorbed too little of the recoil force and thus the entire carriage rolled back when the gun fired; in order to control this, large wooden ramps were built and placed behind the gun-wheels, so that the carriage recoiled up the ramps and then ran back down again after firing. Over a hundred were built, but at 25 tons weight they were far too heavy for convenient movement in the conditions which obtained in France and Flanders, and they were eventually superseded by a lighter equipment. By the end of the war only fifty-four were left, and these were rapidly declared obsolete in 1919.

The lighter replacement was requested in May 1916 and the quickest solution appeared to be to lighten the existing Mark VII gun by rebuilding the outer hoops and jacket, so reducing the gun weight by three tons, building a new cradle and hydro-pneumatic recoil system, and then dropping the result into the carriage of the 8in (203mm) howitzer. This became the 6in (150mm) Mark XIX gun and was first fired in October 1916. It had a maximum elevation of 38 degrees, giving it a range of 18,750yd (17,140m), and it began replacing the Mark VII gun, 108 having been built and issued by the Armistice.

In 1910 the Royal Artillery Committee had asked for a design of heavy siege howitzer and, being familiar with the shell-power of the 9.2in coast gun, suggested 9.2in as a useful calibre for a howitzer. The Coventry Ordnance Works received the contract and set about developing an entirely new design. It was completed early in 1914 and the first pre-production model had been delivered in the summer to the artillery range near Rhyader, in Wales, there to undergo a variety of acceptance tests. Formal approval of the design was given in July 1914, but manufacture of the howitzers had already begun by this time: specimens marked 'RGF 1913', the mark of the Royal Gun Factory at Woolwich Arsenal, have been seen. In August the original was packed up and sent to France. It saw its first major action at Neuve Chapelle in early 1915 and became familiarly known as 'Mother' throughout the Regiment. By the end of 1916 233 complete equipments had been delivered.

The 9.2in (234mm) Mark I howitzer was a robust design which had been well thought out before the first metal was cut. It began with a segment-shaped ground platform built up from steel sections. On top of this was the gun carriage, pivoted to the platform at its front end and traversed from side to side by a spur gear on the rear end coupling into a toothed rack on the ground platform, the weight of the carriage being supported on rollers. The recoil system was a hydro-pneumatic design in which a 'floating piston' kept the oil and compressed air apart; this was the first application of this idea and it proved so successful in the field that it rapidly became the standard British system.

For movement, the equipment broke down into three basic loads, each carried on a separate wagon. The barrel and breech formed the first load, weighing 5.25 tons; the carriage, cradle and recoil

A 6in Mark XIX gun in France. Note the gunlayer and his dial sight well above everything else. The drill book said the ramps were to be laid behind the wheels, but doubtless they had a reason for putting them in front – though I have to say that it escapes me.

system formed the second load, 5.5 tons; and the ground platform the third, at 4.25 tons. The ground platform was removed piecemeal from its wagon and assembled in place. A gyn was then erected over it and the second load brought in beneath. The carriage was hoisted into the air, the wagon removed, and the carriage lowered on to the platform. Then the howitzer wagon was brought into position and locked in place so that the barrel could be winched off and into its place in the cradle.

The principal defect of this weapon from the gunners' point of view was that because of being kept short in order to keep it compact enough for horse draught, the carriage had a distinct tendency to rear up in the air when the howitzer fired, so in order to keep it down an 'earth box' was provided. This steel box was bolted together and bolted to the front end of the platform. It was then filled with nine tons of earth, manually shovelled into it. And when the time came to move on, why, nine tons of earth had to be shovelled back out of it.

Once in action, the 9.2in Mark I fired a 290lb (132kg) high explosive shell to a maximum range of 10,050yd (9,186m). Again, this was quite satisfactory performance by 1913 standards, but by 1915 it was felt that more range would be

The original 9.2in Mark I howitzer during its acceptance trials, which accounts for the ammunition truck and other debris. Note, too, that the earth box has been neatly filled with sandbags.

The 9.2in howitzer in its three transport loads: barrel, bed and carriage. The three are linked together for towing by one Holt tractor.

The 9.2in Mark II howitzer, showing some detail differences from the earlier model and with the earth box filled with earth

A Battery of 9.2in Mark II howitzers in action.

advantageous. Examination of the design did not reveal any convenient short-cut to improving the performance, so a completely fresh design was begun in 1916. However, the Mark I was never supplanted by its successor and continued in service until the war ended.

The successor was the 9.2in (234mm) Mark II howitzer, designed by Vickers to meet a demand for a weapon capable of reaching to 14,000yd (12,800m) range. The significant difference lay in the ordnance, which was 17.3 calibres long (159.16in; 405.4cm) instead of the 13.2 calibres (121.5in; 309cm) of the Mark I. This pushed the range up to 13,935yd (12,740m), close enough to the specified 14,000yd to be acceptable. The carriage was more or less the same as that of the Mark I howitzer, with some minor changes to facilitate manufacture and assembly and a stronger recoil system, and the size of the earth box went up to a capacity of 11 tons.

These, therefore, were the guns actually in being at the outbreak of war and their descendants which

appeared during the course of the war. But they were not enough; other designs were needed. As early as October 1914 orders were placed for thirty-two 12in howitzers and for an unspecified number of 8in howitzers.

The 8in weapons were frankly designed as stopgap weapons, and the 'design' was simply a matter of converting whatever stock of elderly 6in (150mm) guns could be culled from the army and navy reserves of obsolescent designs. These old 6in guns, of various patterns and marks, were cut down in length and bored out to take a 200lb (90.8kg) 8in (203mm) shell. The carriages were equally varied; some were from old 6in (150mm) siege gun mountings, others based on the Percy Scott 6in gun carriage, others assembled from parts of old siege carriages and parts of naval gun mountings. Eventually there were five marks of howitzer and five marks of carriage, all of which were simple box-trail types with two huge 'traction engine' wheels. Every combination had a different weight, but the two common figures were

An early mark of 8in howitzer in its gunpit near Albert, July 1916

On the move; a battery of 8in howitzers, somewhere in France.

An 8in howitzer Mark VI, with a shell on the loading tray.

the maximum elevation of 45 degrees and the maximum range of 10,500yd (9,600m). As they wore out, they were discarded, but many lasted throughout the war and they were all made obsolete in 1919.

Once the immediate need had been filled by the Marks I to V howitzers described above, attention was turned to the provision of something rather more efficient and a little more elegant, and in August 1915 Vickers were requested to produce a fresh design capable of ranging to 10,500yd (9,600m) with the same 200lb (90.8kg) shell. A design was worked out and submitted within two months, manufacture of a prototype was authorized in November, and the first complete 8in (203mm) Mark VI howitzer left the works on 1 March 1916 for its proof firing, after which manufacture for service went ahead.

The design was quite straightforward; a box trail with a top carriage permitting 4 degrees of traverse each side of the centre-line, a cradle with hydro-pneumatic recoil system, traction-engine wheels and 50 degrees of elevation. The howitzer was of the same length as the Marks I–V, but had a faster

and more modern breech mechanism. This combination gave a maximum range of 10,750yd (9,825m), and although it still looked ungainly, it actually weighed some five tons less than the earlier designs.

Although the Mark VI was a more efficient design, it did not show very much improvement over its predecessors in maximum range, and as the war progressed so it was obvious that range was becoming a critical factor, since it either allowed fire deeper into enemy territory or it allowed the guns to be placed further back and out of the immediate hazards of the front line area. And so in June 1916 Vickers were again approached with a request to develop an improved 8in howitzer, this time with a range of 13,000yd One suspects that Vickers, being accustomed to the military tendency to come back periodically for improvements, had already set about forestalling this request; they were asked for a design on 24 June 1916 and submitted one on 8 July, a speed which suggests that the design was already up their sleeves, ready for producing when called for.

Preparing ammunition behind an 8in Mark VII howitzer in France.

The desired range had been achieved by lengthening the barrel to 17.3 calibres, but beyond that there was very little difference between this Mark VII and the earlier Mark VI. The design went into production in late 1916 as the Mark VII howitzer, but there were a number of minor modifications in the construction of the howitzer barrel which led to sub-marks of VII* and VII**, after which there was a major redesign, making the barrel somewhat heavier, which became the Mark 8 howitzer. But the ballistics and performance remained the same, a maximum muzzle velocity of 1,500ft/sec with a 200lb (90.8kg) shell, giving a maximum range of 12,300yd (11,240m). This finally became the 'definitive' 8in howitzer (and the last British design of such), and survived into the years of the Second World War.

The 12in (305m) howitzer was an entirely different matter; there was no existing weapon or carriage which could be cannibalized for this, since nothing of such a size had ever been contemplated before. But there was at least a suitable model, and when Armstrong's Elswick Ordnance Company were asked for a design, they took the short way out and simply scaled-up the 9.2in Mark II howitzer. Eight complete equipments were delivered by August 1916 and were in action in France very soon after that.

The mounting (or siege carriage, as it was still known) was similar to the earlier 9.2in model, with an A-shaped ground platform carrying a front pivot, the gun carriage traversing on a roller race and a curved arc at the rear end. As before, the design had to be transportable, the carriage and

A 12in howitzer under camouflage in France.

platform were therefore short, and an earth box had to be attached to the front end of the platform, demanding no less than 20 tons of soil to be shovelled into it before firing could commence. It was moved in six loads: barrel; cradle, carriage; platform; earth box; and miscellaneous components. Assembly was done in an ingenious system of interconnection of the transport wagons so that the various components could be manipulated by winches. The platform was assembled in place on the ground, after which the carriage was slid down ramps from its wagon into place. Then the cradle wagon was brought close up to the carriage and the cradle slid off and dropped into the trunnion beds. After this the barrel wagon was brought up and attached to the platform; a screw jack beneath the wagon then lifted the barrel weight off the wagon springs until the barrel was precisely aligned with the cradle, whereupon it was winched off its wagon and into the cradle and the gun lugs securely bolted to the recoil pistons. A hand-operated crane was fitted at the rear end of the carriage to lift the shells on to a loading tray which was then pushed along rails until the nose of the shell entered the breech, after which the detachment manned a large rammer and drove the shell home into the bore.

The 12in (300mm) Mark II Howitzer (the Mark I was a railway mounting) fired a 750lb (340.5kg) shell by means of a 36lb (16.3kg) charge of cordite, giving it a maximum muzzle velocity of 1,196ft/sec and a maximum range of 11,340yd (10,360m). The maximum elevation possible was 70 degrees, but loading could only be performed with the barrel at 3 degrees elevation, so the barrel had to be manually depressed after every round had been fired and elevated once again after it had been loaded, a tedious business.

No sooner was this weapon in production than Vickers sat down to design its replacement, well aware that sooner or later there would be a call for more range. Again, they followed the path of the 9.2in design, lengthening the barrel by 4ft (122cm) and increasing the charge to 48lb (21.8kg) of cordite to achieve a range of 14,350yd (13,120m). The carriage was improved by the addition of larger

working platforms for the detachment and a second shell crane. So far as the gunners were concerned, the greatest improvement was the introduction of a power-operated rammer, probably the first such device ever used on a field equipment. This was mounted at the rear of the carriage and worked by compressed air. Sufficient air to ram the first shot was provided by a hand pump; after that an additional cylinder on top of the cradle, with a piston attached to the gun, pumped sufficient air during each recoil stroke to provide the necessary power for the next shell to be rammed. The rammer was aligned so that the gun had only to be brought down to 19 degrees elevation for loading, which speeded up the rate of fire slightly.

The 12in Mark IV Howitzer (the Mark III was another railway version) entered service in mid-1917. With that, the British heavy armoury was complete; heavier weapons were impractical for road use and were placed on railway truck mountings, described later.

The ultimate heavy weapon was the 15in (381mm) howitzer, privately developed by the Coventry Ordnance Works in 1914–15. Having built and tested this weapon, the question of getting it into service was addressed by Admiral Bacon, a director, informing the Admiralty. He probably expected the Admiralty to inform the War Office, but for reasons which doubtless seemed good at the time, Mr Winston Churchill, First Lord of the Admiraltry, elected to man it with Royal Marine Artillery and send it to France as part of the Naval brigade. He also ordered a further eleven howitzers to be built, which, upon completion, went to join the Marines in France. Admiral Bacon became a colonel of the Royal Marines and commanded the force.

By 1916 the Navy decided they had better things to do (Mr Churchill having left the Admiralty) and handed the howitzers over to the army. The army, less than delighted, asked the Ordnance Board for details of the weapons; the Ordnance Board were caustic: 'In view of the poor range achieved it is considered that these weapons are a waste of money and material.' A maximum range of

The 12in Howitzer

A 12in Mark II howitzer in action.

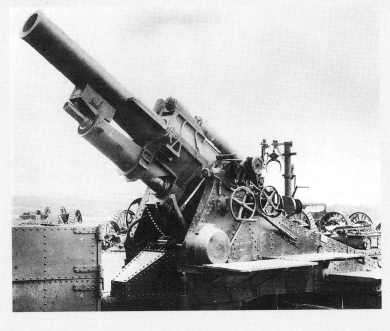

A 12in Mark II howitzer in action.

The 12in Howitzer Continued

Rear view of the 12in Mark IV, showing the shell hoists and loading trolley.

The family resemblance between this and the 9.2in howitzer points the fact that this was simply an enlarged version of that weapon, produced as being the easiest solution when thirty-two 12in howitzers were demanded in late 1914. This short cut allowed the first eight equipments to be shipped to France in 1916, and no time was wasted before getting them into action in the Ypres Salient in late May.

The howitzer travelled in six component parts on wagons drawn by tractors and was erected on site. First, a steel girder baseplate in a segment shape was laid on the ground and dug in. Then the carriage wagon was dragged across this baseplate and the carriage jacked down on to it, the pivot being connected so that the carriage could traverse around the segment through 60 degrees. The cradle was then hoisted into place on the carriage, and the gun wagon brought up behind the cradle and the gun barrel slid into it.

It seems probable that sixteen MarkII howitzers (the Mark I was a railway-mounted weapon) were made and issued, but before that order had been completed, work began on a better model, which was more or less similar but with a longer barrel and the addition of a powered rammer to assist in loading. This became the Mark IV howitzer, a generally 'cleaner' design with an improved breech and recoil system. Both versions had to have an 'earth

The 12in Howitzer Continued

box' bolted to the front end of the base platform and filled with 20 tons of soil to act as an anchor and prevent the platform being pulled out of the ground on recoil.

The number of Mark IV howitzers built is not known; there were twenty-two howitzers in action on the Western Front by the time of the Armistice, and several Mark IVs were retained after the war, the Mark IIs being made obsolete in 1921. They appeared again in 1939, two being sent to France and left there at Dunkirk. The remainder were deployed as invasion defence weapons along the East Coast and saw no further action. However, there was a brief flurry of interest in 1943; events in Italy, where concrete strongpoints proved impervious to field artillery, led to the development of a concrete-piercing shell for the 12in howitzer, but it is doubtful if any were ever made, and the weapon was declared obsolete in March 1945.

DATA: Ordnance BL 12in Howitzer Mk IV, on Carriage, Siege, BL 12in Howitzer, Mk II

Calibre	12in	Total weight	37.5 tons + 20 tons of earth
Weight of gun	20,440lb	Recoil	50in
Length of gun	222.35in	Elevation	+20° to +65°
Length of bore	17.3 calibres	Traverse	30° right and left
Rifling grooves	60	Shell weight	750lb
Rifling twist	RH, 1/15	Muzzle velocity	1,468ft/sec
Breech	Screw, percussion	Max range	14,350yd

One of the 15in howitzers in action. A list of 'battle honours' painted on the side mentions Aubers Ridge, Festubert and Loos in 1915 and 'The Bluff' in 1916.

10,795yd with a 1,400lb shell was really not worth the effort of shifting and erecting these monsters. A study showed that developing a lighter shell might add 2,000yd to the range but at the expense of accuracy, whereupon the army shrugged its shoulders and allowed the 15in to remain on strength, comfined to odd tasks where its short range was acceptable. They were declared obsolete in 1920.

FRANCE

The range of guns in the French heavy artillery armoury was large, due to the urgent demand which arose towards the end of 1914. This resulted in guns being taken from fortifications well away from any likelihood of attack and mounted in all sorts of carriages to act as a stop-gap until manufacture of more modern designs got under way. Inevitably the first such designs were lacking in range or refinement and were superseded by better models until an acceptable design was reached and standardized. But provided the gun could shoot it tended to remain in service, so that by the middle of 1917 there was a vast and varied collection of guns and howitzers in use. Thereafter the older models, as they wore out, were replaced by standardized models and by the end of the war the variety had considerably decreased.

The 145mm gun Mle 1916 was one of the extemporized designs, though it took rather a long time to come into service. The idea was born in early 1915, of taking a powerful 145mm naval gun built in the Naval arsenal at Ruelle, near Angouléme, and marrying it to a carriage constructed by the Forges et Acéries de la Marine et d'Homécourt, better known by their address of 'St Chamond'. The result was an awkward-looking equipment with what appears to be an abnormal amount of breech end behind the trunnions, doubtless in order to balance the 42-calibre barrel. The barrel moves inside a ring cradle, and behind the breech is a supporting framework for the loading tray, attached to the gun so that it recoils with it. Above and below the cradle are the cylinders of the hydro-pneumatic recoil system. The carriage was basically a box trail with dual wheels, but there was a small ground platform which could be planted beneath the gun and connected to the trail by a linkage; the wheels were then lifted from the ground by a wedge arrangement, connected to the front of the trail by a shock absorber, whereupon the trail could be fairly easily swung right and left, pivoting on the ground platform, to point the gun. A pit had to be dug beneath the trail to provide space for the breech to recoil into if the elevation exceeded 30 degrees; the maximum was 38 degrees at which angle the 33kg (72.6lb) shell ranged to 18,500m (20,165yd), a most useful performance.

Canon de 145–155 Mle 1916 St Chamond, an ungainly marriage between a naval gun and a field carriage, but with 18.5km range available nobody complained.

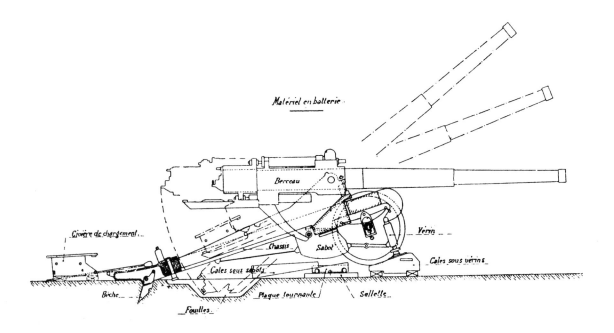

Diagram showing the 145–155mm gun emplaced.

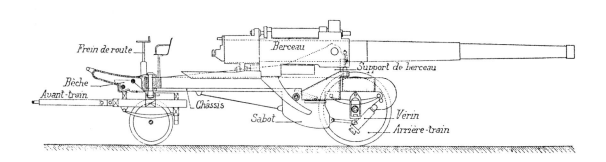

The 145–155mm gun limbered up for movement; note the well-sprung suspension, somewhat novel for 1915.

The 145mm Mle 1916 first appeared in the field during the Somme battles of 1916, and it remained in service throughout the war and for some time afterwards, most being sold to Romania in the 1920s. As the guns in service wore out, so they were taken back to the Ruelle arsenal and bored out to 155mm (6.1in) calibre and then returned to service as the 145/155mm Gun Mle 1916, in which guise it fired the 43kg (94.6lb) shell of the 155mm (6.1in) GPF gun to a range of 21,300m (23,220yd), outperforming the GPF by a considerable amount. But it was a good ton and a half heavier than the GPF and was more of a handful to bring into and out of action, so in postwar years the GPF was retained while the 145/155 was not.

The 6.1in (155mm) calibre first appeared in the French artillery in 1877, a 27-calibre gun built by De Bange, inventor of the obturating screw breech system, and it appears to have remained in service up until 1914. By that time it was quite outdated, but the barrels were still serviceable and they were removed from their non-recoil 1877 carriages, given an improved breech mechanism to permit firing by percussion (instead of friction tubes) and mounted on to a slightly modified version of the Schneider carriage developed for the 105mm gun Mle 1913 TR. In 1877 guise the gun had fired a 40kg (88lb) shell to 9,800m (10,680yd); after Schneider had finished with it, it fired a 43kg (94.6lb) shell to 13,600m (13,840yd).

However, the rebuilding of the Mle 1877 was simply not fast enough to meet the demand, and numbers were taken into service as they were, non-recoil carriage notwithstanding. As the barrels wore out they were replaced by a new barrel, of simpler design and with constant-twist rifling instead of increasing twist (easier to make) and a somewhat better breech mechanism. In this form they were known as the 155 gun Mle 1877/1916, and with a modern streamlined shell they could reach out to 12,700m.

The next pre-war venture into 155mm calibre was the Canon de 155 courte Mle 1904 Tir Rapide, designed by Colonel Rimailho. Rimailho had set out to produce a heavy-calibre gun with manoeuvrability and rate of fire, particularly at high angles, comparable to a field gun. He succeeded, but at the expense of considerable mechanical complication. The weapon itself was a conventional box-trail, two-wheeled carriage with a short howitzer barrel and hydro-pneumatic recoil system. The breech mechanism was of the screw type, using a brass cartridge case, and was officially described as 'automatic opening and semi-automatic closing', and this was the heart of Rimailho's design.

The breech-block carrier was attached to two rods which were fitted into tubes inside the recoil system body. As the barrel recoiled after firing, these rods were withdrawn from their tubes against spring pressure. When recoil stopped, the rods were

Look, no recoil system! The 6.1in Mle 1888 was used as a stop-gap gun until more modern designs became available.

The 155mm court Mle 1904 TR, Colonel Rimailho's masterpiece, is brought into action; first, place the shoes beneath the wheels and lower the trail en abatage.

locked in place by a catch. The barrel now began to return to its forward position, whereupon it drew the breech-block carrier forward on the rods. One rod had teeth, engaging a pinion on a shaft which, on its other end, had a pinion engaged in a semi-circular rack on the breech block. As a result, as the carrier moved forward, the pinion shaft was rotated, and the upper pinion rotated the breech block through a quarter of a turn to unlock the screw. At the instant it was fully unlocked, the carrier was held by another catch and the barrel continued forward to its firing position. The situation now was that the barrel was forward, the rods extended, and the breech block held on the rods sufficiently far back to permit loading. The fired cartridge case was held on the face of the breech-block by the extractor and could be removed by one of the gunners.

Loading was done by hand; the shell was entered into the chamber, its rear end resting on a small bracket formed at the rear of the breech ring and lying between the rods. The cartridge case was dropped on to a semi-circular collar on the face of the breech-block and held by the extractor. The catch holding the rods was then released by hand, and the power of the springs was sufficient to pull the rods back into their housing, so causing the breech block to run forward and ram the cartridge

Loading; the shell is partly into the breech, the cartridge case behind it, and both are in front of the breech screw. The gunner on the right will now release the catch, the round will be loaded and the breech closed.

90

The gun is loaded and laid, all that now remains is to fire it; five rounds a minute was the official claim.

A closer view of the 155mm TR, which illustrates another peculiar feature: the elevating arc is fixed to the carriage and the elevating handle and gears are fixed to the cradle, so that they wind up and down with the gun. Every other gun in the world fixes the arc to the cradle and the handwheel to the carriage. They do things differently in France.

and shell into the gun. As the block entered into its housing in the breech ring, the rods continued their forward movement and this, acting through the pinions as before, caused the breech block to be rotated a quarter-turn to lock.

Should the springs not have sufficient power to ram and close the breech, due to a high firing angle or dirt in the mechanism, a handwheel could be brought into engagement with a toothed rack on the undersurface of the right-hand rod, allowing a man to wind the rods fully home. The same mechanism

was used to open the breech in order to load the first round of a series.

It was a remarkable mechanism, and the most remarkable thing about it is that war experience showed it to be fool-proof and robust. But, as the official history said, it was unfortunate that the tactical theories which held sway when the gun was being designed did not envisage firing at ranges greater than 6,000m (6,540yd). With a maximum elevation of 41 degrees and a 40kg (88lb) shell, it delivered powerful and accurate plunging fire, but

The 155mm Mle 1917 and its detachment. The wheel on the front of the cradle was for a cable to pull the gun into battery from the travelling position.

The mud of France and Flanders caused a number of inventors to study ways of moving heavy equipment; this was a French solution to shifting the 155mm Mle 1917 across shell-torn ground. It appears reasonably practical, but it was never accepted.

The 155mm Longue Mle 1918, which was simply the 1888 barrel mounted on a modern carriage.

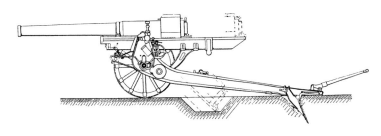

the conditions of the First World War soon showed that the range was insufficient, and whilst the existing howitzers were put to use, no more were built.

Having thus provided some stop-gap 155mm guns, Schneider then set about providing a much more versatile weapon, the 155mm Long Gun Mle

1917. As with most of their designs it was actually a gun-howitzer, being capable of low or high trajectory fire. The gun was derived from the Mle 1877/1914 but lengthened so as to improve the range by some 4,000m, while the carriage was essentially that of the same Mle 1877/1914, a two-wheeled box-trail type with shield. The cradle was extended behind the breech to give more support to the gun during recoil and also to assist in the assembly of the equipment, since it travelled in two sections. The carriage was towed by a horse team as one load, and the barrel on a special trailer by a second team. The barrel trailer was designed to be pushed across the trail of the carriage and connected to the cradle, whereupon the barrel could be winched from its trailer and into place on the carriage. For short-distance moves the barrel was disconnected from the recoil system and pulled back to the full-recoil position and fixed to the trail. This was then supported under the trail end by a two-wheeled limber. The gun could fire a 43kg (94.6lb) shell to a maximum range of 16,000m (17,440yd), a very useful performance.

It was later augmented by the Canon de 155mm Longue M1918, which was simply the barrel of the M1877/194 gun mounted on the carriage of the 155mm Short gun Model 1917. This, due to its shorter barrel, could only reach to 12,000m (13,000yd). with the same 43kg (94.6lb) shell.

Finally, and as a result of studying the performance of all these various 6.1in (155mm) weapons in the field, came the two which were destined to become standard not only with the French but also with the American and several other armies in post-war years: the Schneider 155mm M1917 howitzer and the Filloux 155mm M1917 gun.

It will be recalled that Schneider had developed a useful 4.1in (105mm) high velocity gun, based upon a carriage designed for a Russian 6in howitzer, a design which perfected a number of Schneider features. So it was logical for them to use it once again to produce a 155mm howitzer for the French Army in 1915. This was the Canon de 155 court Mle 1915, a conventional enough short gun placed on the carriage and recoil system of the 105mm M1913TR. This weapon was accepted for

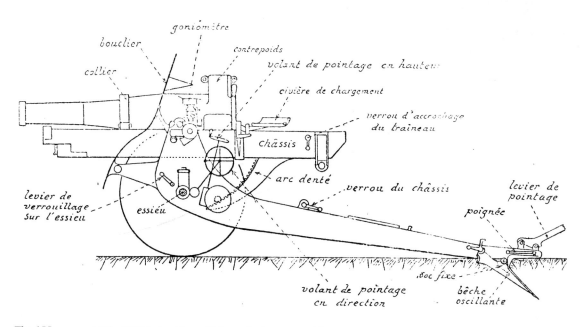

The 155mm court Mle 1915 Schneider, which used a brass cartridge case.

The 155mm court Mle 1917 was the same as the 1915, but used bag charges and gradually replaced the earlier design.

service in 1916 and first entered the war in the summer of 1917. It fired a 43.5kg (95.7lb) shell to a range of 11,500m (12,540yd).

The Model 1915 used a brass cartridge case, and this became something of an economic burden. Not only was it expensive to produce, it used a material which was fast becoming critical – due to the vast quantity of brass cases required for everything from pistols upwards – and packing it was something of a problem; a dented case generally refused to enter the chamber of the gun. There was also the enormous problem of collecting the used cases and sending them back for cleaning, resizing and refilling. It was therefore decided to alter the design to use a resilient pad for sealing the breech and linen bags for the cartridge powder. A second model, known as the Canon de 155 court Mle 1917, was developed and put into production in 1917 and this eventually supplanted the Mle 1915 to become the standard French 155mm howitzer, remaining in service throughout the Second World War.

The Canon de 155mm Longue Mle 1917 GPF marked the entrance of the French government arsenals into the 155mm field. This gun was designed by Lt. Col. Filloux and manufactured first at the Puteaux arsenal, then by the Renault factory under contract. Approved in late 1916, the first of these guns went into action in August 1917 and like the Schneider howitzer it remained in use in various parts of the world until after 1945.

GPF stands for 'Grand Puissance, Filloux' – high power, designed by Filloux – and his aim was to provide the maximum possible elevation and traverse without having to move the gun. He used a split trail, giving 60 degrees of traverse and 35 degrees of elevation. The gun was a completely new design, though using the Schneider breech mechanism, and fired a charge which gave a maximum velocity of 725m/sec and threw a 43.5kg (95.7lb) shell to a maximum range of 16,200m (17,660yd). There was a suggestion, in 1918, to adopt a different form of rifling and

155mm Schneider Howitzer M1917

The 155mm Mle 1917 howitzer; this is an American-made model, in their camouflage paint scheme.

The breech of the 155mm Mle 1917 howitzer. The firing lanyard operates the hammer below the breech-block, which strikes the primer-holder in the block's centre.

Although called a short gun, this is more generally described as a howitzer, and it became the principal heavy howitzer of the French artillery during the war years. It was also adopted by the American Army as the M1917 and later manufactured in the USA. In postwar years it was distributed all over Europe to arm emergent states and replace wartime losses.

This weapon started out as a private design by Schneider to meet a Russian contract, and it became the 6in M1910 howitzer in the Tsar's army. Schneider put a lot of thought into the design and the result was a most serviceable weapon. When war broke out Schneider offered it to the French Army who, in desperate need, accepted it in spite of what they considered to be a drawback – it fired a brass-cased charge, and the French were not in favour of cartridge cases in such large calibres. Nevertheless, they took it on as the 'Canon de 155mm Court, Mle 1915S' but asked Schneider to be kind enough to get

155mm Schneider Howitzer M1917 Continued

busy and design a fresh one using bag charges. The demands on Schneider for every kind of artillery meant that this redesign was delayed for some time, during which production of the 1915S went ahead and the gun went into service. Eventually the new design was completed – it really involved no more than redesigning the breech mechanism to use the De Bange pad system of sealing, and it is practically identical to the breech end of the 6.1in (155mm) GPF – and it was introduced late in 1916 as the Mle 1917S. It gradually replaced the 1915S, most of which went back to the factory to be reworked into 1917s, and such was the production that it almost replaced all the other odds and ends of 155mm howitzers which had been accumulated. One authority quotes wartime production as being, 3,020 howitzers, apart from those converted from the earlier model.

There is little that is novel on this weapon, apart from the Schneider idea of putting a retaining catch in the chamber to hold the shell until the rammer is in place behind it. A loading tray hinged to the left side of the cradle was originally fitted; this was swung over after the breech was opened and the shell placed on it by the two ammunition men. The layer and the breech operator pushed the shell off the tray and into the chamber, by which time the ammunition men had dropped their shell tongs and grabbed the rammer to finish the job. The bag charge was then loaded, and the tray then had to be swung clear before the breech would close. This, though, turned out to be something of a nuisance, and fairly quickly the idea was dropped in favour of a simple loading tray which could be lifted on to the cradle when needed and taken away when not.

How the howitzer travelled depended on how it was drawn; if it had an eight-horse team, then the barrel was pulled back along the trail and the trail end supported on a two-wheeled limber. If it was tractor-drawn, the gun stayed where it was and the trail was simply hooked straight on to the tractor.

In 1939 the French Army still had 2,043 of these weapons in service, and so did many other armies; they could still be found in obscure parts of Europe into the 1950s.

DATA: Canon de 155mm Court, Schneider, Mle 1917

Calibre	155mm	Total weight	3,220kg
Weight of gun	1245kg	Recoil	1.28m
Length of gun	2.332m	Elevation	0° to +42° 20'
Length of bore	11.4 calibres	Traverse	3° right and left
Rifling grooves	48	Shell weight	43.55kg
Rifling twist	RH, 7°	Muzzle velocity	450 m/sec
Breech	Screw, percussion	Max range	11,500m

chamber and a larger charge and better-shaped-shell to achieve 21,000m (22,890yd), but experiments showed that the accuracy suffered and the plan was not pursued.

In May 1917 Lt Col Filloux proposed improving the performance by installing a 194mm (7.6in) barrel on the 155mm (6.1in) carriage. Such were the carriage dimensions that the only alteration required would be to the cradle, to suit the larger diameter of the new gun, and the proposal was accepted, the result being the Canon de 194 GPF. The gun fired a new 80kg (176lb) shell to a range of 18,300m (19,950yd), which was a very satisfactory performance, but the 194mm barrel weighed more than twice as much as the 155mm it replaced, and it proved impossible to move the equipment in one piece. The carriage and barrel had to travel in two loads and be assembled when emplacing the equipment, a slow and laborious business. In fairly static warfare this was perhaps a fair price to pay for the extra range and shell weight, but the 194mm gun was not built in any quantity after the war.

Of the larger guns, some, like the 22cm Mortar M1880 and the 24cm gun M1884, were elderly weapons removed from coast defences or frontier

The 155mm GPF gun

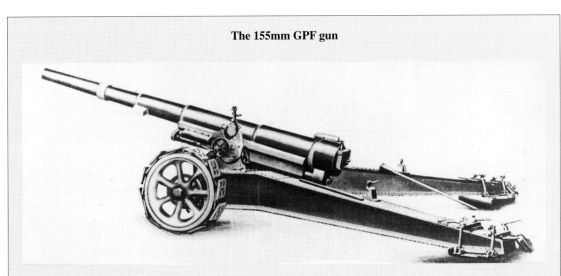

The 155mm GPF gun Mle 1917, the first large calibre gun to use the split trail.

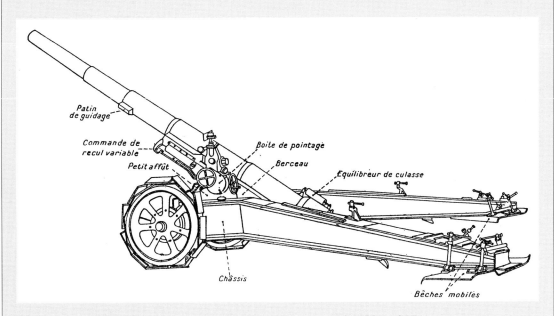

Drawing from the French manual, showing the major components of the 155mm GPF.

GPF means 'Grand Puissance, Filloux', ie. gun of great power designed by [Lt-Col] Filloux', who worked at the Puteaux Arsenal. It was approved for service late in 1916 and manufacture took place at Puteaux and also at the Renault automobile factory in Paris. The first guns of this type went into action in August 1917.

The 155mm GPF gun Continued

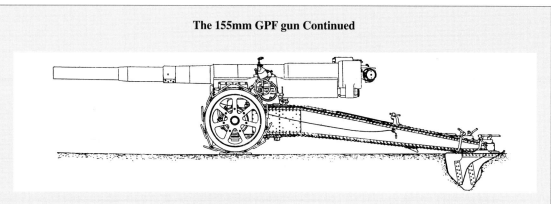

The 155mm GPF emplaced for firing

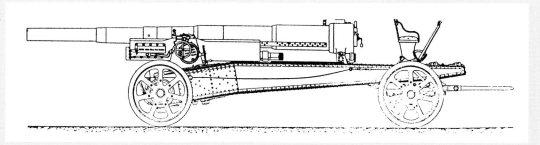

The 155mm GPF with the barrel retracted and limbered up for movement; note the gunner's seat, from where he could operate the brake to avoid over-running the towing vehicle.

The principal novelty about this gun is simply that it was the first big gun to use a split trail; until this appeared, only the 75mm Deport gun had been seen with such a trail, although the British 3.7in howitzer was under development as well. But to jump straight to a very powerful 155mm gun with such a new innovation was considered rather rash in some quarters. Nevertheless, Filloux had the figures at his fingertips, argued his case, won, and produced a gun which, like the earlier 75mm Mle 1897, put the French one step ahead of anyone else. Here was a weapon with 60 degrees of traverse and a maximum elevation of 35 degrees without the need to shift anything; simple arithmetic shows that this amount of elevation and traverse allowed a single gun to command something like 206 square kilometres of ground.

The remainder of the design was more or less conventional. The breech mechanism was the well-proven Schneider screw, and the hydro-pneumatic recoil system was similar to that of the 75mm Mle 1897, although it reversed the action, pulling the recoil block across the fixed pistons. Recoil was variable, giving a full recoil of 1.80m up to 10 degrees of elevation, then shortening until at 28 degrees and above it was 1.10m. For transport the gun was disconnected from the recoil system and run back to lock on to a bracket on the trail legs, so spreading the weight.

Over 700 of this gun were built, of which a number were supplied to the American Expeditionary Force. The US Army adopted it as standard, and produced it in the USA as the M1917. The Poles also adopted it in postwar years. In 1939 all three countries still had it in first-line use, the French with some 450 of them. Once again, their faith in the superiority of their technology led them to keep a gun in service which really ought to have been overhauled. The Americans had already begun their redesign and produced the excellent 155mm M1 gun; the French weapons changed hands and became the '15.5cm Kanone 418(f)'.

The 155mm GPF gun Continued

DATA: Canon de 155mm long, Mle G.P.F

Calibre	155mm	Total weight	11,200k
Weight of gun	3,870kg	Recoil	1.80m
Length of gun	5.915m	Elevation	0° to +35°
Length of bore	30 calibres	Traverse	30° right and left
Rifling grooves	48	Shell weight	43.1kg
Rifling twist	RH, 6°	Muzzle velocity	735m/sec
Breech	Screw, percussion	Max range	16,200m

The 220mm Model 1917 Schneider was designed to combine power with a mobility superior to that of a railway gun; approved in June 1917, it did not go into action until June 1918, by which time the static front had broken and it saw relatively little use.

The Schneider 220mm Mortier Mle 1916 was an improved version of a 9in howitzer built for Russia in 1907. It was first issued to the French Army in October 1916. Note the railway line for the chariot de chargement.

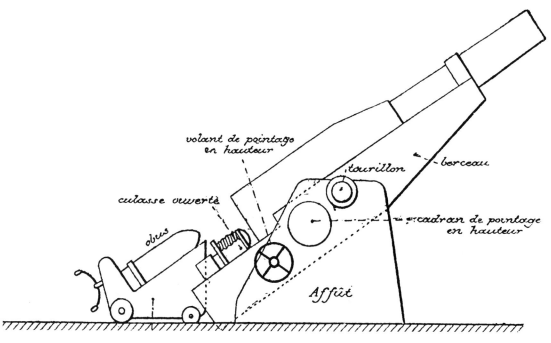

The general layout of the 293mm Schneider howitzer, showing the open breech and the shell on its chariot de chargement.

fortresses, given a rudimentary ground platform carriage, and sent to the front. Others, such as the 22cm mortar M1901 and the 27cm mortar M1885, were survivors of the siege train and were thus portable, though slowly and after much dismantling and reassembling. As such they had no particularly remarkable features. But there were a handful of weapons worth a closer study.

One such was the largest of the field pieces, the 370mm Filloux mortar. This was developed in 1915, but its appearance would suggest a product of the 1880s; Filloux abandoned any technical cleverness and concentrated on getting the heaviest portable weapon in the simplest possible form. The basis was a cast steel platform with spades on its under-surface and with additional *enlargissements* which were bolted on during emplacement. This went into a shallow pit, after which the 'chassis' was lowered on to its pivot. This was a simple steel casting with two sloped sides on which the carriage moved, controlled by two massive hydraulic cylinders, the pistons of which were secured to the front of the chassis. The carriage supported the trunnions of the mortar, a short-barrelled (7.22 calibres) weapon with a simple screw breech with pad obturation. The whole equipment, when emplaced, totalled about 30 tons and there were various hoists and trolleys provided to allow the various parts to be carried on a narrow-gauge railway and then , by running a temporary line to the battery position, assembling the mortar off its transport trucks.

The 155mm Court TR described above had a somewhat unusual breech mechanism, and it is a matter of opinion whether or not the breech mechanism of the 293mm Schneider howitzer surpassed it in complexity. This was another attempt to provide rapid fire from a heavy weapon by automating the breech action, and here we are dealing with a 293mm weapon firing a 660lb (300kg) shell.

The general form of the weapon was conventional: a ground platform, upper carriage and barrel. The piece recoiled in a large cradle, controlled by an hydro-pneumatic recoil system, and this contained an extra cylinder and piston known as the

'breech recuperator'. Attached to this piston rod was a carriage, riding on the cradle, which carried a pivoting arm attached to the breech block. The breech block was a stepped-thread type with three diameters, so that one-sixth of a turn was all that was needed to unlock it.

On firing, the piece recoiled and, since the recoil system block (or 'sleigh') recoiled with it, the apparatus of the breech block carriage went back as well. Also attached to the sleigh was a steel plate with a curved track cut into its surface, into which an arm of the breech-block carrier fitted. At the limit of recoil a spring stop came out and held the breech-block carriage; thus, when the piece and sleigh began to go forward, propelled by the recuperator, the carriage stayed still. The piece, naturally, pulled on the breech block; this pull drew the supporting portion of the block through its housing in the carrier arm. The two parts were threaded, so that pulling the block forward caused it to rotate the necessary amount to unlock, and once it was unlocked it stopped moving and the piece moved forward, into battery. The breech had thus opened automatically.

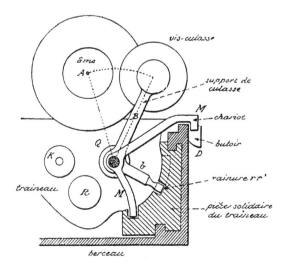

Rear view of the 293mm breech, showing how the breech screw is swung sideways by the arm riding in a groove in the cradle.

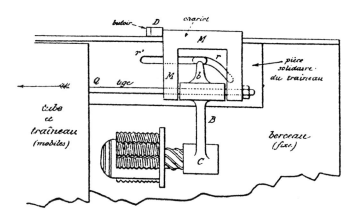

Top view of the 293mm breech arrangements, showing the 'chariot', M, the groove r–r, and the position of the breech screw on its own slow-thread screw carried on the chariot arm.

The forward movement of the sleigh was also carrying the steel plate forward and drawing the groove over the arms of the breech-block carrier. This groove was straight for most of its length, then sharply curved. The result was that during the unlocking and withdrawing movement of the breech block the arm moved in the straight portion of the groove and the carrier stayed in line with the axis of the piece. Once the block was open and clear of the breech ring the arm went into the curved section of the groove, so forcing the breech-block carrier end into the air and out of alignment with the chamber so that the gun could be loaded.

Once the breech was open and the piece back in battery the *chariot de chargement* was wheeled up, with the 300kg shell on board. This trolley carried the shell on a sloping trough which was of exactly the same angle as the loading angle of the piece. It also carried a chain rammer, behind the shell, driven by a rack and pinion device on the side. The trolley was firmly anchored in the correct position behind the cradle and breech, so that the rack and pinion was aligned with yet another piston system in the sleigh, the *recuperator de chargement*. The loader then pulled a lever and this piston, under pressure, was driven out so as to strike the rack on the trolley; this drove the pinion and made the chain rammer unwind and ram the shell into the chamber. The trolley was removed and the propelling charge loaded by hand.

To close the breech, the spring stop was disengaged; the breech recuperator piston was thus allowed to pull the carrier forward. The arm riding in the slot first lowered the breech block until it was aligned with the bore, after which the block entered the breech ring. As soon as it was fully entered and stopped, the continued forward movement of the carrier rotated it to the locked position and the howitzer was ready to fire as soon as a primer had been loaded into the vent.

One benefit of all this complexity was a rate of fire of one round in two minutes, which is not at all bad for a weapon of this calibre.

Self-propelled guns are not generally thought of when the First World War is being discussed, but nevertheless two of the heavy French pieces were mounted on self-propelled carriages. The idea was born in 1917 and the two major manufacturers, Schneider and St Chamond, set about it with their own very different ideas.

The Schneider design was truly self-propelled, A simple steel chassis carried tracks on each side driven by rear sprockets, and the petrol engine and transmission were mounted in a raised compartment at the rear of the chassis. The body was decked, and on this was mounted a fixed top carriage upon which the cradle, recoil system and piece of a new 240mm gun were installed. The

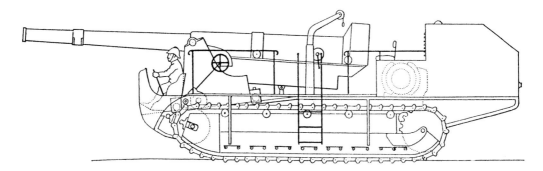

The Schneider self-propelled carriage with a 220mm Mle 1917 gun mounted.

A rare photograph of the Schneider 220mm gun carriage on test in 1918.

driver sat in front of the gun mounting, and there was sufficient room on the deck to allow the gun detachment to work, with railings to prevent them falling off, and ladders to mount and dismount. The whole thing was a practical and workable design, but by the time it had been perfected the war was close to its end; the gun went into production and it is believed that a few were used in the St Mihiel salient in 1918, in support of American troops, but production stopped at the Armistice and barely a dozen were ever made.

St Chamond approached the propulsion problem from a different direction and adopted the Crochat-Collardeau electro-mechanical system. This involved two vehicles; the *avant train*

chenille was a tracked load carrier which contained a petrol engine driving an electrical generator which delivered power to two electric motors, one driving each track through the usual rear sprocket. There was also room for thirty rounds of ammunition in racks at the rear of the vehicle. This machine was then connected to the *affut-chenilles* another tracked vehicle mounting either a 240mm gun or a 280mm howitzer. It, too, had two electric motors driving the tracks, but the power was supplied by a cable from the leading generator vehicle. All the driver of the gun carriage had to do was steer in sympathy with the leader; speed was controlled by the driver of the front vehicle. The gun (or howitzer) was mounted so as to point over the

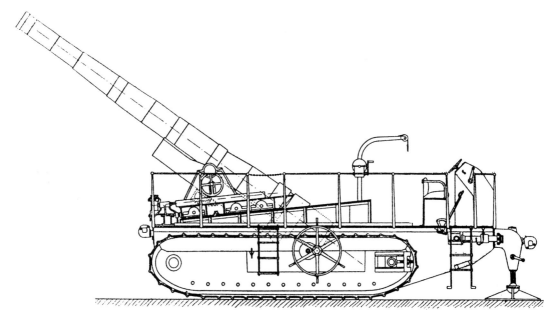

The St Chamond solution was to mount a 240mm gun on a carriage moving up an inclined plane, and drive the vehicle by electric power supplied from outside.

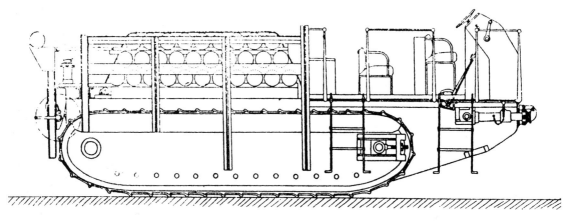

The St Chamond avant-chenille *tractor which used a petrol-electric generator to propel itself and also supply power to the gun carrier. It also carried a useful load of ammunition.*

rear of the vehicle and was on a simple sliding mount with the recoil controlled by pneumatic buffers and run-out performed by gravity, the gun carriage sliding up and down an inclined plane.

How many of these were actually built is in some doubt; certainly prototypes were built and tested, but it is believed that only one or two complete equipments were put into service before the

One of the few remaining examples of the St Chamond carriage is at Aberdeen Proving Ground.

This 1918 picture shows how the gun barrel was retracted for travelling; not for the usual reason of balance, but so as to make the vehicle shorter and more manoeuvrable.

Another view of the Aberdeen Proving Ground specimen, mounting a 194mm gun.

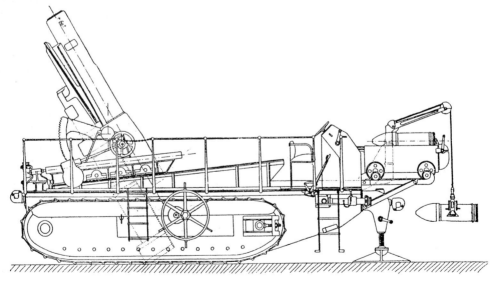

The St Chamond chassis with 280mm howitzer, showing the rear jack which holds the mounting steady under recoil, and the ammunition supply arangements.

The St Chamond 280mm howitzer under test in 1918.

Armistice. There is also evidence that a number were completed in the 1920s and fitted with the 194mm GPF gun, since some appeared on the Russian front in German hands during 1942–43.

USA

American heavy artillery was non-existent in 1917 and, as already stated, it was agreed that the AEF would be provided with light artillery by the French and with heavy by the British. As a result numbers of 6in Mark VII and Mark I9 guns, 8in and 9.2in howitzers were provided for the troops in France, and these were taken back to the USA and remained in service until the late 1930s. The Midvale Steel Co in the USA had been making 8in (203mm) howitzers on a British contract and were therefore given a fresh contract to make them for the US Army, but it was to be ten months before the first one reached the hands of the troops.

The US government also contracted with Schneider for a 9.5in howitzer, to be produced in the USA under licence. It existed only on paper when the idea first arose and was, in fact, a scaled-down version of a 11in weapon which Schneider had built for the Russians in 1912. Schneider built one, it was inspected by a US mission in France

American troops loading a 6.1in M1917 howitzer.

107

The ill-fated 9.5in M1918 howitzer.

An interesting American project, mounting a British 8in howitzer. One has the feeling that the driver's view of the road ahead was somewhat impaired.

early in 1918, and the drawings were then sent to the USA for production to be organized. Schneider were most helpful and even sent specialist mechanics to America to assist, but the Armistice came before any production had been achieved. The 9.5in M1918 howitzer was eventually built, taken to a proving ground and fired, and blew up at the first shot. This was repeated several times before all the wrinkles were ironed out and the equipment finally got into service in the late 1920s.

RUSSIA

Russia had a varied mixture of medium-to-heavy guns in 1914, some of Russian origin but most either purchased from abroad or foreign designs built under licence. From Britain there had come the 5in 60-pounder gun, the '127mm Model 1904'; from Krupp of Germany the 152mm M1910 howitzer; from Schneider the 152mm M1910 gun and its partner the 152mm M1910 howitzer which, as we have seen, introduced a number of Schneider design features and went on to form the basis of a number of French wartime designs. During the war the shortage of heavy guns and howitzers led to the placing of orders with manufacturers in France, Britain and the

USA but none of these produced any results until late in 1916 since all these firms were already inundated with orders from their own armies or, in the case of the USA, from Britain and France, and Russia came a long way down the priority list.

Two howitzers had come from the Putilov factory, the 152mm Model 1886 and the 6in Model 1909. The former was satisfactory in 1886 but was long obsolete by 1914, even though numbers were still in use. It had the gun trunnioned directly on to the front end of the trail, which was curved up to form a top carriage, had no means of traverse, and the only recoil control was by means of a spring spade. It could fire a 30kg (66lb) shell to no more than 3,400m (3,700yd) range, which limited its utility in modern warfare.

The Model 1909 was intended to replace the M1886; it certainly improved on its performance, firing a 41kg (90.2lb) shell to 8,700m (9,480yd), and was well up to date, using a hydro-pneumatic recoil system and having a shield. But for some reason the maximum elevation was only 41 degrees, whereas the 1886 design had reached 47 degrees; had the M1909 had those extra few degrees it could have had an even better range.

The Schneider and Krupp 152mm howitzers which went to Russia in 1910, and which were thereafter built in Russia under licence, fired the

The Putilov 152mm M1909 howitzer.

same ammunition as the Model 1909 and gave about the same performance; where they improved on the local design was in the matter of weight, since they weighed some 600kg less, which made a significant difference when it came to hauling them about in the spring thaw. It seems obvious that the foreign designs were bought not to replace the Model 1909 but to supplement it and bring the army's gun strength up to date as quickly as possible.

The 152m M1910 gun, on the other hand, was to be a complete replacement for the Obuchov company's 6in 200-pounder Model 1904. Whatever had possessed Obuchov to produce this antique in 1904 is long forgotten, but it was a remarkable product for its year. It had no on-carriage recoil system, and was merely an old-style two-wheeled solid-sided box trail with the gun trunnioned into the front end. Below the axle was a horizontal hydraulic buffer cylinder which could be connected to a ground anchor. Two large wedges were then placed behind the wheels, and when the gun fired it ran back up these wedges, and pulled on the hydraulic buffer. Recoil having stopped, the entire carriage then ran down the wedges and back into the firing position. It could have been thought a trifle daring in 1880, but by 1904 it was obsolete before it started. But the replacement by the Schneider 1910 gun never got far enough to make a complete sweep, and several of these ancient warriors were still in use until 1917.

The 1910 gun was advanced for its day, with all the Schneider refinements we have already examined. It was moved in two parts, the barrel on a four-wheeled wagon and the carriage on its own two wheels and a limber. This made two horse loads, but in later years when tractors became available it was common to pull both loads behind one tractor.

The 1910 models of gun and howitzer were both manufactured in Russia under licence, and this continued after the 1917 Revolution. In 1930 both were overhauled, given pneumatic tyres and improved ammunition, and as the M1910/30 models, continued in service until the 1950s.

Guns and howitzers of greater calibre remain something of a mystery; we know that Schneider produced a 28cm howitzer for Russia in 1912, but how many, and whether any more were made under licence in Russia, we cannot say. The basic defect of Russian heavy artillery organization was that the artillery staff had concentrated their expenditure on arming fortresses, to the neglect of the field armies. At the outbreak of war the various forts on the western frontier were armed with 2,813 modern guns plus 3,000 older ones; the field armies, on the other hand, had but 240 heavy guns and howitzers between them. The establishment was eight heavy brigades, each of three six-gun batteries, five brigades stationed in Russia and three in Siberia. The brigades existed on paper but were seriously under-strength in both men and guns. The number was, of course, increased during the war, and four-gun batteries were instituted so as to increase the number of available batteries, but it was never increased to anything like the proper amount. During the course of the war every one of the forts fell to the Germans, most of them with their entire stock of guns and ammunition, while the field armies operating around them had insufficient heavy weapons to withstand the German attacks and had perforce to retire.

ITALY

Italy benefited from the Terni factory operated by Sir William Armstrong, which had originally been set up to provide naval guns but later supplied a number of 6in guns of their own design, taken into service as the Canone da 149/35 M1900. This was designed as a siege gun, and had no on-carriage recoil system. Instead, it was wheeled on to a prepared timber platform and connected to a ground anchor by means of a hydro-spring recoil strut built and supplied by Krupp. The usual wedges were placed behind the wheels to aid in checking the recoil and assisting the run-up; these came in useful when it was deployed as a field-piece during the war.

An Italian 149/35 gun on the Austrian front.

Once Italy entered the war more guns were forthcoming from Armstrong, via the British government; numbers of 6in 26-cwt howitzers were supplied, becoming the 'Obice da 149/13'. (The Italian system of notation includes the calibre-length of the barrel; thus '149/13' means 149mm calibre and 13 calibre-length (1,937m) barrel.) Other guns supplied included the 155mm Schneider Mle 1917 gun and the British 12in Mark II howitzer.

Heavier weapons had been acquired in small numbers prior to 1914. From France came the Mortiao 260/9, a siege howitzer firing a 220kg (484lb) shell to 9,000m (9,810yd). (It is not at all clear where the dividing line between 'mortar' and 'howitzer' falls; the 12in how was a howitzer but the 260mm how was a mortar.) The Mortiao 210/8 di Stefano appears to have been built by the Ansaldo company and was another solidly emplaced siege weapon using a top carriage recoil system. There are records of other 305-, 310-, 360- and 380mm howitzers but it is difficult to discover details; it seems probable that a small number of 36cm and 38cm howitzers were acquired from Skoda in the early 1900s, and these were certainly used in the mountain campaigns in 1916/17. It is also possible that others could have been captured from the Austrians during the course of the war and put to good use.

Another view of the 149/35 gun revealing the absence of a recoil system and the use of heavily braced ramps, up which the gun wheels moved on recoil.

Italian 305/12 howitzer firing in the Carnatic Alps.

Italian 310mm M1910 howitzer.

Italian Mortiao da 210/8 Mod 1910 emplaced in Val Dogno in 1915.

4 Railway Artillery

The idea of putting artillery on special railway wagons in order to provide mobile heavy artillery appears to have been first suggested in the 1850s, when a Mr Anderson published a pamphlet in Britain called 'National Defence' in which he 'proposed a complete plan of wrought-iron protected railway carriages', but nothing came of it. The first practical move took place in the American Civil War when guns and mortars were placed on railway flatcars, protected by simple wood and iron shields, and used to bombard Petersburg in the siege of 1864–65. These weapons were rigidly attached to the railway car and in order to aim them at their targets the track was laid in a gentle curve. Pushing the car along the curve gradually altered the pointing of the bore and it was stopped when it was correctly aligned with the target. On firing, the recoil caused it to roll back along the track for a few feet, after which it was pushed back once more.

A few 6in naval guns were placed on railway trucks in South Africa, with the intention of using them to bombard the forts around Pretoria, but Pretoria fell before they could be deployed and the guns were returned to their proper places on the ships. The French firm of Schneider-Canet examined the idea in the late 1880s and eventually produced a 120mm gun mounted on a flatcar so as to give all-round fire. They failed to interest the French Army in the idea, and then touted it around the world as a possible coast defence system, by which a handful of guns placed at strategic junctions would be able to move to threatened points at short notice. The Danish government bought a few in the 1890s, and the Peruvian government bought some 20cm howitzers on rail mountings, also for coast defence, in 1910. And there the matter rested until 1915.

By late 1914 the French had realized that they had a drastic shortage of heavy artillery in their field army and were withdrawing guns from coastal and inland fortresses in order to fill the gaps. All these weapons were on static ('garrison') mountings which were entirely unsuitable for field use. They had to be made mobile in some way, and, given the proliferation of railway tracks which existed and which were being rapidly laid in all directions behind the front line, putting them on railway mountings seemed to be a quick and simple solution.

But moving the weapon is only part of the business; there is an old maxim among artillerymen that 'guns on wheels are useless', meaning that a gun in the process of being moved from place to place is not available for firing and is therefore lost so far as the commander is concerned. Only when the gun is sited in its correct place and is capable of firing can it be considered part of the effective force. And so the railway gun has to be fired, and this brings problems.

The principal problem is that of stability. Early (and primitive) designs of railway-mounted guns had shown that the recoil shock could be alleviated by allowing the gun some movement on its truck, and the truck some movement along the track. But this was only applicable if the gun fired in a direction in prolongation of the track. Should you wish to fire at right-angles to the track, then there was a considerable likelihood that the recoil force would simply overturn the entire equipment because of the narrow wheelbase. Moreover, the downward force of the recoil, acting through the limited areas of contact between the wheels and the rails, was likely to hammer dents into the rails and ruin them very rapidly, especially since the average piece of rail laid by battlefield engineers was not very substantial. All these, and other, considerations led to the gradual adoption of three distinct types of railway mounting – the sliding mount, the rolling mount and the platform mount.

With the sliding mount, the weapon is brought to its firing position and then the frame of the mounting is lowered so that it rests either on top of the track or on a prepared surface; the wheels are entirely relieved of any weight. On firing, the portion of recoil not absorbed by the normal type of recoil mechanism attached to the gun – if one is fitted – will be translated into a sliding movement of the entire mount along the rails or the prepared base.

With the rolling mount, the weapon goes into action with the weight still on its wheels. The brakes are applied, but when the gun is fired any recoil force not absorbed by the recoil system is expended by rolling the entire equipment back on its wheels, overcoming the brakes until the movement is reduced to a point where they begin to take effect once more. This type of mounting obviously has to be provided with sufficient wheels to spread the load, otherwise the first shot would simply produce a set of flattened wheels and a severely damaged set of rails. The distance moved is not very great – ten to fifteen feet at the most; The old soldiers' tales about railway guns which recoiled down the track and into a convenient tunnel to conceal themselves, or which recoiled down to the next station and brought up the rations and mail on the return trip, are just that – old soldiers' tales.

In the platform mount, the weapon is not rigidly aligned with the mounting, as in the two previous cases, but is free to rotate on a turntable or pivot so that it can be pointed in any direction independently of the orientation of the mount. The mount itself can be a sliding or rolling type, either

being satisfactory so long as the gun is firing in prolongation of the track; but once the gun is trained away from the line of track, the across-track recoil force introduces complications. It becomes necessary to brace the mount so that it will not be driven off the track, and this is generally done by placing outriggers – strong beams – extending from the sides of the mount and supported by screwjacks, so as to spread the base. The outriggers are augmented by rail clamps – hook-like metal grips which are anchored around the rails and screwed tight so as to hold the mount firmly down to the track and resist any tendency to lift under the recoil or jump of the gun. A further aid to stability might be steel cables attached to ground anchors, holding the mount securely in place. Any or all of these devices might be used, depending upon the amount of recoil energy to be absorbed.

With the recoil question attended to, other problems now have to be solved. Obviously, when the mount runs back under recoil, it has to be repositioned after recoil has stopped. Usually the amount of movement is small and often more than one shot can be fired before the mount has moved so far that aiming becomes impossible and the mount must be replaced in its starting position. This can be done most easily by pushing it back with a locomotive, but this is not always convenient – one does not like having a locomotive in steam standing idly on the track waiting to be bombarded by the enemy – and sometimes the return is performed by winches on the mounting pulling in a rope attached to a ground anchor, or by 'translating gear', by means of which movement of a hand crank by several men was connected to a set of wheels. Moving a sliding mount usually meant that the whole thing had to be jacked up off its base and back on to its wheels, though with some lighter weapons it was possible to drag it along its platform.

Another problem was that of providing the weapon with the necessary amount of traverse to allow it to be pointed accurately at its target. As a general rule a railway gun was not emplaced with a view to firing all over the battlefield; it was usually sited with a specific target or group of targets in view, and thus a restricted arc of fire was acceptable. But as anyone who has ever aimed a rifle will appreciate, some delicacy of control was needed in order to adjust the fall of shot precisely on to the target. A curved track provides an answer for guns which are rigidly attached in their mountings; 88ft of track on a 500ft radius gives about 5 degrees of traverse, equivalent to a movement of the fall of the shell of some 1,450yd sideways at a range of 15,000yd. But attempting to lay a heavy gun accurately by shouting and arm-waving to a locomotive driver is a time-consuming and frustrating business, and it became normal practice to provide some degree of traverse, be it ever so small, on the mounting itself so as to avoid too much fussing back and forth on the track and give a fine degree of adjustment under the gun-layer's control.

One of the simplest methods of adding traverse is to permit a sideways movement of one end of the mounting across the supporting bogie beneath it, using the attachment to the other bogie as the pivot. This could be done by some simple gear or screw mechanism, hand- or power-actuated, or, even more simply, by loosening the attachment to the bogie and then heaving the mount to one side or the other by means of 'warping winches' set out at right-angles. Such a system is obviously restricted by the construction of the mount, and rarely allows more than one or two degrees of movement, but in conjunction with a curved track is usually sufficient.

Another method is to mount the gun and its cradle into a 'top carriage' and allow this some movement around a pivot on the mounting itself. Obviously this will not allow very much movement either, but, as with the cross-bogie system, one or two degrees is all that is necessary. These systems also allow for the misalignment which follows after firing and recoiling on a curved track, allowing the gun to be re-aimed and fired perhaps three or four times before it becomes necessary to push it back to its original position. But where more on-mounting traverse is required, then the only solution is the platform mount and there is an upper limit of gun size and power which can be accommodated on such a mount before the stability problem becomes too great to be overcome.

BRITAIN

When war broke out in 1914 the British Army was in no rush to consider railway guns. The demand did not arise until 1915, when the front had stabilized , and the reaction was the standard one for the time – look to see what coast and naval guns could be spared and find a cheap and quick mounting for them. In those days it was customary to manufacture an excess of gun barrels over requirements, and put them in store against the day when the in-service barrels wore out. This source of supply was tapped, and in order to mount them the usual British system was adopted: throw the problem at the professional gunmakers and let them get on with it in their own way, a system which generally produces the best guns. The Elswick Ordnance Company was approached with a request to mount some 9.2in guns, and they produced a design using a well-base double-bogie truck carrying a standard naval Vavasseur slide mounting. These mountings were readily available, since many naval broadside and coast defence guns had used them and numbers which had been replaced by more modern mountings were lying in store. A suitable design was quickly put together from stock components; the rolling mounting was little more than a normal commercial well wagon, suitably strengthened. The resulting 9.2in (234mm) Mark I gun weighed about 60 tons and fired a 360lb (163.4kg) shell to a maximum range of 12,900yd (11,790m).

The equipment was reasonably successful, if somewhat lacking in refinements; the principal drawback was a lack of range due to the limited elevation of 28 degrees, the maximum possible with the Vavasseur mounting. Early in 1916 the company was asked to redesign the mounting so as to reach a higher elevation and thus more range, and in a matter of days a fresh design was produced in which the front end of the recoil slide was raised by inserting packing pieces, allowing the gun to elevate to 35 degrees. The necessary components for modification were made up into kits and sent to France, where the mountings in service were rebuilt to the new pattern on the spot. This improvement increased the maximum range to 16,000yd (14,600m).

After producing this modification, the Elswick Ordnance Company knew very well that in a short time the customers would be back demanding an improved model, so they set about designing a fresh pattern of Mark III 9.2in gun mounting from the wheels up, a double-truck straight-back platform truck with an improved Vavasseur mounting carried on a circular racer to give all-round traverse. A variety of guns were made available to fit this mounting (see box) and eventually the maximum range was raised to 26,000yd (23,800m).

Once the 9.2in guns were completed, the next task the Army threw at Elswick was the production of a heavy howitzer. The standard heavy howitzer was a 9.2in weapon, but this was not considered sufficiently powerful to be worth the trouble of mounting on rails. Elswick were therefore asked to develop a 12in railway howitzer, while Vickers were given the task of developing a road-mobile version.

Elswick did the sensible thing in the circumstances – they simply took the existing 9.2in howitzer, which was a Coventry Ordnance design, and more or less scaled it up to 12in calibre. Details of the recoil system and breech mechanism differed, since Elswick had their own ideas about what constituted good design, and also appear to have been influenced by what they happened to have in store, but the result was a simple and workmanlike job. A well-base truck carried a roller race, upon which revolved the 12in howitzer. Jacks were provided to

The 9.2in gun Mark XIII on Mark III mounting gave all-round fire.

An Elswick factory picture of the first Mark III 12in howitzer.

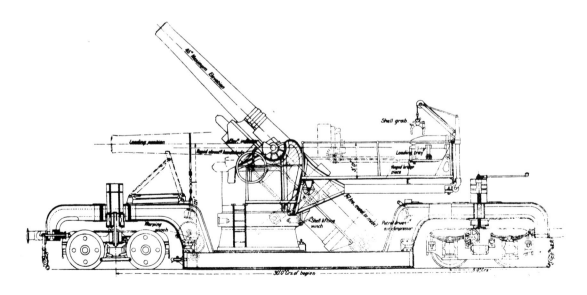

Handbook diagram of the 12in Mark V howitzer.

Elswick factory picture of the 12in Mark V howitzer with outriggers extended and firing jacks in place, allowing all-round fire.

steady the mounting, but firing had to be conducted within 20 degrees each side of the centreline, so avoiding the need for outriggers and stabilizers. This Mark I howitzer gave a maximum range of 11,132yd (10,170m) with a 750lb (340.5kg) shell.

While these were being built, Elswick set their drawing office to design its replacement, knowing that the army would soon demand more range. This became the Mark III howitzer, and was simply the same as the Mark I but with a longer (17.3 calibres) barrel. The truck had to be strengthened to take the greater recoil forces, and the maximum range went up to 15,000yd (13,710m).

Although the Army was impressed by the improvement in performance, they were not particularly pleased with the restriction to firing within a 40 degree arc of the end of the mounting; they

wanted a weapon with all-round traverse so that it could be fired in any direction. So the Elswick designers set to work once more and produced the Mark V howitzer. The barrel was of the same length as the Mark III, but with a lighter breech; a platform was fitted to the mounting so that loading could be conveniently done at any angle of traverse; and outriggers and cable anchors were provided to stabilize the truck when firing across the track. But due to the design, the barrel could only elevate to 45 degrees, which slightly reduced the maximum range to 14,350yd (13,120m).

The 12in Guns

The story of the 12in (305mm) railway guns in British service forms a curious combination of

The 12in Mark III howitzer in France, concealed by a camouflage net.

The 9.2in Guns Mks X and XIII

9.2in Mark XIII gun on Mounting Mk IV on Railway Truck Mark II.

The 9.2in Guns Mks 10 and 13 Continued

This was the improved design developed by the Elswick Ordnance Company in advance of the army's requirement. The base component was a new straight-back truck designed for its job and supported on two six-wheel bogies. On to this went a roller-bearing racer ring, on top of which was a platform carrying the gun mounting. This was the same Vavasseur (inclined plane and hydraulic buffers) type as before, though with minor improvements to permit the required elevation.

Outriggers could be attached to the mounting, with heavy spades at the outer ends, and the truck body was secured to the track by rail clamps for firing. A screw mechanism in the bogie bolsters could be used to lower the truck body to rest on baulks of timber laid on the track bed, so as to remove all firing stress from the wheels. A platform behind the gun allowed the detachment to serve the breech and load at any position of traverse, and a small hoist on the platform was used to lift up the ammunition. A rack at the rear of the platform carried a few shells and cartridges, and the shell was hand-rammed into the breech.

The guns which found their way on to this mounting were an odd collection. The 9.2in (234mm) Mark I0 gun was the 'approved pattern', this being the most modern and powerful type available, but since most of them were earmarked for use by the Royal Navy not all the mountings could be supplied with them. The Elswick company had two 9.2in coast guns which they had built for the Australian government and had been unable to deliver, and these were appropriated as the 'Mark XT'. The Vickers company had another four 9.2in (234mm) guns which they had built for overseas sale in prewar days, and these were also adapted to the railway mounting, though since they were considerably different to any British service pattern they became the 'Mark XIV' guns. Finally the Elswick company produced a fresh design of 35-calibre gun especially for the railway mounting, in that the breech end was made thicker and heavier. This allowed the trunnions to be placed closer to the breech, giving less overhang and allowing the gun to elevate to 40 degrees without fouling the platform on recoil. This gun became the Mark X111, and when the mounting was modified to allow the extra 10 degrees of elevation it became the Mark 4. The details of these various weapons varied according to the type of gun used. All weighed about 90 tons; the Mark X fired the standard 380lb (173kg) shell to 21,000yd (19,190m), and the Mark X111 to 22,600yd (20,660m).

Numbers of these equipments managed to survive the 1919-39 period in out-of-the-way depots and were resurrected as anti-invasion defences in 1940. They were declared obsolete in 1948, the guns, if serviceable, being placed into coast artillery reserve stock.

DATA: Ordnance BL 9.2in Gun Mk XIII on Mounting, Railway Truck, BL 9.2in Gun Mk III, on Truck, Railway, BL 9.2in Gun Mk II

Calibre	9.2in	Total weight	87 tons
Weight of gun	24t 4cwt	Recoil	34in
Length of gun	335.025in	Elevation	0° to +30°
Length of bore	35 calibres	Traverse	360°
Rifling grooves	48	Shell weight	380lb
Rifling twist	RH, 1/30	Muzzle velocity	2,100ft/sec
Breech	Screw, percussion	Max range	22,600yd

private enterprise and interservice buck-passing. The story opens in September 1915, when a somewhat surprised Director of Artillery informed the Ordnance Board that he had just been presented with a *fait accompli*; the Admiralty had informed him that they had taken two 12in guns from the reserves of HMS *Cornwallis* and given them to Vickers with instructions to place them on suitable railway mountings. They had then waited until the weapons were almost complete and then informed the Director that he was about to receive two railway guns for the army to use in France. Just what prompted the Admiralty to this course of action is by no means clear, but one tends to see the hand of Winston Churchill in there somewhere. (It might be thought that the Navy were taking something of a risk in donating two reserve guns of a ship, but in the long run it was justified, since the *Cornwallis* was torpedoed off Malta in 1917 and its reserve guns were never needed.)

The Vickers mountings were quite unique in appearance. The design was basically the usual girder frame carried on a front sixteen wheel bogie and a rear twelve-wheel bogie, but the axles were carried on inside bearings so that the entire wheel was visible and the girder body was in skeleton form, rather than being of solid appearance like

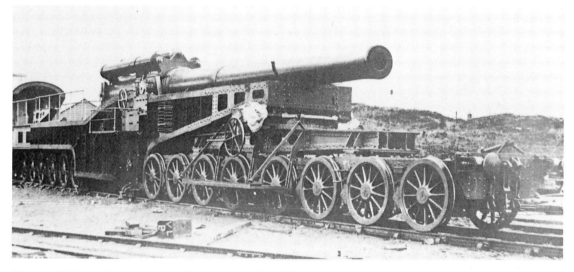

12in gun Mk 9 on railway mounting Mark I, designed by Vickers.

The second 12in gun Mark IX, on the Mark II mounting designed by Armstrongs.

Firing the 12in Mark II near Meaulte, France, in August 1916.

every other railway gun. There were also shock-absorbing springs between some of the frame girders, presumably to cushion some of the firing shock and give the structure some elasticity over quickly laid battlefield railways. There were small but distinct differences between the two mountings, particularly in the arrangement of the main girders, which suggest that the first model, test fired late in September 1915, revealed the need for modifications.

The guns mounted were the 12in Mark IXW, and they were carried in ring cradles with a hydro-spring recoil system. The guns weighed 50 tons and fired an 850lb (386kg) shell to a range of 32,700yd (29,890m). The entire gun and mounting weighed just over 171 tons complete with its attached ammunition car.

Both guns were delivered to France and given into the care of 53rd Siege Battery RA, the Commanding Officer of which rendered a report on 14 January 1916 bringing to light one or two deficiencies but, in general, praising the accuracy and reliability of the guns. This decided the War Office to manufacture another pair, and two more Mark IXW guns were delivered to the Elswick Ordnance Company, together with the comments on the existing guns, and they were invited to produce their idea of a 12in railway mounting.

The '12in Mark IX on Mounting Mark II' was rather more conventional in appearance, using a solid-sided girder body supported on a front fourteen-wheel double bogie and a rear eight-wheel bogie; these were outside-bearing types but, again, rather unusual in having solid sideplates. The gun was in a ring cradle, trunnioned to the side girders, and had the recoil system beneath the cradle, rather than above it as in the Vickers design. The first gun was proved at the Elswick firing range on 6 May 1916 and by August of that year both were in action in France.

The 12in Howitzer

12inch Mark V howitzer on Mounting Mark III on Truck Mark III

The mounting was a well-base vehicle with a racer ring which allowed the howitzer to traverse through 360 degrees, but in order to avoid complicating the issue with outriggers, it was restricted to firing within a 40 degree arc over either end of the mounting. The platform was carried on two four-wheel bogies which were connected to the platform by screw jacks, so that the entire platform and howitzer could be lowered until it rested on the sleepers or on a prepared platform, and no weight rested on the wheels. Rail clamps were then applied to hold the platform tightly down to the track.

The resulting 'BL 12 inch Howitzer Mark I on Mounting Railway Truck 12 inch Howitzer Mark I' weighed 58 tons and fired a 750lb (340.5kg) shell to a range of 11,132yd (10,175m). The Army seemed quite pleased with it, but Elswick felt that there was insufficient performance for such a large equipment, and they were quite sure the

The 12in Mark V Howitzer in travelling order.

The 12in Howitzer Continued

The 12in Mark I howitzer in travelling order.

Army would be back before long, demanding a more powerful weapon. So they immediately set about designing a new howitzer which would give more range. The mounting was little changed, other than to strengthen it against the heavier firing shock, and the complete equipment, known as the Mark III howitzer, was ready in late 1916 and rapidly replaced the Mark I. The new model weighed 61 tons and fired the same 750lb shell to a maximum range of 15,000yd (13,710m).

The Mark III, though, was still restricted to firing within the 40-degree arcs and the Army wanted all-round fire, so Armstrongs now designed the Mark V howitzer. The barrel of the Mark III was given a lighter breech end and a new recoil system to provide a better balance and also to lower the silhouette and the centre of gravity, making the whole equipment more stable in movement and easier to camouflage. The mounting was a turntable on the same well-base platform, but with a loading platform carried round with the gun so that the detachment had somewhere to stand and load while the gun was across the line of rails. At the rear of this platform was an ammunition hoist and a loading tray, and the platform itself also counter-balanced the gun barrel on the pedestal. So that the howitzer would be stable when firing at any angle of traverse, outrigger spades were provided, though some versions used ground spades located by steel cables, relying on the tension of the forward cables rather than the compression of rear outrigger girders.

The howitzer could elevate only to 45 degrees, whereas the previous models had been able to go up to 65 degrees. This slightly restricted the maximum range. Although, theoretically, a gun's maximum range is achieved at 45 degrees, in real life this is not always the case, and the Mark III howitzer had reached its maximum at a slightly higher angle. Restricting the elevation to 45 degrees, due to the design of the mounting, meant that the maximum range dropped slightly to 14,350yd (13,120m), but the Army felt that this was a negligible loss in exchange for unrestricted all-round fire and they were happy with the barter. Both the Mark III and Mark 5 howitzers were to remain in service for many years, being declared obsolete in 1945.

		The 12in Howitzer Continued		

DATA: Ordnance BL 12in Howitzer Mk V, on Mounting BL 12in Howitzer Mk III, on Truck, Railway, BL 12in Howitzer Mk III

Calibre	12in	Total weight	76 tons
Weight of gun	10t 11cwt	Recoil	60in
Length of gun	225.3in	Elevation	+20° to +45°
Length of bore	17.3 calibres	Traverse	120° right and left
Rifling grooves	60	Shell weight	750lb
Rifling twist	RH, 1/20	Muzzle velocity	1,468ft/sec
Breech	Screw, percussion	Max range	14,350yd

The 14in Guns

The Elswick Ordnance Company had built guns for many overseas customers in the years before the war, some of which the war had prevented being delivered, so that they had a useful collection of guns in their factory. Moreover, being long connected with the British services they had their contacts from which they could ascertain what the Army and Navy were thinking. In 1916, with the 12in guns almost completed, they discovered that the Army was already thinking about even longer-ranging weapons, and so Elswick turned out its store to see what could be adapted. Just prior to the war the

The 14in 'H.M.Gun Boche-Buster' in camouflage paint scheme.

The other 14in 'H.M.Gun Scene-Shifter'. Note the left-handed breech mechanism.

Japanese government had ordered a number of 14in (350mm) naval guns, and the last two guns of this contract had not been delivered. The company now approached the War Office, offering these two weapons as potential candidates for railway mounting; the offer was accepted, and Elswick were asked to design suitable mountings.

As it turned out, they were to be the last railway mountings ever built for the British Army, though no one could have known this at the time. They were simple and elegant designs, representative of the best ideas on the subject, and they were not surpassed until some of the German developments of the 1930s and 1940s. The mounting consisted of the usual box girder structure suspended between two sets of double bogies, two eight-wheel at the front end and an eight-wheel and a six-wheel at the rear end. The gun was carried in a trough cradle trunnioned to the side girders, and was allowed only 34in (864mm) of recoil movement.

A total of 4 degrees of traverse were provided by sliding the end of the mounting across the front truck bolster, movement being controlled by a warping winch laid out to ground anchors on either side. To obtain a greater arc of fire, a curved track was generally laid. A 30hp Siddeley petrol engine on the front end of the mounting drove a generator to provide power for the ammunition hoists, but the rest of the operation of the gun was by hand.

Photographs of these guns reveal an unusual feature for an army weapon; it is usual for gun breeches to swing open to the right, but one of the 14in guns had a left-ward opening breech block. This is because the guns were of naval origin and were a 'handed pair' for mounting in a turret where, for convenience in operation, the breech-blocks opened towards the outside of the turret.

Although the idea had begun in 1916, it was not until early 1918 that they were completed and sent to arm 471 Siege Battery RA in France. One gun, named 'HM Gun Boche-Buster' and commanded by Major S.M. Cleeve went to the Arras sector; the

The 18in howitzer, which used the same mounting as the 14in guns, but which was not ready for service when the war ended.

other, named 'HM Gun Scene-Shifter' under Capt. M.B. Elderton, went to the Bethune area. 'Boche-buster' was later to be distinguished, on 8 August 1918, by a visit from HM King George V, while the gun was in position at Mareuil. Under His Majesty's eye the gun opened fire on Douai railway station at a range of 18 miles and scored a direct hit with the first round, a feat which went into regimental history as 'The King's Shot'.

The 18in Howitzer

It is a common practice with towed artillery to produce a carriage which will take two weapons interchangeably, one a long-range gun and the other a howitzer firing a heavier shell than the gun, though to a lesser range. This practice was now to be applied to the 14in mounting, and a design for an 18in (458mm) howitzer was called for in 1917. At that time no weapon of this calibre existed in service so the howitzer would have to be designed and built from scratch. Since a howitzer is less stressed than a gun it was possible to built the greater calibre into an exterior size which would still fit the 14in mounting, the only major difference being in the breech mechanism which was necessarily larger and thus some two and a half tons heavier.

The howitzer was not completed until after the war ended, and was introduced into service some time in 1919. Four barrels were built, mounted in turn, on one of the 14in equipments for test firing, and then dismounted again and placed in store.

At the same time as the 18in howitzer project was begun, a project for an 18in long-range gun was mooted; work began on this in 1917 but the idea was dropped early in 1918. Three guns were eventually made, but by that time the project had been passed across to the Royal Navy and the three weapons ended up arming three monitors of the *General Wolfe* class. There was also discussion, in 1918, of developing a 20in (508mm) naval gun and, inevitably, somebody suggested railway mounting for this. But the post-war Washington Conference on Naval Limitations knocked the 20in idea on the head, and that was the end of that.

FRANCE

The Schneider-Canet company of France were the private-enterprise pioneers of railway artillery, having developed a 16cm platform-mounted gun in the 1880s, some of which were sold to Denmark as coast defence weapons, but the French Army remained unimpressed and no railway gun was taken into military service. The French Army had spent the years after the 1870 war in developing a philosophy of attack and rapid movement, and the railway gun, or indeed any heavy gun, played no part in it. As we have seen, French Army artillery rested on a firm base of 75mm M1897 field guns, which were among the best of their kind in 1914, and the remainder of the armament was a collection of lighter weapons for horse and mountain artillery and a leavening of heavy support.

The events of 1914 soon showed that the theorists had got it wrong. Heavy artillery *was* necessary, and it had to be scraped up from somewhere, and quickly. By raiding the stocks of reserve naval guns, removing guns from fortresses distant from the fighting and milking the coast defences, guns were made available and Schneider were asked to provide mountings so that this collection would be put to practical use at the front. The drawback was

that most of these guns had been designed to fit into coast and naval carriages where the recoil system formed a component part of the mounting; the guns were fitted with trunnions which rested in top carriages which recoiled on a slide, the recoil system being interposed between top carriage and slide. This meant that the guns did not come provided with suitable cradles and recoil systems which could be adapted to mobile carriages. And the design and manufacture of suitable recoil systems in sufficient numbers would take months, if not years, given the state of French heavy engineering industry in 1914.

The solution finally adopted was startling in its simplicity and would not have been given two minutes' hearing in peacetime before being thrown out; the guns were to be placed on railway mounts *without* recoil systems.

The design developed by Schneider was a simple steel box with reinforced trunnion bearings into which the gun was secured. The box was then supported at the ends by however many wheels were necessary to take the weight, and pulled into its firing position. Since the front line, by the end of 1914, was relatively static, time taken to prepare a firing site was of little importance. Having laid track to the chosen site, the track bed was

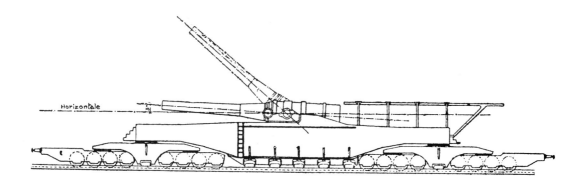

Drawing showing the Schneider sliding mount; the five box-girder units beneath the body rested on girders emplaced in the ground and took the weight from the wheels.

reinforced by four rows of 10in I-beam girders laid parallel to the track. The gun mounting was positioned over the girders and cross-beams beneath the mounting were lowered by screw jacks until the weight was taken from the wheels and completely transferred to the I-beam foundation. When the gun was fired the recoil force passed from the gun via the trunnions to the side members of the steel box and attempted to move the whole equipment backwards. Friction between the I-beams and the cross-beams absorbed the recoil force. Movement between gun and platform varied from one to four or five feet, depending upon the size of gun and amount of elevation of the barrel. After recoil stopped, the screw jacks were again operated until the gun was on its wheels, and a hand crank mechanism operated a train of gears to rotate one axle of the mounting and thus propel the mounting back to its original position, whereupon the cross-beams were lowered and the whole business started again. It was scarcely the fastest gun on the Western Front but it worked, it was cheap, it was simple, and it could be manufactured quickly, and those were the factors which counted most at that time. The only people who failed to be impressed by the simplicity were the unfortunate *poilus* who had to manipulate the hand crank; it took 100 turns of the crank to make one turn of the mounting's wheels.

The only drawback to the system was that after a few hundred rounds had been fired, the enormous hammering of the recoil force would eventually have its effect on the trunnions and the side girders, which would begin to crack and break away at the trunnion bearings. But by that time the gun barrel would probably be worn beyond its limit of accuracy, so the whole weapon could be withdrawn and scrapped. Apart from that they had the unquestionable merit of being virtually maintenance-free, there being nothing to maintain except the elevating gear and the gun breech.

In addition to these *glissement* mountings, a number of other odd patterns appeared in 1915, most of which were either guns which Schneider and other makers had built in pre-war years as speculative sales ventures, or were improvisations of one sort or another to make use of smaller weapons. After this emergency provision of elderly guns was completed, there was a more deliberate period of design which produced one or two platform mounts for small guns, followed by the Batignolles mount. This, designed by Creusot, was considered to be the best limited-traverse design produced during the war due to its simplicity and robustness. Special steel cross-ties with integral spades were inserted between the normal track sleepers, and two heavy girders were bolted on to the ends, parallel with the track. These girders were provided with twelve sets of flanges which matched similar sets on the bottom of the mounting. Once the basic platform was laid, the mounting was run into place and, by means of a hand crank geared to one of the axles, was precisely positioned so that the sets of flanges matched. The mount was then locked to the girders by driving in

A wartime picture of the 340mm Mle 1893 gun showing the box girder supports beneath the body.

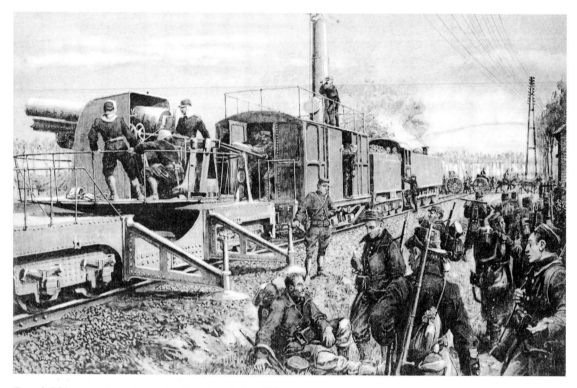

French 164mm gun in action on the Yser front in late 1914.

wedges between each set of flanges until the weight of the mounting was directly on the base and no longer on the wheels. The interlocking of the flanges, and the integral spades of the cross-ties, ensured that both the downward and rearward thrusts due to firing were carried into the ground and the mounting never moved. Some Batignolles mounts were built using guns with cradles and recoil systems, but a number were also built on the Schneider non-recoil system.

The last French railway gun to be built during the war was, frankly, a waste of effort. After the Germans had battered Liège, Maubeuge, Namur and Verdun with their 42cm howitzers, public outcry in France demanded French prestige be restored with a bigger and better howitzer. The designers got to work and came up with a 52cm howitzer. Developing a road-mobile mounting for this monster would probably have been beyond the

state of technology at that time, and would certainly have taken far too long, so a railway mounting was chosen as the quick solution. It was first intended to take the quickest way out and use a Schneider non-recoil mounting, but the recoil energy of this enormous weapon was too great to be comfortably accommodated and it was necessary to develop a suitable recoil system. Two of these weapons were built and duly paraded for visiting politicians, but little other or warlike use was made of them.

The number of different designs of French railway gun, due to the hurried construction of emergency equipments in 1915, is legion, and space cannot be spared to cover each model in detail. Since, in many cases, the same mounting was used for a variety of barrels, a description of one will have to suffice for all, though the various weapons mounted will be found in the Table of Equipments.

Among the earliest designs were the 164mm guns; these were naval weapons and were fitted to simple platform mountings on a straight-back truck. The mounting was shielded, and magazines for ready-use ammunition were provided at each end of the platform. Two hinged working platforms were attached to the sides of the main platform and could be lowered to provide room around the gun for the gunners. The gun was a naval pattern fitted on a rotating base in the centre of the car and protected by a shield. Four screw jacks, two on each side, were lowered to rest on iron caps on top of wooden floats, and eight clamps anchored the car firmly to the track before firing commenced. This gun and a 194mm of very similar appearance, were not normally used as railway artillery of position on the Western Front, since they had insufficient range, but they formed part of special armoured trains used for coast defence against the possibility of a German attack in an attempt to outflank the seaward end of the front line.

An elderly 194mm howitzer was also railway mounted in limited numbers early in 1915. This, the Model 1875, was a coast defence gun complete with mounting which was simply lifted bodily from its emplacement and bolted down to the bed of a small four-wheeled or six-wheeled flat-car. The gun mounting had an inclined top surface,

up which the small sub-carriage carrying the gun would ride when it recoiled, controlled by a hydraulic buffer. Counter-recoil was by gravity, the sub-carriage and gun simply sliding back down the incline to the firing position. The usual arrangement of screw jacks and rail clamps was used, augmented by a wire rope led to a ground anchor planted in front of the mounting.

This seemed to work in a reasonable manner – it was not a very powerful weapon and the mounting was able to take the strain – so a number of other coast defence antiques were removed and similarly mounted. These included the 24cm Mle 1876 howitzer, the 24cm Mle 1884 and 1903 guns, the 27.4cm Mle 1870/81 howitzer and the 27.4cm Mle 1893 gun. The railway cars used for these were a miscellaneous collection of two-, three- and five-axle models, the latter being specially built from existing rolling stock components so as to take the weight of the larger weapons.

The 24cm gun was available in some numbers, having been a preferred French coast defence and naval calibre for many years – very much like the British 9.2in gun – and the next application of the Mle 1884 gun was a much more efficient equipment. The standard coast mounting was lifted bodily and dropped on to a racer ring set into a reinforced well-base truck to make a platform

194mm Mle 1893 gun on Creusot mounting.

The 285mm Mle 1917 gun, another Schneider sliding mounting, with an overhead trolley to carry the shell to the breech.

mounting with 360 degrees traverse. Two small ammunition magazines were placed at each end of the car, similar to the arrangement used with the 164mm guns. The gun mounting was of the Vavasseur pattern using a similar sloped-top mounting with sub-carriage but with both recoil and counter-recoil controlled by hydraulic cylinders. It was simply an improved variation of the gravity mount used with the older guns, but the improved buffer arrangements kept the recoil-stroke down to about 1.5m and absorbed more of the firing shock.

As is usual with artillery development, successive models of the 24cm gun became heavier and more powerful, and the 24cm Mle 93/96 demanded a somewhat more robust mounting so as to deal with the greater weight and energy, but apart from an increase in size it was essentially the same basic design as the earlier type, a 360 degree platform on a well-base wagon supported on two twelve-wheel bogies. This had, in fact, already been developed for the 305mm 93/96 gun, though it was found to be insufficiently strong in that role and the 305 was given a different type of mount. In the 240mm case, the central portion of the vehicle was raised by screw-jacks on the bogies; on arriving at its firing site steel girders were then laid, the vehicle body lowered, and steel wedges driven in to anchor the vehicle to the ground. This was, in effect, the first steps in the development of the Batignolles platform system. For firing across the track, outrigger struts and ground pads were used to resist the overturning force on the vehicle.

The 27.4cm Models 1887, 1893 and 1917 guns were the smallest calibres adapted by Schneider to their type of non-recoil sliding mount, and they can be taken as representative of the class. The basic structure consisted of two heavy side-plates rigidly connected by an elaborate system of cross-transoms to make a very rigid box. The side-members were shaped to accept the gun trunnions in a reinforced area, with solid steel bushings to take the recoil blow, and the basic box was supported at each end by a multi-axle bogie. An arrangement of cross-beams and screw-jacks was fitted to the underside of the centre section and platforms as required for the service of the gun were provided. Since the whole equipment slid back on firing it was not possible to keep an ammunition car permanently attached, and a shuttle car, called a *transbordeur*, was provided. This was pushed to the ammunition car, some distance from the gun, and a 216kg projectile was lowered from an overhead trolley on the ammunition car to a small rolling trolley on the *transbordeur*. This was then pushed back to the gun, a hinged 'drawbridge' lowered, and the rolling trolley pushed on to the gun mounting and up to the ammunition table, where the projectile was rolled off. The empty trolley was withdrawn

The French 240mm Gun Mle 1903

The carriage car of the 240mm Mle 1903 gun.

Gun car and carriage car coupled together.

The French 240mm Gun Mle 1903 Continued

The gun is lifted off the gun car by the A-frames and lowered on to the mounting.

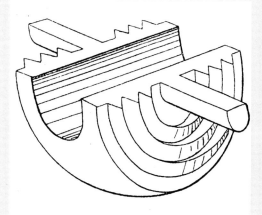

The unusual breech-block of the 240mm gun.

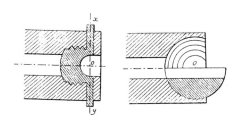

Vertical and horizontal sections, showing how the breechblock functions.

One of the more remarkable equipments was this 240mm gun Mle 1903. In the first place the gun itself used a most unusual breech mechanism known as the 'Canet', in which the block was semi-circular and rotated down through 90 degrees to open. Because of this shape and its weight, it had to be securely

The French 240mm Gun Mle 1903 Continued

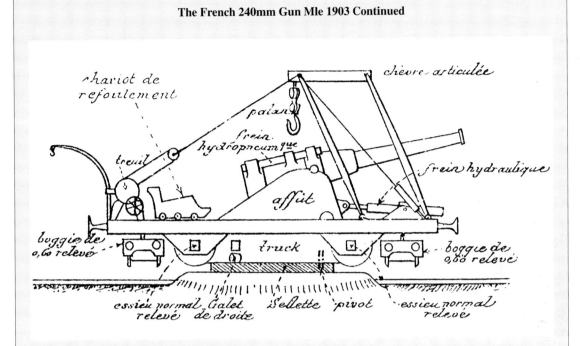

A handbook drawing showing the use of the A-frames in mounting the gun.

locked closed, but during the run-out after recoil the lock was tripped and thus the block opened automatically and ejected the spent case. The mounting was equally idiosyncratic; the gun was trunnioned in a ring cradle directly into a top carriage which rode on the bed of the railway car on a set of inclined planes, so that as it moved backward, so it rose, this giving additional resistance to the movement; there was also an hydraulic recoil cylinder anchored to the front of the vehicle, with its piston rod attached to the gun mounting, giving more resistance. There was thus a dual recoil system, probably the first such system ever employed. The gun recoiled and ran out inside its cradle and the top carriage also recoiled on its incline; run-out was taken care of by the weight of the mounting running back down the inclined planes.

The vehicle was fitted with four wheels of standard gauge, plus two narrow-gauge four-wheel bogies, one at each end of the car. For normal running and covering major journeys it travelled as a standard-gauge vehicle as close to its firing site as could be arranged. After that it could be jacked on to a set of road wheels and pulled by a traction engine, or shifted to a 60cm narrow-gauge track by lowering the narrow-gauge bogies by means of screw-jacks. It was then run to its firing position, which was a prepared bed of earth and timber through which the narrow-gauge track ran. Once the car was straddling this bed the jacks were used to lower it into a firm contact.

In order to lighten the equipment when travelling by road or narrow gauge, the gun could be lifted from the carriage to a separate transport car, and so could the carriage; this was done by a large A-frame with lifting tackle, permanently fitted to the carriage vehicle. All in all, this was a very complicated piece of equipment which involved a great deal of hard work to get it into place; once emplaced it was satisfactory enough. However, relatively few appear to have been built.

The French 240mm Gun Mle 1903 Continued

DATA: Canon de 240 Mle 1903 sur affut-truc St Chamond et Schneider

Calibre	240mm	Total weight	47.8 tonnes
Weight of gun	17.8 tonnes	Recoil	Dual: 620 mm/1 m
Length of gun	6.474 m	Elevation	+15° to +40°
Length of bore	20.6 calibres	Traverse	7° right and left
Rifling grooves	72	Shell weight	140kg
Rifling twist	RH, 7°	Muzzle velocity	526m/sec
Breech	Canet, percussion	Max range	17,300m

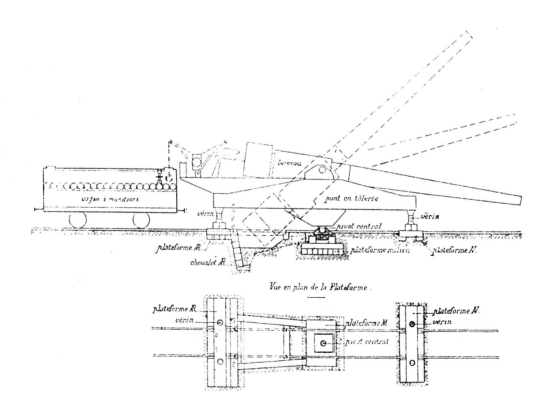

Diagram of the 340mm Mle 1912 in cradle mounting, showing how it was supported on jacks, centrally pivoted, and braced by two arms connected to a buried platform.

and the shell then rammed; the four-part cartridge was passed up by hand.

In addition to the 27.4cm guns, 28.5cm guns, 30.5cm guns and howitzers, 32cm and 34cm guns and 37cm guns and howitzers were similarly mounted, the only significant change being the size and strength of the basic box and the size of the bogies upon which it was supported. Five or six axles were usual, but some of the 34cm and 37cm weapons used two four-axle bogies at each end, tied together by a span bolster to which the mounting was pivoted. Such an arrangement, as well as distributing the weight, gave better articulation to the mounting and allowed it to be manoeuvred on the somewhat sinuous tracks laid behind the lines. It may be noted here that the European standard loading gauge imposed a weight limit of 17,000kg per axle, which, by simple arithmetic, accounts for the varying wheel arrangements.

The 34cm gun Mle 1912, after being installed in a sliding mounting was also placed in a cradle mounting. Two very similar models of this gun existed, one with a 4 degrees rifling twist (giving the projectile one complete revolution in 45 calibres of travel) and the other with a 6 degrees twist (one turn in 30 calibres). The change in rifling gave the projectile better stability in flight and allowed the development of some better-shaped

shells, and together with a slight increase in the propelling charge, these seemingly minor changes increased the power of the gun from a muzzle energy of 18,900 tonnes to 20,550 tonnes and added about seven kilometres to the range. But this additional power meant a far heavier recoil blow, which the sliding mount was adjudged insufficient to withstand, so a cradle mounting had to be made. In effect it was the Schneider sliding mount but with the gun carried in a ring cradle trunnioned to the mounting side plates. Four hydraulic recoil cylinders and one hydro-pneumatic recuperator cylinder were built on to the cradle; the latter cylinder was operating at a pressure of 2,300lb per square in, an exceptionally high pressure indicative of hurried design.

With the perfection of the Batignolles mounting in 1917, the 30.5cm Mle 93/06 gun and the 37cm Mle 87 howitzer were constructed to this pattern, and become more or less the preferred types, replacing the earlier Schneider sliding mounts as they wore out – although some managed to survive into the postwar years.

In order to produce a really heavy weapon, the St Chamond company took a worn-out 34cm Mle 1887 naval gun, shortened it and rebored it to 40cm calibre to make a heavy howitzer. The mounting was of their own design and was

The 320mm Mle 1893 gun on Schneider sliding mounting.

a simple flat-topped girder bearer mounted on bogies and carrying the gun in a cradle and top carriage. The unit was pivoted at the rear to give a limited top traverse. Operation was based on the Batignolles system, the mounting being lowered to the ground before firing, although most of the recoil force was absorbed by the hydro-pneumatic recoil system. It was a very clean and efficient design, but the weapon was insufficiently powerful for its size and only eight were built.

The largest French rail gun was the Schneider 520mm (20.5in) howitzer. In truth this was a political weapon rather than a military requirement, built mainly to demonstrate that it was possible and to rehabilitate the French gunmakers in the eyes of their countrymen after the shock of the German 42cm howitzers early in the war. Only two were built, neither was ever used in action, and in the summer of 1918 one was destroyed by a premature detonation of its shell while firing some experimental ammunition at the Quiberon proving ground.

The howitzer was 16 calibres long and was mounted in a cradle slung by its trunnions into the side girders of a simple box structure. This was carried on two double-bogie sets, each bogie having four axles. The cradle had four hydraulic recoil cylinders and two pneumatic recuperator cylinders, allowing a recoil of 945mm (37in). Elevation and ammunition handling were powered by electric motors, the power coming from a special generator car which was located about 100m from the gun and connected by cables. The mount was of the sliding type, with five supporting beams beneath the body and one beneath each bogie span bolster. On firing, the entire mount slid back about one metre; it then had to be raised from its beams and two electric motors connected to the two outermost axles were used to drive it back into position, after which it was lowered again. There was no traverse, aiming being done by motoring it along a curved track.

The design was well done, but dragging 255 tons around the countryside and spending three hours emplacing it in order to fire only nine miles was scarcely cost-effective.

USA

As soon as America entered the war, the Ordnance Department, realizing that heavy artillery would be needed, made a survey to discover what heavy guns could be obtained from coast defences, the Navy, or from private gun manufacturers. A total of 464 weapons were earmarked in this way, ranging from a dozen 7in Navy guns to a solitary 16in howitzer currently under test for the Coast Artillery. The next question was that of what to mount them on, and railway mountings seemed to be the quickest and simplest solution and, moreover, a solution which was particularly appropriate to the kind of warfare then being conducted in France.

But before they could think of putting guns into operation in France, it would be necessary to raise and train an army, which gave the Ordnance Department some breathing space; guns without men to operate them are useless. And thus the first design of railway gun was not for France, but for use in the USA: in an extension of a pre-war idea, it was decided to mount a number of guns on rail so that they could be moved rapidly around the coastline in case of a shelling attack by German submarines against areas without fixed defences.

The 7in Guns

For this role the 7in (178mm) guns were selected, since there were only twelve – insufficient to make their journey to France worthwhile – and they were the smallest of those available and would thus make a good test-bed for the designers. Firstly the designers set about developing a standard railway car, the M1918, upon which the 7in and 8in guns and the 12in mortars could be mounted. Once that was done a circular pedestal was bolted to the floor of the car and on top of that the standard 7in navy pedestal mount was fixed. The first pedestal was used to lift the navy mount-

7in (178mm) railway gun acted as the test-bed for various ideas which were put to better use in other designs; it led to the standard M1918 car, gravity loading, tubular outriggers and other devices.

ing sufficiently high so that the gun could traverse all round without striking the raised ends of the car, and also to allow the gun to be depressed for loading. The 7inch was usually loaded by hand ramming the shell, but there was insufficient room on the ends of the car for men to move with the rammer, so gravity loading was adopted. The shell was placed on an elevated trough on one end of the car, slightly higher than the gun breech. The gun was lined up with the tray and depressed to –5 degrees and a 'spanning tray' fitted between the trough and the open breech. Then the shell was shoved off the trough, down the tray, gathering speed as it went, to coast through the gun chamber and into the rifling with sufficient force to cause the driving band to bite into the grooves. The powder bag was then slid down the tray, the tray removed, the breech closed and the gun was then elevated and pointed. The height of the pedestal also allowed the gun sufficient depression to permit it to be fired from elevated positions on the coast down upon low-lying submarines. The maximum range, firing a 165lb (75kg) shell, was 17,000yd (15,540m) and the entire equipment weighed 76 tons. Assembly was by the American Car & Foundry Co. at Berwick, Pennsylvania.

The 8in M1918 Gun

For the 8in (203mm) guns the Ordnance Department designed what they termed a 'barbette mount'. This was a pedestal in the well of the M1918 car, on which a gun pedestal and platform was fitted so that the gun could traverse through the full circle. The gun were M1888 coast defence models removed from forts, or the Navy Marks I,II, III or IV removed from the reserve warship stocks. A total of ninety-six guns were available, and so as to have a reserve of barrels, forty-seven were taken for mounting. The first was tested in May 1918, and by June the tests were completed and the design approved. Contracts were given to the Morgan Engineering Co. of Alliance, Ohio; the Harrisburg Manufacturing & Boiler Co. of Harrisburg, Pennsylvania, and the American Car & Foundry Co., and by the end of the war twenty-four equipments had been completed. Eventually thirty-seven were made before the contracts were terminated in 1919.

Operation of the 8in guns was similar to that for the 7in, the same method of gravity loading being adopted, though in this case the loading table was actually on the gun platform and thus always revolved with the gun and was always in position

The 8in M1918 gun set up for firing across the track, braced by four outriggers. Note the unusual combination of American coupler and European buffers.

behind the breech. Two davits were provided for hoisting the 200lb (91kg) shells onto the gun platform. Another interesting feature was that the mount was designed so that by changing the bogies it could be run on standard or narrow-gauge track, and each car was provided with a set of 23.6in (60cm) narrow-gauge bogies for use on the forward area railways in France. The complete equipment weighed 77 tons and had a maximum range of 20,000yd (18,280mm).

The 10in M1918 Gun

No fewer than 129 10in (254mm) guns were available; these were all M1888 models which had been removed from coast defences around the turn of the century and replaced with the more powerful M1895 and M1900 models. Firing a 510lb (232kg) shell they would be perfectly satisfactory for rail use, and it was decided to put thirty-six of them into the simplest kind of mount, the French Schneider sliding mount. In fact the construction became a joint American-French venture, the heavy castings and guns being prepared in the USA and shipped to France, there to be finished and assembled in the Schneider workshops. General Pershing asked that the entire thirty-six sets of parts be delivered by March 1919, by the end of the war eight sets had been shipped. Work continued, though on a slower priority, and eventually parts for twenty-two guns were manufactured. The components shipped to France were completed, then sent back to the USA, and the other sets were finished in the USA, but since the sliding mount was considered to be a wartime expedient, they were little used and were scrapped in the late 1920s.

The mounting simply consisted of two massive side girders secured together by transoms and cover plates. Two sets of twelve wheel bogies supported the mount for travelling. The gun was held in the side girders by its trunnions, so that it could elevate but had no traverse; direction of fire could only be controlled by using a curved track. There was no form of recoil system; the recoil force of the gun acted through the trunnions on to the entire structure, and recoil was absorbed by building a platform of wooden beams beneath the centre of the mount, around the railway track. Steel I-beams attached to the bottom of the mount were then lowered by screw-jacks until they pressed on the wooden beams and took the entire 180 ton weight of the mount. On firing, the recoil force pushed the entire mount back across the wooden beams, the friction absorbing the firing stresses.

This sounds a simple method, but in fact it had one drawback; as an American commentator observed after the war, wooden beams 14 x 16in (350 x 400mm) and 15ft (4.6m) long were not something to be found lying around anywhere, and the gradual destruction of these beams by firing meant their frequent replacement, which led to a supply problem.

The 12in M1918 Gun

A total of forty-five 12in (305mm) coast defence guns were available for use, together with six 12in 50-calibre naval guns which had been built for sale to Chile for mounting in a battleship, but which had not been delivered. These, it was felt, demanded something rather more efficient that the Schneider sliding mount, and it was decided to adopt the French Batignolles mount which had been developed by the Creusot company. This consisted of a strong girder frame supported by two sets of eight-wheel bogies. On top of the girder was a 'top carriage' supporting the gun in a hydro-pneumatic recoil system, and this top carriage was pivoted at its front end and fitted with a traversing screw so that it was possible to move the gun 2 degrees either side of the centre-line so as to obtain fine control of pointing. The gun was be initially set on a curved track, but the ability to traverse allowed for easier pointing.

The gun would be placed in action by first building a platform of girder steel on the trackbed; the gun was then run across until its centre section was above the platform, with a few inches clearance between the two. Steel wedges were then driven in along both sides of the mounting, lifting the gun weight from its wheels and placing the entire 144 tons weight on to the platform. Firing shocks would be absorbed by the recoil system and the mounting would not move. The 12in M1895 gun fired a 712lb (323kg) shell to a range of 30,000yd (27,420m).

12in M1895 gun on Mounting M1918 Creusot which used a cradle mounting and a top carriage to give some 4 degrees of traverse.

At the same time, it was thought that some of the spare 10in guns could also be placed on this type of mounting, and the entire project was given to the Marion Steam Shovel company, with orders to produce eighteen 10in and twelve 12in guns. But they had considerable trouble in converting the French drawings of the mountings to American standards and in obtaining supplies of suitable steel, and the Armistice arrived before any of these guns had been built. The contract for the 10in guns was immediately cancelled, but that for the 12in guns remained in force, since most of the component parts had been made, and the contract was eventually completed some time in 1920.

As mentioned above, there were also six 12in naval guns available, and it was decided to fit these to sliding mounts, there being some doubts about the speedy provision of a suitable recoil system for such a powerful gun. But by this time the American manufacturers were somewhat wary of French designs, which seemed to give them nothing but trouble, so the Ordnance Department set about redesigning the Schneider mount, first to simplify manufacture and secondly to incorporate some ideas of their own. Three mounts were to be built, so as to keep three gun barrels as reserves; the contracts were placed in the early summer of 1918, and all three were completed before the Armistice, which testified to the simplicity of the Ordnance Department design; the French mount, it was estimated, would have taken eighteen months to build. The three mounts, with guns and with all their ancillary ammunition and fire control cars were completed in 1919 as the '12in Sliding Mount M1918'

The 12in M1918 Mortar

The US Coast Artillery had long been advocates of using 'mortars' – what other people would call howitzers – for coast defence, their role being to drop heavy piercing shells almost vertically on to the thinly protected decks of warships. This was felt to be more likely to cause vital damage than firing flat-trajectory guns at the more heavily armoured sides of the ships. The 12in M1890 Mortar fired a 700lb (318kg) shell to a range of 15,300yd (13,980m), and appeared to be a useful weapon for land warfare, so 150 were made available for railway mounting. An ambitious programme was begun (see box) and, unlike so many ambitious programmes of that time, although the war ended before it could be completed, it had advanced so far that cancellation would have been a gross waste, so that ninety-one howitzers were completed in 1920. They were largely dispersed around the continental USA as coast defence weapons, though a number were deployed in Hawaii and the Philippine Islands, using the 23.6in (60cm) narrow-gauge bogies to allow them to run on plantation railways.

The 14in Guns

Two separate 14in (350mm) gun programmes were initiated in 1917, by the Army and the Navy. The Army did not have any 14in guns which it could spare from the coast defences, since these were the very latest coast defence weapons and were all mounted in vital positions. The Ordnance Department, therefore, had to begin by setting up a programme to build sixty new 14in guns. This proved difficult, since there were no gunmaking facilties which could be spared, and an entirely new plant at Neville Island, on the Ohio River near Pittsburgh, was planned. This was to be equipped so as to manufacture fifteen 14in guns and 40,000 shells monthly and was to cost $150 million. In the event, the war ended long before the planned factory was ready and the project was abandoned early in 1919.

Before this, though, in May 1918 the US Navy offered to give the Army a quantity of 14in guns which they had under construction, estimating that thirty would be available by March 1919. The Army agreed to this and made plans for mounting sixteen of them, giving a contract to the Baldwin Locomotive Works. But within six months, and long before the equipments could be built, the war ended and the contract was cancelled.

The 12in Railway Mortar

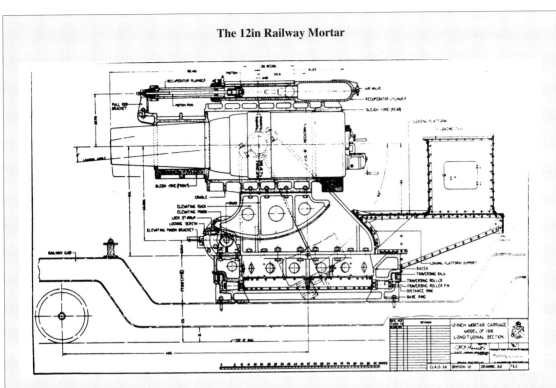

The US 12in M1918 howitzer; longitudinal section drawing.

Front view of the 12in M1918 howitzer

The 12in Railway Mortar Continued

Side view of the 12in M1918 howitzer in camouflage paint

A post-1918 picture of a 12in howitzer emplaced for coast defence. Note the overhead trolley track extending from the magazine car to the gun.

The 12in Railway Mortar Continued

Since these weapons weighed less and had less recoil force than the 12in guns, the M1918 car which had been used for the 7 and 8in guns was quite adequate and ninety-one complete equipments were ordered from the Morgan Engineering Company, leaving fifty-nine spare barrels for replacement when the originals wore out.

This proved to be one of the largest projects of the whole American artillery programme. The Morgan company built a complete new factory, costing $1.7 million, and the US government footed the bill for another $1.8 million worth of special machine tools. Construction of the factory began in November 1917 and was finished in June 1918, and the first complete equipment was ready for testing on 22 August. By the time of the Armistice, every casting, forging and structural part for every one of the ninety-one mounts was prepared. General Pershing had asked for forty-five to be available for the spring 1919 offensive, and forty-five were actually delivered in April 1919, the remainder of the ninety-one being assembled by 1920.

The M1918 car was adapted for the 12in mortar by giving it six-wheel bogies, and the mounting was a barbette type similar to that of the 8in gun, which allowed the mortar 65 degrees of elevation and 360 degrees of traverse. The mortar was carried in a hydro-pneumatic recoil system with a large cast ring cradle. As with the guns on this mount, the bogies were interchangeable with 23.6in (60cm) narrow-gauge bogies. The potential field use of these weapons also led to development of plain high explosive shells, since the generally issued armour- and deck-piercing projectiles used in the coast defence role were ineffective for anti-personnel work.

DATA: Mortar 12in M1890, on Carriage, Mortar, 12in M1918, on Car, Railway Mount, M1918M2

Calibre	6in	Total weight	78.9 tons
Weight of gun	12.9 tons	Recoil	30in
Length of gun	145.25in	Elevation	−5° to +65°
Length of bore	10 calibres	Traverse	360°
Rifling grooves	72	Shell weight	700lb
Rifling twist	RH, Inc to 1/20	Muzzle velocity	1,500ft/sec
Breech	Screw, percussion	Max range	15,290yd

The Navy had begun building these guns in January 1918, their intention being to use them against the German naval bases on the Belgian coast from positions within the Allied lines. It was a simple and effective design, instantly recognizable by the enclosed bodywork which covered the breech end, and it was put into service in a remarkably short time (see box). Although the Navy thought that thirty guns might be ready by 1919, the Baldwin Locomotive Company were only able to build eleven before the Armistice ended the contract. Of these eleven, five were placed on mountings and went to the US Navy, while the other six guns were given to the US Army in 1919 where they formed the basis for the Army's subsequent development of their 14in M1920 guns.

The Navy guns, and their trains, were shipped in pieces to France in July 1918, and the gun crews had first to assemble them at St Nazaire. By mid-August two trains were ready and were moved to French proving grounds for test firings and then sent to the front. The three remaining trains were assembled and tested, and arrived at their battle positions in September. Guns Nos 1 and 2 operated with the French army, while guns 3, 4 and 5 operated with the US Army. To Gun No 2 went the distinction of being the first American gun manned by an American crew to fire an American shell against Germany during the First World War; this was fired on 6 September from a point in the forest of Compiegne against Tergnier, an important German rail junction. Between that shot and the end of the war a total of 782 rounds were fired, all at ranges between 30,000 and 40,000yd (17 to 22 miles; 27km–35km).

14in US Navy Railway Gun

The US Navy 14in gun crossing a wartime bridge en route to the front.

The 14in gun in action at Soissons, 1918.

14in US Navy Railway Gun Continued

A cloud of smoke which must have been hard to camouflage, as the 14 inch (305mm) gun fires.

The US Navy's own involvement with railway artillery began when their reading of reports from France disclosed the German use of long-range guns to bombard Dunkirk from 25 miles range. It was felt that unless some powerful guns were provided to neutralize these weapons, their number might increase until the Channel ports became unusable. Since the US Army had no weapon capable of such ranges, in November 1917 Rear-Admiral Earle, of the US Navy Bureau of Ordnance, suggested mounting 'several naval 14 inch guns' along the French coast to bombard the German guns. The Navy had a number of suitable guns in reserve, and plenty of ammunition, and a railway mount seemed to be the most feasible idea. The Naval Gun Factory in Washington DC was given the job, and by 10 December they had submitted a design. Approval was given for the construction of five guns and the necessary train equipment, and by 15 January 1918 the manufacturing drawings were ready. After some problems with bidders for the contracts, that for the guns and locomotives was awarded to the Baldwin Locomotive Works on 13 February 1918 and that for the cars and other equipment to the Standard Steel Car Company. The first mount was completed on 25 April 1918, seventy-two days from the award of the contract.

The mounting was relatively simple in design, consisting of two longitudinal side girders built up from steel plates and structural shapes, joined by suitable transverse stiffeners. This was supported upon two front and two rear six-wheel bogies. The gun, cradle and recoil system were largely Navy standard patterns, and the cradle was trunnioned into the side plates so that it could reach 43 degrees elevation to give a maximum range of 42,000yd (23.9 miles; 38,390m).

At such a high angle much of the recoil force would be directed downward and place great strain on the running gear, and the mount was therefore designed so that a pit mounting could be used. A large pit was excavated in the ground and into this a foundation of steel girders and timber baulks was lowered by a small crane. On top of this a heavy cast 'transom bedplate' was bolted. The rail track was then laid across the pit area and the gun run over until a cast pivot pin beneath the mounting was aligned with a socket in the transom bedplate. Jacks were then placed under special I-beams at each end of the mounting and lifted the mounting until the weight was removed from the bogies, after which the bedplate was raised by screw jacks until socket and pivot were engaged. The forward jacks were then removed and the weight of the gun rested on the bedplate and the two rear jacks. The track and girders at the rear of the pit were then removed so as to leave a clear space into which the gun breech could recoil below the mounting.

14in US Navy Railway Gun

The gun proved to be completely stable on this mount, and although it took some thirty-six hours to excavate the pit and install the mounting, it was considered well worth the effort for the accuracy and ease of pointing the gun. A special installation team moved ahead of the guns, preparing pits for future use.

The gun could also be fired off the track in the usual way, but in this case the maximum elevation was only 15 degrees, giving a maximum range of 23,000yd (21,000m). Pointing, on either form of site, was done by using a curved track and, for fine adjustment, the rear end of the mounting could be moved across the I-beam by a screw mechanism, giving 2 degrees traverse each side of the centre line.

The guns were ordered back to the USA within a few days of the Armistice, arriving there by the first days of January 1919. One gun is preserved at the US Navy Yard Museum in Washington DC.

DATA: Gun, 14in M1919, on Carriage, Railway, Mk I

Calibre	14in	Total weight	238.8 tons
Weight of gun	85.9 tons	Recoil	44in
Length of gun	560in	Elevation	0° to +43°
Length of bore	50 calibres	Traverse	2½° right and left
Rifling grooves	?	Shell weight	1400lb
Rifling twist	RH, Inc to 1/25	Muzzle velocity	2,800ft/sec
Breech	Screw, electric	Max range	42,000yd (23.9 miles)

The 16in Howitzer

In pre-war days the Ordnance Department had developed a 16in (400mm) gun for coast defence purposes, and was reviewing the design with a view to recommending this as the standard heavy calibre coast gun. In order to achieve a measure of standardization, they had also prepared a prototype 16in coast defence mortar, but since the provision of heavy coast defence guns had fallen to a low priority with the advent of war, it was decided to mount this, too, on a railway car and send it to France. This would throw a 1,660lb (754kg) shell to a range of 23,000yd (21,500m), and the Army was so impressed with this that it gave orders for another sixty-one to be built. The design of the mounting was completed in February 1918 and one was built and test fired, but that was as far as the programme had got before the war ended, and the contract was forthwith cancelled.

The 16in howitzer mount was a simple girder structure supported upon two twelve-wheel bogies. The howitzer was carried in a ring cradle with a hydro-spring recoil system trunnioned into a top carriage which allowed 5 degrees of traverse. Behind the howitzer was a raised platform with loading table and spanning tray for the usual gravity loading system. The howitzer could be fired from its wheels at any elevation up to the maximum, and the mounting could also be anchored to a ground platform similar to the type used with the 14in Navy gun. When fired from its wheels the recoil stress was partly absorbed by the recoil system and partly by rolling the mounting back some 20 to 30 feet (6–9m) along the track; the recoil blow amounted to a force of 338 tons, and it was a tribute to the design that this enormous blow did not spread the tracks or flatten the mount wheels.

5   Anti-Aircraft Artillery

The Wright brothers made their first flight just eleven years before the outbreak of war; no sooner had they done so than minds turned to possible military applications for aviation. The general view was that aircraft or balloons would be capable of employment for reconnaissance purposes; the Hague Convention of 1907 had addressed the question of the bombardment of open towns and had stipulated that 'the bombardment of undefended places by any means whatever is forbidden' and it was generally conceded that the phrase 'any means whatever' was deliberately chosen so as to include aircraft. This left military and naval establishments open to attack, and by 1909 people were contemplating guns for shooting at aerial targets.

It is difficult for us, at the other end of the century, to appreciate the magnitude of the problem which confronted would-be anti-aircraft gunners. First, the plain fact was that on 1 January 1909 there was no such thing as a gun capable of shooting at that sort of elevation apart from howitzers, which were far too cumbersome to track a moving target. Secondly there was the problem of detecting the target, then of assessing its range and height. Then there was the question of what sort of projectile to use: high explosive? shrapnel? incendiary? or something entirely new? And how did one adjust the fire? Viewed from the gun one could perhaps see the burst of the shell and identify it as being 'right' or 'left', but how much right or left? And was it this side of the target or the other side? And how could you hope to hit a target moving at perhaps 50 or 75 miles an hour by aiming off? And if the shell took 20 seconds to get to the aircraft, and in that time the aircraft had

travelled a third of a mile …? And so on, and so forth, *ad infinitum*.

In 1909 an industrial exhibition in Frankfurt displayed a variety of 'anti-balloon cannon', exhibited by Krupp and the Rheinische Metallwarenfabrik, 5- and 9-pounder guns mounted on lightly armoured vehicles. The tactic suggested was to deploy these vehicles in likely places and then, on the appearance of an aircraft, drive them rapidly to some point of interception and there open fire; or perhaps, as a last resort, dash after them if the roads ran in a convenient direction.

From 1910 to 1914, therefore, the various military authorities in the major European countries began to examine the prospect of anti-aircraft weapons; most of them passed the problem to the gunmakers and solicited suggestions. Vickers produced a 3-pounder quick-firer mounted on a Daimler car chassis; France, as might be expected, took their 75mm Mle 1897 and developed a high-angle mounting on the back of a DeDion Bouton car chassis. Woolwich, prompted by the Admiralty, who felt that naval bases might be a prime target for scouting aircraft, began developing a 3in high-angle gun, and under the Army's guidance, a more powerful 4in weapon. The United States looked at the problem and decided that their forthcoming 3in split-trail gun, capable of 45 degrees traverse and 53 degrees elevation, would make a perfectly sound dual-purpose field/AA gun. And at about that stage in the development, war broke out.

There were two schools of anti-aircraft thought in 1914; those who looked for a light rapid-firing weapon capable of putting up sufficient metal in a short time to virtually guarantee at least some of it

One of several exhibits at Frankfurt in 1909 was this motorized Erhardt 50mm 'anti-balloon cannon'.

striking the target; and those who insisted that a single well-aimed shot from a larger gun would be a better and more economical solution. Events were to show that they were both right, in different areas of the sky and against different types of target, but for the moment Britain was content to allow both to have their say. As a result, in pre-war days the Royal Garrison Artillery had shown that a Maxim 1-pounder pom-pom was a capable rapid-firing weapon and they had developed a suitable high-angle mounting. This now became the standard air defence gun; largely, one suspects, because the Army could see little use for it elsewhere.

Shortly before war broke out the Admiralty, anxious for the safety of the enormous Naval magazines at Chattenden and Lodge Hill, north of Chatham, asked the Army to Do Something. The only weapon the army had which could elevate to the necessary angle was the 6in 30-cwt howitzer on its siege platform, so four of these were installed around the magazines. The chance of

their actually hitting an aircraft was fairly remote, but at least the Army had Done Something. But in fact the single-shot school of thought were now to be given their chance, and in March 1914 the 3in 20-cwt high angle gun was approved for 'common' (land or sea) service. It was rapidly followed by the 4in Mark V gun, which the Army had started but which was eventually introduced as a Naval weapon. But only a handful of these had been put into manufacture by August; the solitary 4in was sent to Portsmouth to protect the dockyard. Four 3in guns had been made, and two were immediately sent to Chattenden to replace the howitzers, one to the Royal Gunpowder Factory at Waltham Abbey, and one to guard the Army's cordite magazines at Purfleet.

The 3in (76mm) 20cwt was a beautifully designed and built weapon, the best of its class used by any nation in the war, and one which was to stay in service well into the Second World War. The original Mark I version used a semi-automat-

The British 3in 20-cwt gun on Peerless lorry mounting; several of these survived to fire in anger during the Second World War.

ic vertical sliding breech mechanism, one of the first of its kind. The gun fired and recoiled, and as the gun then 'ran out' and returned into the firing position, a cam opened the breech, ejecting the spent cartridge case, so that when the gun came to rest the breech was open and the chamber empty ready for a fresh cartridge. This not only speeded up the rate of fire but it removed one man from the gun detachment, since there was no need to have a man to open and close the breech for each shot. This was just as well, because the sighting system devised for use with this weapon required two gunlayers, one on each side of the gun, and so the right-hand gunlayer was able to occupy the space which would otherwise have been taken by the breech-worker.

Unfortunately, the breech mechanism was a precision job; the block, for example, had multiple bearing surfaces on each side, all of which had to be carefully scraped, ground and hand-fitted in order to spread the pressure from the gun chamber equally over all the surfaces. This became a major bottle-neck in production and a redesign (Mark II, introduced in early 1916) was eventually done, changing the breech mechanism to a hand-operated rotating screw; this was selected because there

was more capacity available for a screw breech, and more experience in making them, than for the complex block breech. But this, of course, meant that the breech-worker had to come back into the detachment, and the right-hand gunlayer found his position somewhat cramped.

Two gunlayers were used because it was considered best to have one man concentrate on elevation and one on bearing. They were backed up by two assistant gunlayers who fed information into and reset the sights as demanded by changing information from range-finders and other sources. The gun fired a 12.5lb (5.7kg) shrapnel shell fitted with a powder-burning time fuze, so another man was needed to keep setting and resetting the fuzes as the range changed. One man actually loaded the gun, one man passed the fuzed round of ammunition from the fuze-setter to the loader, and one man passed ammunition from the box in which it came to the fuze-setter. The gun detachment commander, usually a sergeant, oversaw everything that went on, checked sights and gave orders. So we arrive at ten men, four of whom – the breech-worker, loader and passers – were actually firing the gun, while the remaining six were worrying about fire control. And there, in a nutshell, was the greatest dilemma

The 3in 20-cwt Gun

3in 20-cwt gun on lorry mounting, showing the fitting of the outriggers and stabilizing jacks.

The 3in 20-cwt Gun Continued

Maintenance of the 3in 20-cwt gun, showing the multiple bearing faces of the original semi-automatic sliding breech.

This gun was first suggested by the Royal Navy in 1911, and the development was entrusted to the Royal Gun Factory at Woolwich Arsenal. The resulting gun, approved for service in March 1914, was a masterpiece, and without doubt the best anti-aircraft gun used by anybody in the war. It was originally provided with the 'Mounting, High Angle, Mark I' which was a simple structure of two side-plates rotating on a roller race and supporting the cradle trunnions. These were not set at the same height, the axis of the trunnions being tilted 2½° down to the left so as to provide automatic compensation for the drift of the projectile due to its right-handed spin. The elevating gear had a two-speed gearbox so that a fast rate could be employed to get close to the target, then the fine rate could be engaged for precise aiming.

The gun had a vertical sliding block breech with multiple bearing surfaces and with a selective semi-automatic mechanism which opened the breech on recoil and closed it as the cartridge was loaded. Firing a 12.5lb (5.7kg) HE shell it could actually reach up to an altitude of 37,200ft (11,300m), the 'maximum ceiling'. but the time fuze fitted to the shell would not function long enough to reach that distance, so the 'practical ceiling' was 23,500ft (7,170m). But, of course, this is only true when the gun is elevated to 90°; as soon as it moves away from that position the ceiling drops, and so an arbitrary condition has to be imposed such as 'the maximum height at which an aircraft can be engaged continuously for 30 seconds', and this brings us to the 'effective ceiling', which in this case would be about 20,000ft (6,100m).

The somewhat luxurious specification was abandoned when mass-production became necessary. The two-speed elevation went, and the complex sliding block breech was abandoned for a simpler interrupted-screw type. The static mounting was now supplemented by a mobile mounting, which was simply the static unit bolted to a four-wheeled trailer which had four outrigger arms which could be extended to the sides and thus form a wide and stable platform. Then came a self-propelled mounting, with the same static unit fitted into the cargo bed of a 4-ton Peerless truck.

The 3in 20cwt gun gradually became the inter-service standard (for the Navy was fitting them on to warships) and replaced many of the improvised guns which had appeared in 1915. It continued in service throughout the Second World War, not being declared obsolete until 1946.

of the anti-aircraft world in 1914–15. It was labour-intensive, and the most intensive part was not the heave and fire part of the operation, but the highly skilled and complex business of aiming the gun and calculating all sorts of aim-offs, fuze lengths, elevations and so forth. The shortage was not simply of men, but of fairly intelligent and highly trained men. However, since the Royal Navy was the

The 3in 20-cwt Gun Continued			
DATA: Ordnance, QF, 3in 20-cwt Mk I on Mounting, 3in AA, Mk IV			
Calibre	3in	Total weight	13,318lb
Weight of gun	2,250lb	Recoil	11in
Length of gun	140in	Elevation	+10° to +90°
Length of bore	45 calibres	Traverse	360°
Rifling grooves	20	Shell weight	16lb
Rifling twist	RH, 1/30	Muzzle velocity	2,500ft/sec
Breech	Block, percussion	Max ceiling	37,200ft

source of both the 3in and 4in guns, they had priority; in the meantime, the Army made do with about thirty 1-pounder pom-pom guns, which were distributed around central London on roof-tops and which needed no more than two or three men each to operate them. Their sights were rudimentary, so there was no need for a large team of specialists.

The army, though, considered that their priority was providing protection for the troops in the field, and as a result the protection of London was given to the Royal Navy, that of the rest of the country remaining an army responsibility. And since the production of the two specialist guns was slow, and the supply slower, the next move was to cast around for any guns which were available and which could be converted into anti-aircraft weapons. Woolwich Arsenal were quick off the mark here and, after considering the matter chose the 13-pounder horse artillery gun. This fired a useful 3in shell at a good velocity, and a pedestal mounting to allow 70 degrees elevation was easily designed. The only modification needed was to fit a 'cartridge retaining catch' into the mouth of the chamber so as to retain the round of ammunition in place after it had been loaded at a high elevation and while the breech was being closed, and to fit an additional spring recuperator above the gun in order to assist in pulling the gun back into battery after recoil. At the low elevations used in the field role the normal recoil system was perfectly adequate, but pulling the gun 'uphill' needed the additional spring. This modified equipment was then

fitted into the cargo bed of a Peerless motor lorry and on 16 October 1914 was approved for production and issue as the '13-pounder Mark III'.

(It is worth noting that those guns which survived the war in good condition had the retaining catch removed and were refitted to field carriages and returned to duty with the Royal Horse Artillery. Some survived, to be declared obsolete in 1944, were placed in store to await disposal and were then rescued and issued to the King's Troop RHA for ceremonial purposes. The guns which today fire salutes in Hyde Park may well have fired in a more serious role in Hyde Park in 1915–18.)

Another likely weapon was the coast artillery 12-pounder QF gun, and numbers of these were put on a pedestal mounting, given the same retaining catch and additional return spring, and fitted to two-wheeled trailers with girder legs which could be folded out to give a firm platform. However, experience showed that the ballistics of the 12-pounder were not well suited to anti-aircraft work, and relatively few of these guns were adopted.

Next came the idea that if the 13-pounder was good, the 18-pounder field gun might be even better, and it, too, was modified in the same manner as the 13-pounder, placing it on a pedestal and then anchoring this in concrete to provide a static gun for permanent emplacement. But, again, the ballistics proved unsuitable; the muzzle velocity was not sufficiently high to give the desired short time of flight, the slow flight of the shell making

The Royal Naval AA Division being inspected by Grand Duke Michael of Russia, Admiral Sir Percy Scott and Cdr Rawlinson, the latter's aide, in December 1915. The gun defies identification but was probably a Vickers 3-pounder on a made-over ship's mounting fitted to a trailer; the searchlight in the background is also of interest.

aiming-off something of a problem. Moreover the sectional density of the 18-pounder shrapnel shell was poor, leading to inaccuracy at high angles of fire and a low effective ceiling. After a handful of guns had been converted, second thoughts were had and a better solution presented itself. If the barrel was given a new 3in liner it would be able to fire the 13-pounder shell propelled by the 18-pounder cartridge; this would give a high velocity with a proven projectile. The idea was examined, tried, proved to work, and in August 1915 fifty equipments on motor truck mountings were ordered. To call this an 18-pounder would have been somewhat confusing, so it became the

The 13-pounder Mark 3 gun on Mark 1 mounting; this had an extra spring casing above the normal recoil system. The Mark 2 mounting had a fresh design of system which compressed everything into one casing.

The 13-pounder 9-cwt gun on high-angle mounting. The large dial on the side indicates the fuze length to be set.

The 10-pounder Russian. Close examination shows that the various scales are all provided with electric lamps for night-firing.

'13-pounder 9-cwt Mark I' and eventually proved to be the backbone of the field AA defence system.

Another 13-pounder, the Mark IV, also appeared early in 1915. This was a 76mm (3in) gun developed by the Elswick Ordnance Company for commercial sale; it differed from the service 13-pounder in having a slightly shorter barrel and a lower muzzle velocity, and it also used the Nordenfelt screw breech (as used in the French 75mm Mle 1897). These were lying unclaimed in the Elswick factory so they were rapidly fitted to motor trucks and offered to the army. They were first used around London, notably around the Royal Gunpowder Factory, but later all six went to France.

The last 'scratch' gun to be taken into service was another commercial design from Elswick, a 2.95in gun originally developed for the Russian

Navy. A dozen of these were lying in the Elswick factory, their delivery having been prevented by the war, and in 1915 Elswick placed them on improvised pedestal mountings and offered them to the Royal Navy. They accepted them, but on second thoughts decided that the logistic problem of supplying these twelve guns with special ammunition at sea might be more trouble than they were worth, and so they passed them across to the Army. As the '10-Pounder Russian', they were taken into use in 1916 and are believed to have spent their lives in the AA defences of London (the Army having taken back the responsibility for London by that time).

The QF 4in (102mm) Mark V gun had been approved for Naval use on the last day of 1913, and the Navy was placing them on ships as fast as

The 13-Pounder

13-pounder Gun Mark IV on Mounting, Motor Lorry, Mark III. This side view well shows the additional spring casing, needed to drag the gun 'uphill' after each shot.

A 13-pounder 9cwt in action; the two figures in front of the platform appear to be Serbians, suggesting that this gun was in Salonika.

157

The 13-Pounder Continued

The absence of anti-aircraft guns in 1914 led to a hurried examination of available ordnance and the selection of the Horse Artillery's 13-pounder on the grounds that they were available, that the course of the war so far suggested that it might not be the best divisonal gun, and that it had a respectable shrapnel shell capable of damaging aircraft. Study of 'the anti-aircraft problem' indicated that one of the prime requirements had to be a high velocity in order to reduce the shell's time of flight and thus ensure that the target had not moved too far during that time, so simplifying the calculation of the target's future position and the associated fuze length and fire orders. The simplest answer was to move up in power and use the 18-pounder, but against this was the desperate need for these guns in their proper divisional role and, as experiments showed, the unarguable fact that the ballistic coefficient (or 'carrying power') of the 18-pounder shrapnel shell was unsuited to vertical gunnery.

On 10 August 1915 the Director of Artillery suggested boring out the barrel of an 18-pounder gun, inserting a liner of 3in (76mm) calibre, and then using the 18-pounder cartridge to fire the 13-pounder shell. His staff must have made some rapid and satisfactory enquiries, for on 15 August orders for fifty equipments on motor trucks were given. Calling such a gun an 18-pounder would have been confusing, so in October it was formally named the '13-pounder of 9 cwt.'

It took time to get these guns manufactured and into service, and it was also necessary to set up special production for the ammunition, the 18-pounder cartridge case having to be reworked and 'necked' so as to accept the 13-pounder shell. It was thererfore mid-1916 before the new gun made its appearance in worthwhile numbers, but once established it soon built a sound reputation.

The construction of these equipments was kept simple; a pedestal on the back of a Peerless or other motor truck supported the standard 18-pounder cradle and the modified gun. Indeed, the first design was a little too simple, being that of the earlier 13-pounder Mk 3 gun, and it had to be strengthened to take the extra recoil force of the converted weapon. The recoil system was adjusted for a constant 35in stroke, making the mounting quite steady.

Since it was purely an interim gun, due to the slow production of the 3in 20-cwt gun, the 13-pounder was not kept in service after the war, being declared obsolete in April 1921, though a number appear to have remained in service with the Canadian Army until about 1930.

DATA: Ordnance, QF, 13pr 9cwt Mk I on Mounting, Motor Lorry Mk III or Mk IV

Calibre	3in	Total weight	16,800lb
Weight of gun	1,008lb	Recoil	35in
Length of gun	96.96in	Elevation	0° to +80°
Length of gore	30.9 calibres	Traverse	360°
Rifling grooves	18	Shell weight	13lb
Rifling twist	RH, 1/30	Muzzle velocity	2,150ft/sec
Breech	Screw, percussion	Max ceiling	19,000ft

they came from the factory. But in 1915 the army were building two armoured forts out in the estuary of the Humber, the vast lagoon of water behind Spurn Head, and felt that the high velocity of the Mark V gun (2,350 feet per second, as compared with the standard Mk III gun's 2,090ft/sec) was a desirable feature to allow a relatively lightly armed artificial island to deal with enemy raiders. The Army successfully applied to have the Naval gun approved for land service use, which was done in May 1915, and duly installed two into Haile Sand Fort. Once having seen what the gun could do, and having got the necessary authority to use them in land service, the army was not slow to organize some of the production for anti-aircraft use, for which the Navy's original dual-purpose (high angle and surface) mounting was apparently adequate. The gun fired a 31lb (14kg)

The 3.6in Gun

GHQ France, in spite of being well-provided with 13-pounder 9-cwt guns, spent much of 1916 bewailing the lack of a high-performance anti-aircraft gun, and so in 1917 the development department of the Ministry of Munitions set about preparing a fresh design. They started this in the traditional manner, looking to see what existing gun could be cannibalized into fitting the demand and picking on the naval 4in high-angle gun. After several months of trying to design a mobile mounting without success, everything was torn up and a fresh start made in early 1918. The result was the 3.6in (91mm) gun which fell neatly between two stools: technically, it was ahead of its time; tactically it was just too late, the war ending before the design could be perfected. Although officially introduced on 20 September 1918, and although a production order for 100 equipments was given, in the aftermath of the Armistice this was cancelled and only five equipments, solely for trials purposes, were authorized.

Had the war continued, the 3.6in would have been an excellent weapon. It had a semi-automatic breech and what appears to be an integrated sighting and fuze-setting station, and the peformance was good. Two mountings were developed: one, a static pedestal, was never formally introduced, and the other, shown here, was an ingenious tracked trailer with stabilizing legs which well shows the contemporary concern with transporting guns in the Flanders mud.

One of the drawbacks was the difficulty of loading at extreme elevation

However, after trials had been completed, the 3.6in was scrapped. Which was, on reflection, just as well, since it left the way clear for the subsequent development of the 3.7in in the 1930s. Had the 3.6in survived, it is probable that the newer gun might never have been demanded.

DATA: Ordnance, QF, 3.6in Gun Mk I

Calibre	3.6in	Total weight	?
Weight of gun	2,790lb	Recoil	22–40in
Length of gun	168.6 in	Elevation	0° to +85°
Length of bore	45 calibres	Traverse	360°
Rifling grooves	28	Shell weight	25lb
Rifling twist	RH, 1/30	Muzzle velocity	2,000ft/sec
Breech	Block, percussion	Max ceiling	20,000ft

The 3.6in Gun Continued

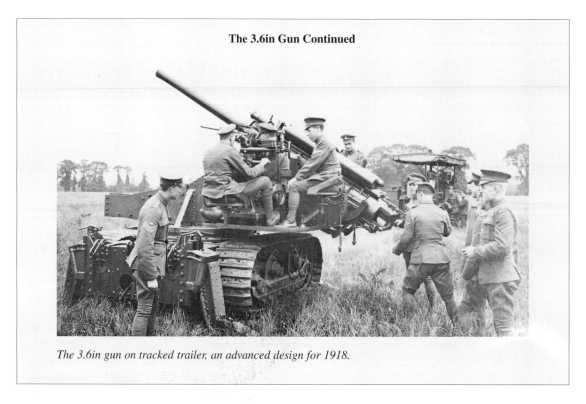

The 3.6in gun on tracked trailer, an advanced design for 1918.

A 13-pounder 9-cwt AA Section in France.

shell to an effective ceiling of 28,000ft (8,540m) and was, so far as performance went, one of the best air defence guns of the war. But it was a bad design insofar as it could not be loaded at angles greater than 20 degrees of elevation, so that when firing at high angles it had to be wound down, reloaded, and then wound all the way back up again, giving it a poor rate of fire. Nevertheless, a number were installed around coastal towns and harbours where the navy could supply ammunition, but as soon as the war was over they were all (except the two guns at Haile Sand, which were on special low-angle coast defence mountings) handed back to the Navy.

With this collection of ordnance in place and being strengthened by the improving production of the 3in 20-cwt and the 13-pounder 9-cwt, the next question to be tackled was that of the ammunition.

At the start of the war the standard projectile for light artillery was, as we have already seen, the shrapnel shell. On the face of it, this seemed to be a suitable projectile for anti-aircraft purposes, since the shower of lead bullets would shred the sticks-and-string aircraft of the day and puncture balloons and airships. But experiment showed that, in fact, a shrapnel strike on a balloon or airship was not immediately fatal, since the bullet-holes were relatively small and the elasticity of the material and the gas pressure tended to make the holes contract, so reducing the loss of gas. On aircraft they were a little more effective, but the major drawback, which was complained of with some force by the troops on the Western Front, was that after the shrapnel shell had functioned at the target, the empty shell then fell to the ground. And a six or seven-pound lump of cast steel falling from several thousand feet was a dangerous missile.

This had, in fact, been foreseen; and disdained. In 1910 a Colonel Bethell, writing on *Modern Guns and Gunnery*, observed that:

It has been objected to balloon guns in general that our own troops would be endangered by the shells falling on their heads. This objection is, however, unsound; even if the balloon is attacked by a rival dirigible or aeroplane, it has to be destroyed by projectiles of some sort. And it matters little to the soldier below whether a shell which falls on his head from a height of 5,000 feet weighs one pound or twelve. Moreover the Krupp 12-pounder, for instance, ranges some 8 miles at 45 degrees elevation, so that at any rate the troops in the vicinity of the gun would not suffer. Finally, since the object in view is to bring down some tons of balloon or some hundredweights of aeroplane from the sky, the incidental fall of a few 12-pounder shells would appear to be a minor matter.

Some two years later another writer, Major Hawkins, in the *Proceedings of the R.A. Institute,* also expressed doubts:

A great disadvantage of shrapnel is the unavoidable return to earth of its bullets and pieces, a serious matter when we consider the number of shells that will certainly be necessary to get a hit, so that except in great emergency it will not be possible to fire in directions that will damage our own troops. Moreover, officers and NCOs must have an instinctive acquaintance with the vertical trajectories of their guns so as to decide promptly where the debris will return to earth.

When theory turned to practice, Hawkins' view prevailed over that of Bethell, particularly in the eyes of the soldiers on the ground beneath the bursting shrapnel. It was therefore decided that high explosive would be a better projectile. It would certainly dispose of anything it hit; it would ignite the hydrogen then used to inflate balloons; its radius of effect would provide some degree of damage from a near miss; and the individual fragments would be less likely to cause severe damage when they returned to earth. The problem was that no high explosive shell was yet in production, because there were some technical problems which had demanded solution.

Several writers in the post-1919 period, generally in the interest of promoting their own causes, asserted that the problem was simply that the authorities were incapable of designing a time fuze for use with explosive shell. There was rather more to it than that, however. True, time fuzes for HE shell were not something contemplated by many people in pre-war days; there seemed to be little point in it. The HE shell was for use with howitzers, to destroy field works, and an impact fuze was all that was needed. Shrapnel shell did use a time fuze, but the design of the two types of shell was considerably different; the shrapnel shell had a 2in hole in the nose and the time fuze screwed into this. Moreover, the fuze was designed to deliver a flash to the gunpowder expelling charge in the shrapnel shell. The HE shell, on the other hand, had a hole in the nose about 1in in diameter, into which the impact fuze screwed. So the current time fuzes would not fit any high explosive shell nor would they detonate a high-explosive shell.

A further complication was added by the demand that any fuze used with a high explosive shell needed to be 'bore-safe'; the detonation train must be physically interrupted or blocked while the shell was inside the gun barrel, so that should the fuze be faulty and initiate its action as soon as it felt the jolt of firing, the explosive in the shell would not be detonated. A bore premature with a shrapnel shell was embarrassing, and could possibly damage the gun's rifling; a bore premature with an explosive shell would undoubtedly wreck the gun and probably kill some of the detachment as well.

The Royal Laboratory at Woolwich Arsenal, at that time the design authority for almost all service ammunition, had appreciated the problem shortly before the war and had developed a serviceable solution. They designed an HE shell using a similar body to the shrapnel shell, a parallel-sided body with a separate nose bush. The forward end of this bush had a 2in hole for the standard shrapnel time fuze, while the lower end had a threaded hole to suit the standard howitzer impact fuze. The shell was filled with Lyddite, and a cavity left in the

front of the charge. The nose bush was fitted, and a howitzer fuze screwed down into the Lyddite filling. The time fuze was then screwed on top. After firing, and at the set time, the time fuze exploded and delivered a blow to the top of the howitzer fuze sufficient to drive in its firing pin and, in effect, cause it to function on impact. The shell detonated. The howitzer fuze also contained a 'shutter', a blocking device actuated by centrifugal force which would prevent the detonation passing into the shell unless the shell was spun at speed for a short period of time to open the shutter, a condition which only applied when it was in flight and some distance outside the muzzle.

This 'Fuze, Time and Percussion, No 80/44' was approved for service on 29 October 1914, but the combination of fuze, shell and filling had to be rigorously tested, after which production had to be organized – and by that time there were a lot of other things demanding priority of production. So it was to be shrapnel only for the anti-aircraft guns for some time to come.

Other innovations undergoing trial in 1915 were incendiary shells, for shooting at Zeppelins, and various types of tracer to allow the trajectory of the shell to be seen and thus permit corrections to be made. Tracers fell into two groups, those for day use and those for night use; a night tracer was a pyrotechnic substance fitted into a tube attached to the base of the shell; the pyrotechnic was lit by the flash of the propelling charge and it emitted sparks as it flew through the air. For daylight use, these sparks were insufficiently bright, and until the pyrotechnic scientists of the Royal Laboratory solved that problem the daylight tracer was a container of a thick black ink attached to the shell base, with a hole off-centre. A wax seal in this hole was melted by the propellant flash, and as the shell spun through the air the ink was flung out by centrifugal force and traced a black line in the sky for long enough to allow a quick observer to pick up the trajectory.

The general public, particularly after German Zeppelins began raiding, were not slow in bombarding the Ministry of Munitions, and its

Another photograph from France; this one appears to be more authentic – the figure behind the breech and the gesticulating man in front of the sights suggests a degree of urgency.

Munitions Inventions Department, with their own ideas. Late in 1915 the Secretary of the Ministry of Munitions informed the War Office that he had over 200 designs of anti-aircraft shell which had been submitted by members of the public, and would the War Office kindly lend him an 'expert artillerist' to sort the wheat from the chaff. The War Office replied that they, too, had been inundated with designs. They listed them: shells which contained bullets or segments joined together, to be expelled by an explosive so as to carve their way through the target; shells filled with discs or boomerangs, to be expelled as sub-missiles; shells built in sections, joined by wire, to be blown apart; shells filled with lengths of chain and, most common of all ideas, shells fitted with large knife-blades which sprang out on contact and cut the aircraft or airship to pieces. One or two of the more promising ideas had been tried, but all had failed. Moreover, they all suffered from the same basic defect: they demanded that the shell hit the target. If this minor requirement could be met, of course, then a simple cannon-ball would have done all that was necessary.

Which brings us back to the fundamental fact at the root of all anti-aircraft fire: that the target is free to move in three dimensions, at speed. In such conditions it is obvious that gunnery becomes a game of chance. The only way to approach the problem is to make one firm assumption: that the target will continue flying straight and level on its present course for the duration of your attack, or at least for the time it takes for your shell to reach him. Once granted that assumption it becomes possible to design sights and plan tactics. Of course, the enemy may not continue to fly straight and level; but, strange as it may seem, the assumption holds good for most of the time – it is very difficult to drop a bomb or fire a gun with any semblance of accuracy if the aircraft is being hurled all around the sky – which is why anti-aircraft artillery eventually proved to be successful.

A second point is worth stressing. It is not necessary to shoot aircraft down for anti-aircraft artillery to succeed. If the hostile aircraft can be persuaded to go away, or is so disturbed that his bombs fail to hit his target, then the defence has succeeded. No matter that the bombs may have fallen somewhere else and done damage, the target was not hit, so the enemy attack was a failure. It has to be admitted that this point of view stretches credulity, but it is factually correct; if air defence keeps the enemy from his target, then it can claim to be a success. Unfortunately the general public (which includes much of the remainder of the Army) does not always see this point of view. To them the only sign of a successful anti-aircraft defence is an enemy aircraft falling in flames.

The first step in shooting down an aerial target is to detect it. And one should realize that the aircraft of 1914/15 were mostly small – the Bleriot monoplane had a wingspan of only 30ft – and under-powered – aero-engines were of the order of 75 to 100 horsepower. So they were small, and, by today's standards, fairly quiet. There were no dedicated aircraft sentries or spotters, so there was a good chance that a high-flyer could escape detection. The only hope was the sound of his engine; this may have been detectable in a quiet countryside, but it was a different matter in a battle zone where the grumble of gunfire was fairly constant. Nevertheless, it was all there was, and sound detection began to form the first tripwire in the defensive line.

The sound detector took two forms; first a large horn which would collect the sound and deliver it to a straining ear, and secondly a microphone placed at the focus of a parabolic mirror. Given reasonable conditions of quiet and calm, and a moderately noisy aircraft, it was possible to detect a machine at 15km range with the latter. It also had the advantage of giving some reasonable indication of direction and elevation. The horn, by itself, merely indicated that there was a target out in the general direction; it was improved by mounting two horns side-by-side and feeding the information to the operator's right and left ears, so that he had a stereo effect to aid him in pointing towards the target. By adding a third horn, above the other two, and coupling it to one below, and giving this pair to a separate operator, he was able to come up with a reasonable assessment of elevation.

But brutal physical facts come into it. Suppose the target to be flying towards the locator at 150 kilometres per hour, and that he is first detected at 6km distance. Sound travels at about 330 metres per second, so it would take the sound 18 seconds to reach the listener, during which time the target has flown 750 metres closer to him. So that when the locator hears a target noise from 6,000 metres range, the target is actually 5,250 metres away from him. If we now sound the alarm, and assume an alert gun detachment, ammunition ready and everything generally favourable, we can say that in 30 seconds

Sound detection; an early German example of the technique.

By 1918 the technology had advanced; Americans with a French four-horn detector explain the mysteries to a bunch of orphans.

from the alarm the gun will fire. When the gun fires, therefore, the target is only 4,000 metres away. The shell, let us say, takes 20 seconds to reach the assumed position of the target. And where is the target? At 3,150 metres range, well this side of the bursting shell. Assume the first shot missed, and allow 20 seconds to calculate a fresh point of aim and 20 seconds for the time of flight, and the target is now 1,480 metres away. If the second shot misses, the target will be 200 metres past the gun by the time the third shell gets up into the sky.

RANGEFINDING

Having detected the target, the next problem was to determine the range to it. The only field rangefinding device in 1914 was the 'telemeter', which required a measured base on the ground and an operator with a telescope capable of measuring angles at each end. They compared results, did some trigonometry, and produced a range. Satisfactory for a stationary target, but impossible against a moving target. One-man optical rangefinders had been introduced for use with machine guns in 1912, but these were only capable of ranges up to about 3,000 metres, and were not particularly accurate at that range.

A further point, not appreciated at that time, was that even if a range had been deduced, it would not have been of much use. Gun sights were calibrated on the assumption that the gun and target were more or less on the same level, give or take a few hundred feet. Given a range, setting this on the sight elevated the gun so that the trajectory dropped the shell at that range. But the trajectory of a shell is not a fixed curve which can be elevated into the sky and waved about. Once the target is considerably higher than the gun, the trajectory deforms under the effects of air density and gravity, and this deformation must be analysed and taken into consideration in the design of an anti-aircraft sight.

What the trajectory did when shooting at ground targets was also upset by another factor when shooting at air targets; the air density changed rapidly with height and the shell's flight performance close to the ground did not necessarily bear much relationship to its performance in the upper air, one of the factors which prevented the 18-pounder from becoming a useful anti-aircraft gun. Moreover, experience was to show that time fuzes, which relied upon the carefully regulated burning of a length of gunpowder inside the fuze, performed very erratically at high altitudes, often extinguishing due to a shortage of oxygen.

Then came the question of aiming off to compensate for the movement of the aircraft during the flight of the shell. As we saw above, the 150km/hr target could move over 800 metres in 20 seconds, and aiming ahead of it by 800 metres meant pointing about 9 degrees ahead of it, which demanded some ingenious design in the sight as well as considerable faith on the part of the gunlayer.

And, finally, having got the shell up there and burst it, there was the question of assessing where it was in relation to the new position of the target and deducing what correction to make for the next shot.

By trial and error suitable sights were developed, and the practice grew of opening fire and then continuing to fire as fast as possible without waiting for the results of the shot. As corrections were deduced from observing the bursts, the sights were altered, usually by a second gunlayer while the first maintained his aim at the target. And in order to reduce the complication, two sets of sights were used, one for elevation and one for line, so requiring four men. A fifth man set the fuzes on the shells, while a command post observed the shooting, deduced corrections and fuze lengths and called them out to the guns. But, as we have already observed, this demanded a high proportion of skilled operators, and gradually the general opinion came around to having one central device for determining range, elevation, bearing and fuze length and then ordering this to all the guns. This reduced the number of gunlayers and allowed the actual loaders more freedom around the gun. The second major change was to do away with the idea of correcting fire on observation. Each burst of fire

Two American gunners operating the Brocq Tachymetre.

Provided the basic assumption held and the target flew straight and level, the shell stood a good chance of arriving in roughly the same place as the target. A similar instrument, the Wilson-Dalby tracker, was developed in Britain and rapidly brought into use. Optical rangefinders also appeared, so that by 1916 the central post system was in general use and the accuracy of anti-aircraft fire began to improve.

Improvement, in this case, is comparative; after the war a senior officer calculated that the expenditure of anti-aircraft ammunition throughout the war years gave a figure of 4,500 shells fired for every aircraft brought down. But this figure is somewhat distorted by the fact that not every shell fired at an aircraft was carefully aimed at one. At night, searchlights were used to pick up targets and illuminate them for the guns, but in many cases this proved impossible due to cloud or bad weather, and the guns then resorted to barrage fire, putting up a curtain of bursting shells in the estimated path of the raider. This no doubt had some effect, but it tended to skew the statistics.

FRANCE

The French, as we observed earlier, did little in the way of gun development. They had a serviceable weapon in the 75mm Mle 1897, and it was merely a matter of developing a suitable mounting to allow it the desired elevation and all-round traverse. The first guns, following the fashion, were mounted on DeDion Bouton chassis to become the 'Autocanon', but these were expensive, slow to manufacture, and had only 240 degrees of traverse. A simple centre-pivot mounting was rapidly developed to allow guns to be mounted in static positions, particularly around Paris and other towns close to the front. These 'Postes fixes de DCA' (DCA – Division Contre Aérienne) allowed up to 85 degrees elevation and 360 degrees traverse. Finally the 'Canon de 75 sur voiture remorqué' was developed, a two-wheeled trailer with four outrigger arms which were lowered to

would be entirely independent of anything which had gone before and would be based upon the most recent information available on the target's position, course and speed.

The French were the first to move to the 'central post' system, using an instrument known as the Brocq Tachymetre. This had two telescopes each manned by an observer, one tracking the target's course and the other its height. Each kept on target by turning handwheels which were also connected to electrical generators which produced a current proportionate to the speed of tracking, allowing speed and height to be displayed on dials. By setting in a resistance equivalent to the shell's time of flight an artificial answer appeared which corresponded to the calculated future position of the target by the time the shell got there. This was now converted into an elevation angle, a direction and a fuze length and the data was ordered to the guns.

the ground to give a stable platform for firing. This also allowed the gun 85 degrees elevation and all-round traverse.

A handful of 75mm Autocanon were sent to England in late 1915 to augment the AA defences of London and, using these as a pattern, the Coventry Ordnance Works built a suitable mounting which was then fitted to a variety of Daimler, DeDion and Lancia trucks, the guns and recoil systems being purchased from France. One significant difference was that whilst the French design had the gun trunnioned close to the breech, the British design was trunnioned at the centre of balance. This was because the weapons supplied were simply the barrel and cradle of M1897 field guns and not the specially-designed cradle for the Autocanon; it made for easier manufacture since no balancing springs were needed, but it made loading difficult when the gun was pointed in a direction which placed the breech over the driver's seat.

75mm Mle 1897 on Postes Fixes de Division Contre Aérienne, as used in the static defences of Paris and other cities.

The British equivalent of the Postes Fixes de DCA was this revolving mounting somewhere in the London defences. It was never graced with an official nomenclature.

75mm Autocanons used by the Royal Naval Mobile Anti-Aircraft Division in London, 1915.

The 75mm Autocannon

The French 75mm Mle 1897 Autocanon on De Dion chassis.

The 75mm Autocannon Continued

This version, built by Coventry Ordnance Works, trunnioned the gun at the centre of balance, simplifying manufacture but at the expense of convenience.

The gun was trunnioned beneath the breech, so as to give ample clearance for loading and recoil.

Like Germany and Britain, the French were attracted to the concept of putting anti-aircraft guns on trucks, so that they could be placed in convenient centres from which they could rapidly deploy in the path of an oncoming air attack. There was also the possibility that they could even chase something as slow as an airship hampered by a headwind, though this idea rapidly evaporated when it was actually attempted

As a result, their first major anti-aircraft weapon was the 75mm Mle 1897 field gun mounted on the rear end of a De Dion Bouton car or truck chassis. The gun itself was completely unchanged from its field application. The mounting was a rotating turntable with a platform for the gunlayers and which supported the gun by means of a new design of cradle which had its trunnions as far back as they could go, so that they were a few inches in front of the gun breech. This allowed the maximum elevation but with the gun set far enough from the ground to allow the full recoil stroke. The loading gunners stood on the ground and had ample room to set fuzes and load the gun, following it around as the platform turned. Because of the recoil, it was not possible to fire the gun if the breech was towards the body of the vehicle, and so its arc of fire was restricted to 120 degrees on each side of zero, the zero position being with the gun pointed forward over the engine. Four stabilizing arms with screw-jacks were fitted to the rear end of the vehicle so as to give a firm platform for firing.

The 75mm Autocannon Continued

A dozen of these guns were acquired by Admiral Sir Percy Scott in 1915 to augment his defences of London. They performed well, and more were requested; but the French were hard enough pressed to make enough for themselves. They therefore supplied a number of guns, and ammunition, but the British would have to mount them as best they could. The Coventry Ordnance Works were invited to produce a mounting and did so; it differed in one major respect from the French because the guns had been supplied complete with cradles and recoil system, so the COW design supported the cradles with their trunnions in the same position as on the field guns. This demanded a somewhat different design of mounting in order to keep the breech off the ground in recoil, but the result was successful and in addition to using De Dion chassis, several were fitted to Daimler chassis.

The American Expeditionary Force was also supplied with a number of Autocannons, though they never formally adopted them, preferring to wait until their own M1917 gun came along.

DATA: Autocanon de 75 (antiaérien automobile)

Calibre	75mm		Total weight	3,995kg
Weight of gun	460kg		Recoil	140m
Length of gun	2.72m		Elevation	0° to +70°
Length of bore	36.6 calibres		Traverse	120° right and left
Rifling grooves	24		Shell weight	5.56kg
Rifling twist	RH, 1/25.6		Muzzle velocity	550m/sec
Breech	Screw, percussion		Max ceiling	5,000m

RUSSIA

Little is known about Russian air defences at this time, and the only gun known to have been specifically developed was the 76.2mm (3in) Model of 1915. This appears to have been a naval coast defence gun on a pedestal mount allowing 75 degrees elevation, and the equipment was transported on a two-wheeled platform. Whether this was lowered to the ground for firing, or whether the pedestal and gun were removed from the platform and attached to a prepared holdfast is not clear. The gun fired a 14.3lb (6.5kg) HE shell with a muzzle velocity of 1930ft/sec (588m/sec) to an altitude of about 18,000ft (5,500m). However, given the limited facilities for gun manufacture in Russia in 1915–17, and the interservice rivalry for what facilities there were, it seems unlikely that many of these guns were produced.

ITALY

The principal Italian anti-aircraft gun was the '75mm Gun 75/27 1906/15' which, as the nomenclature suggest, was a 1906 vintage field gun modified into a high-angle gun. The 75mm field gun Model of 1906 was, in fact, a Krupp design, numbers of which were bought from Germany and more assembled in Italy from components purchased from Krupp. It was augmented, in 1911, by a new Krupp design and also by the split-trail 3in (75mm) of Deport, a French designer at the Forges de Chatillon. These two 1911 models were built in Italy under licence, and once production was stepped up in 1915, it allowed numbers of the 1906 gun to be converted into a fairly straight-forward two-wheeled trailer weapon.

In addition, though, the 75mm Mle 1911 Deport, due to its then-revolutionary split trail, was capable of 65 degrees elevation and 54 degrees traverse without moving the trail, and this made it into a useful secondary anti-aircraft gun, particularly on the battle-fronts where it virtually became a dual-purpose weapon. Although not much use against high-flyers, it was still quite effective against balloons and front-line reconnaissance aircraft.

USA

The United States Army was, of course, hamstrung by lack of funds prior to 1916 and therefore nothing was done to establish an anti-aircraft capability. There was a general belief that the M1916 3in gun, being a split-trail design, would prove to be an effective dual-purpose weapon once it was perfected. The Ordnance Department, however, studied the question in 1915 and reached the conclusion that the best solution would be to take an existing coast gun and simply develop a pedestal mount which would allow the maximum elevation. A design was drawn up, using the 3in M1903 coast gun, and once war was declared it was soon put into production as the 3in M1917. A total of 116 of these were made and issued to various defensive posts in the USA and possessions by April 1919.

The M1917 was a static mounted gun, primarily conceived for the defence of ports and naval bases. But once war was declared it became apparent that a mobile gun would be needed for the field armies, and here it was felt that the M1903 gun was

US 3in M1917/18

The US 3in M1918 was the 1898 coast gun given a new lease of life; it was to survive into the late 1930s before being replaced.

US 3in M1917/18 Continued

As already indicated in the text, American anti-aircraft gun development took two distinctly different lines, according to whether the gun was to be static or mobile; this decision was due entirely to the availability of suitable guns at the critical time. When the question of an anti-aircraft gun was first raised, in 1915, the Ordnance Department took the usual attitude and looked to see what was in the stock-room that could be adapted. The Model 1903 3in coast gun was a suitable candidate, and since anti-aircraft defence was decided to be a responsibility of the Coast Artillery Corps, selection of a gun with which they were already familiar was obviously a good thing.

The M1903 seacoast gun, when mounted upon a fresh design of pedestal mount which allowed the maximum elevation, became the AA Gun M1917 and was specifically intended for the air defence of harbours and naval bases. It was a powerful 55-calibre gun, and used a cartridge case of 4.18 litres capacity.

When, in April 1917, it became obvious that mobile AA guns were going to be needed by the AEF, the instant reaction was to put the M1917 on wheels. A little calculation, however, soon showed that the M1917 was far too powerful and would need a very substantial trailer to stand up to the firing shock. Adopting a less powerful gun, albeit one powerful enough for the job, would allow a simpler, quicker to manufacture, and cheaper trailer platform to be made. The M1903 seacoast gun had been developed to replace an earlier model, the M1898 Driggs-Seabury gun; these had been withdrawn and were now in reserve store awaiting disposal. This was a 50-calibre gun, using a cartridge case of 3.47 litres capacity, but it still gave sufficient performance to make a useful AA gun and it was lighter, and delivered a lesser firing shock, than the M1903 gun. So with no further ado it was transformed, by adopting a high-angle mounting, into the AA Gun M1918.

The mobile mounting was a relatively simple design, no more than a four-wheeled flat-bed trailer with the gun on a pedestal in the centre. Four levelling jacks, two inclined stabilizing jacks and four outriggers, a box to hold the sights and tools, and that was that.

In the years after the war the two guns went through various modifications, and fresh mountings were developed until two designs were standardized in 1931. Work continued on improving the 3in guns, but in 1938 an improved 3.5 in design showed promise, and work on the 3in ceased. Numbers of both static and mobile guns were employed in the Pacific in 1941-42 and as training weapons, until eventually being replaced by the 90mm gun in 1943

DATA: Anti-Aircraft Gun, 3in, M1918, on Mount M1918

Calibre	3in	Total weight	15,000lb
Weight of gun	1,782lb	Recoil	24in
Length of gun	154.5in	Elevation	−5° to +85°
Length of bore	50 calibres	Traverse	360°
Rifling grooves	24	Shell weight	15lb
Rifling twist	RH, Inc to 1/25	Muzzle velocity	2,600ft/sec
Breech	Screw, percussion	Max ceiling	22,000ft

too powerful. A gun of somewhat lesser performance would still be adequate for anti-aircraft work and would simplify the design of a mobile mounting, and since there was an ample supply of the elderly 3in Seacoast Gun M1898 on hand, this was selected for the mobile role.

However, although this was a good solution from the mechanical viewpoint, it was less satisfactory from the logistic angle. The M1903 was a 55-calibre gun with a cartridge case of 255 cubic inches capacity; the M1898 was a 50-calibre gun with a 212 cubic inch cartridge case. This meant that two

The American static mounting for the 75mm which took the name of 'Modified Improved AA Gun Carriage M1917' and was intended to be transportable.

entirely different rounds of ammunition were required, one for static guns and one for the field army. Moreover, in subsequent years, as these two basic designs of gun were developed into improved models, this difference in ammunition remained, and unless this is understood there seem to be inexplicable differences in ballistic performance when the various 3in designs are compared.

The M1898 was adapted to anti-aircraft work by producing a fairly basic pedestal mount to carry the gun and cradle, and placing this on a simple flat-bed trailer with four solid-tyred wheels. Outriggers

were fitted to stabilize the platform for firing. An order for 612 of these equipments was given in July 1917, and the first was delivered for test in August. Assembly of complete equipments was then suspended until the testing could be completed, though manufacture of components went ahead so that production in quantity could begin once the design was approved. But approval did not come until after the Armistice, so the M1918 mobile 3in gun never appeared in service during the war.

Instead, two quicker expedients were adopted. Since the French were using the 75mm gun as an anti-aircraft weapon, and since the US Army had decided to standardize upon the 75mm gun, it seemed reasonable to fit it into the air defence role as well, and as a first solution the 'Modified Improved Anti-Aircraft Gun Carriage M1917' was approved. This was a simple structural steel contrivance, set upon a revolving turntable, into which the cradle and barrel of a 75mm Mle 1897 gun could be fitted. This was no better or worse than similar devices erected around London and Paris as part of their static defences, but the American equipment was intended to be mobile. In fact, 'transportable' would have been a better word, for it had to be carried partially dismantled on a special trailer and then erected at the chosen site. But fifty were built and shipped to France in late 1917, there to be fitted with 75mm guns supplied by the French.

Something with better mobility was obviously necessary, and was, in fact, in the pipeline when America entered the war. This was a trailer-mounted 3in M1916 field gun, but, as we have already observed, the M1916 was something of a

millstone. Orders were given for the manufacture of fifty-one of these 3in M1916 equipments in July 1917, and almost immediately the order was modified because of the change of calibre of the M1916 gun to 75mm. Then the manufacturers were handed the contract for the 3in M1918 mounts, which threw their production schedules into disarray, and, of course, the manufacturing problems of the M1916 gun caused more delays. The end of this story is somewhat clouded; the official account merely says that the fifty-one mounts were completed in 1918 and twenty-two had been delivered to France by the time of the Armistice, but it does not expand upon what guns were fitted – if any. It seems most probable that the mountings were shipped to France and provided with 75mm Mle 1897 guns there. Certainly there has never been any evidence that 75mm M1916 guns ever functioned in the air defence role in France; all the US Army anti-aircraft batteries appear to have used either 75mm Mle 1897 or British 13-pounder 9-cwt guns.

Meanwhile, Battery B of the 1st AA Regiment get to grips with the Autocanon near Montreuil, June 1918.

6   Coast Defence Artillery

When war broke out in 1914 the coast artillery of the combatant nations leapt to their posts and waited for the enemy; for the most part they were still waiting when the Armistice was signed four years later. Only two British actions against German warships are recorded, and one of those was actually by a troop of field guns; no American, French, Italian or Russian coast artillery action is known, though it is possible that the guns defending Kronstadt fortress, outside St Petersburg may have occasionally warned-off German patrol boats, and they were certainly in action in Bolshevik hands against British patrols in 1919/20. Turkish coast defence guns and minefields in the Dardanelles saw off the Allied fleet in 1915 and completely ruined the Allied attempt to force a passage through the Dardanelles strait into the Black Sea.

The reason for this inactivity is simply that the Royal Navy seized the initiative from the Germans early in 1915 and retained it thereafter so far as surface warfare was concerned. And once the Germans settled on submarine warfare as their principal naval effort, there was nothing for coast artillery to do.

The first of the two anti-ship actions was the repulse of the German commerce raider *Emden* at Madras on 22 September 1914. The *Emden* was a 3,600 ton cruiser armed with ten 4.1in guns which had been despatched into the Indian Ocean to harry British merchant shipping. Her captain, von Müller, conducted a gentlemanly campaign, ensuring that the crews of his prizes were safely into their lifeboats and clear of their ship before he sank it, and a cheeky one too, since he actually called at the British coaling station of Diego Garcia in 19 October and refuelled; the inhabitants of this remote island, without communication, were not yet aware that war had broken out, and von Müller wasn't going to be the one who broke the news to them.

However, on the evening of 22 September he sailed up to the entrance of Madras harbour and began shelling the Burma Oil Company's storage tanks. Local defence was in the hands of the Madras Volunteer Artillery, with two wheeled 4.7in guns. These they quickly manned and began shooting, causing the *Emden* to withdraw and abandon her raid, though not before half-a-million gallons of oil had gone up in smoke.

In the North Sea, action was anticipated from the first day of war; after all, the growing power of the German fleet was one of the factors which, in many eyes, had accelerated the move to war. So it was to be expected that the German fleet would be out and about, making a nuisance of itself. In fact nothing happened until late in November, when a German squadron of three battle-cruisers, three heavy cruisers, three light cruisers and a flotilla of destroyers swept across the North Sea with the intention of bombarding the coastal towns of East Anglia. But in the early morning mist they were met by two British destroyers and a minesweeper making their morning patrol; these three promptly turned about and, assisted by a smokescreen, vanished back into the mist to report the presence of the German squadron. The Germans, fearful that the British fleet would have been warned and might appear at any moment and cut them off from their bases, decided to open fire on Great Yarmouth and Gorleston, but since the mist had not risen their aiming marks were indistinct and all their 28cm shells fell either on the open beach or into the sea. They then departed rapidly for home, losing one heavy cruiser to a mine *en route*.

The next raid was better organized. Four battle-cruisers (*Seydlitz, Von der Tann, Moltke* and *Derfflinger*), one heavy cruiser (*Blücher*), four light cruisers and two flotillas of destroyers set out to bombard the north-east coast towns of Scarborough and Hartlepool, and the raiders would be followed by the German High Seas Fleet which would cover its return across the North Sea from any British naval interference which the bombardment might stir up. Unfortunately for the Germans, by this time the British Admiralty had a copy of their fleet code book, taken from a beached German warship in the Baltic a few weeks before, and by decoding German radio traffic they were aware that an operation in the North Sea was about to take place, though the exact details were not clear. Nevertheless, extra patrols were set in motion, and at dawn on 16 December 1914 one of these patrols found the German squadron some six miles off the coast near Hartlepool. The alarm was given, and the German force split into two groups, one heading south to bombard Scarborough and the other north to Hartlepool.

The attack on Scarborough was carried out by the *Derfflinger* and *Von der Tann*. The town, of no military or naval importance , had no defences and the two ships were able to cruise slowly back and forth, firing their 28cm and 30.5cm guns into the town, destroying the coastguard station, an empty barracks and the Grand Hotel and killing eighteen people. After half an hour they ceased fire and sailed off to the north-east to rendezvous with the other ships of the squadron.

Hartlepool was a defended port; to the north of the bay, on a headland, was a lighthouse, and on the north side were the two 6in guns of Heugh Battery and on the south the single 6in gun of Lighthouse Battery, both manned by the Durham Royal Garrison Artillery, Territorial Army. (The intention was to build a three-gun battery but the available land and the position of the lighthouse forced the two-battery layout.) A third battery, South Gare Battery with two 4.7in guns, lay at the southern end of Tees Bay about five miles away.

A warning that German forces were at sea had been received the previous night, and the guns were, as routine, manned for an hour at dawn every day. Shortly before 8am guns were heard at sea, and South Gare battery reported seeing large warships sailing north. A Naval signal station in the Hartlepool lighthouse then saw three unidentified warships heading towards them. Minutes later, at 8.10am, the German flag was broken out and the three opened fire. Their intention was first for all three to bombard the coast guns, after which two (*Seydlitz* and *Moltke*) would bombard the town and harbour while the third (*Blücher*) concentrated on keeping the coast defence guns occupied.

The first shell to land fell between the two batteries and destroyed the telephone line from the fire control centre, which meant that the two batteries were now completely independent of each other and the control centre and had to rely upon their own observation. Thereafter the shells rained down, the warships being no more than about 4,000 yards away. Most of their shells were armour-piercing and ricocheted across the guns to land in the town behind, causing considerable damage. The two guns of Heugh Battery engaged the *Seydlitz* and *Moltke*, that of Lighthouse Battery took on the *Blücher*, but as *Blücher* sailed northwards to add its weight of shells to the bombardment of Heugh Battery, the lighthouse obstructed the gun in Lighthouse Battery and it was unable to fire for long periods. Eventually the two battle-cruisers sailed further north, out of the arc of fire of Heugh Battery and both guns therefore concentrated on the Blucher, obtaining several hits and putting some of its guns out of action.

The two battle-cruisers now fired once again into the town, from the north, then sailed south, fired a few more rounds at Heugh Battery as they passed, collected the *Blücher* and sailed off in the direction of Germany to meet their companions from Scarborough and then return to their base. A total of 1,150 shells had been fired into the town, killing 112 people, wounding over 200, and destroying the railway station, waterworks and gasworks and damaging about 500 houses. And although several

British naval patrols scoured the North Sea, the raiders were able to get back to their base at Cuxhaven without further damage.

The damage to *Blücher* was not serious, and the results of the raid were so encouraging that the German fleet decided to repeat the performance in January 1915. By this time the Admiralty's wireless interception service and code-breaking department had got the measure of the German fleet signals organization and knew of the German plan almost as quickly as did the German fleet. As a result, the raiding force met the Grand Fleet near the Dogger Bank on 24 January and in the ensuing battle *Blücher* was sunk, *Seydlitz* crippled and *Derfflinger* damaged. The destruction might have been greater but for Admiral Beatty's flagship being crippled by a German shot, causing him to lose touch with the rest of his fleet for some time. As it was, the High Seas Fleet made for home and coastal raiding was no longer on their agenda.

Coast artillery was unique in one respect: it knew precisely what its targets would be and it could tailor its equipment to suit. Its targets were classified by their size, armament and tactical employment, and the artillery was graduated so as to be able to deliver a projectile capable of defeating the armour at a range at which the battleship guns would be at a gross disadvantage: they would be bobbing up and down on the waves, while the coast guns were securely anchored in concrete. The layman might think this advantageous to the ship, because it had a fixed target. But the point was that the coast gun was a tiny target – the shield of a 6in gun was no more than about six feet square, and that was the only part of it visible from the sea – and the chance of a ship's gun, constantly moving, hitting such a target at long range was remote. On the other hand the ship was a large target – the *Seydlitz*, for example, was 656 feet long, 93 feet broad and displaced 25,000 tons – and with a solidly anchored gun and a skilled gunlayer it was hard to miss at any range. Recall that the German ships at Hartlepool were less than 4,000 yards from the batteries but never achieved a hit on any gun, while the guns achieved hits on the ships. But the affair also shows up the defect in the coast

defence arrangements; the 6in gun was meant to deal with light cruisers; the armour and gun power of full-sized battle-cruisers was out of their league. But 6in guns were installed at Hartlepool, and scores of other places, because logic said that the place was not sufficiently important to attract the attention of a capital ship. And logic was right; the German fleet acted illogically in using a sledgehammer to crack a nut.

A British committee, in pre-war years, had looked hard at the coast artillery's organization and tactics and had recommended that the likely patterns of attack were, first, bombardment at long range by battleships or heavy cruisers; second, bombardment at medium range by light cruisers; third, attempts to enter harbours and sink blockships so as to seal the entrance or otherwise demolish naval obstacles; and lastly, the use of light, fast craft to enter harbours at night and torpedo moored ships. To deal with these, four types of gun were selected: the 9.2in (234mm), firing a 380lb (173kg) shell, for counter-bombardment against capital ships; the 6in (152mm) firing a 100lb (45kg) shell as a close defence gun against light cruisers, boom-smashers and blockships; the 4.7in (120mm) to assist the 6in against boom-smashers and blockships and also take on light torpedo-boats; and the 12-pounder to deal with the light torpedo-boat threat, assisted by searchlights ('fighting lights') or floodlights ('defence electric lights') at night. And, together with a handful of hangovers from previous armament eras, these were the four guns which armed British and Empire coast batteries.

The 9.2in had first appeared as a naval gun, a direct response to the Krupp 24cm gun issued to the German Navy, but on the principle that if the coast defences were to deal with warships then they should have the same armament, it was adopted for Army use. (The same philosophy governed the selection of tank and anti-tank guns in the 1930s.) When the navy moved on to 10, 12 and 13.5in guns the army began to follow suit but it was soon realised that the additional power of these larger guns was unnecessary; the methods of observation and fire control then in use could not even take advantage of the maximum range of the

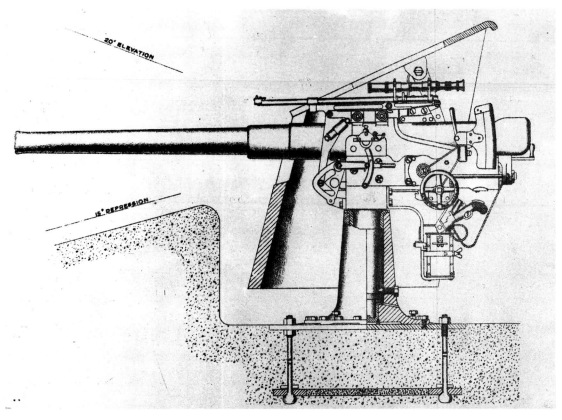

The 12-pounder anti-torpedo-boat gun was on a 'free' mounting – the gunner pushed it round with his shoulder against the pad near the breech instead of using a traversing gear. It was fired electrically from the pistol grip below the breech.

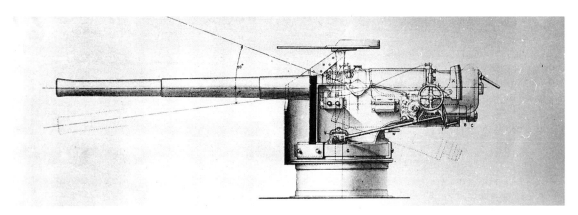

An Armstrong 4.7in on central pivot mounting.

The 4.7in Anti-Torpedo-Boat Gun

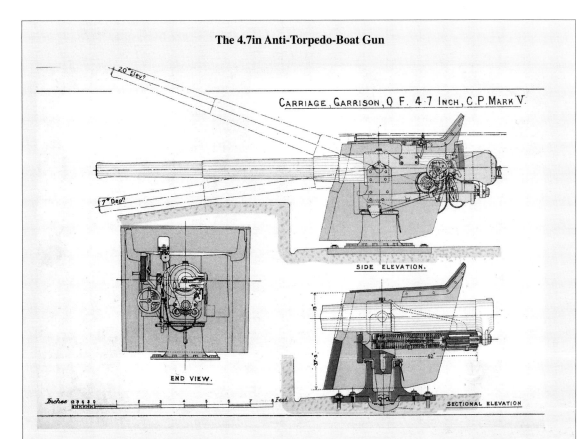

The 4.7in Mark V gun.

As we have seen, as a field-piece the 4.7in (120mm) gun was not an outstanding success; there was nothing wrong with the gun, but it had never been designed with field service in mind and was therefore a fairly substantial piece of equipment. A Naval weapon in the first instance, it appeared in 1888 and was soon appropriated to coast defence. A number were removed from their forts during the South African War and mounted on field carriages, but they were all returned once the war was over. Whatever its failings in the field, on the coast it was a superb weapon, combining a useful weight of shell with rapidity of fire and accuracy.

There were four marks of gun in service at various times; the Marks II, III and IV differed only in their method of construction; they all had similar ballistic performance, firing a 45lb (20kg) shell at 2,150ft/sec

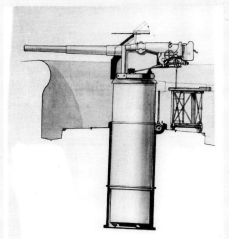

An Armstrong balanced pillar mounting with 4.7in gun, as used in Australia.

The 4.7in Anti-Torpedo-Boat Gun Continued

to 11,800yd (10,790m). The Mark V, for which data are given below, was a longer and more powerful gun, but few of these went into coast service since it was only in some special locations that their longer range could be utilized.

The various mountings were all pedestals with the gun carried in a cradle and protected by a simple shield. The differences were largely in the sights, design of cradle and other detailed fittings. The Mark III was unusual in having a pedestal 8ft 9in high, so that the gun could be placed in deep pits previously built for older guns.

Ammunition for the 4.7 was originally an armour-piercing shell loaded with black powder for attacking light armour and a common pointed shell, also black powder, for dealing with less protected targets. These were later augmented by a common Lyddite shell and a shrapnel shell for local defence.

DATA: Ordnance QF 4.7in Gun Mk V on Carriage, Garrison, Central Pivot Mk V

Calibre	4.7in	Total weight	19,432lb
Weight of gun	5,936lb	Recoil	8in
Length of gun	212.6in	Elevation	−7° to +20°
Length of bore	45 calibres	Traverse	Up to 360°
Rifling grooves	26	Shell weight	45lb
Rifling twist	RH, Inc to 1/30	Muzzle velocity	2,350ft/sec
Breech	Screw, electric	Max range	16,500yd

The 9.2in Counter-Bombardment Gun

A 9.2in Mk X gun on Mounting Mark V, the standard counter-bombardment gun from 1895 to 1956.

The 9.2in Counter-Bombardment Gun Continued

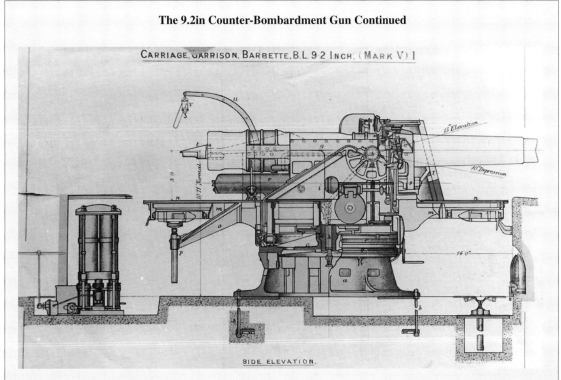

Handbook drawing of the Mark V mounting, showing the shell hoist (lower right) which lifts the shell to the under-shield trolley, from where it is sent round to the hoist 'P' which lifts it to the breech for ramming. The accumulator (extreme left) provides hydraulic power for the first few shots, and the hoist 'V' is there in case the power supply fails and the shells have to be manually lifted.

The 9.2in (234mm) gun was developed in the 1880s as a naval weapon in answer to Krupp's 24cm naval gun, and if ships were to be armed with it, then it followed that the coast defences should have the same power. The Mark X gun appeared in May 1899 and, together with the Mark V mounting, was by 1914 the standard counter-bombardment gun throughout most of the British Empire, India electing to adopt a 7.5in gun. The gun was to remain in use until 1956, even though later models were developed, since there was no real need to replace it. The mounting was improved in post-1918 years, giving it more elevation and hence a longer range, but in most cases the existing gun was simply lifted clear and replaced when the new mounting had been assembled. There was quite enough performance to deal with any major warship at a useful range; and besides, money was short.

The Mark V barbette mounting can best be described as a steel drum bolted to the floor of a concrete pit 35ft in diameter and 10ft deep. On top of this drum, revolving on a roller race, was the gun mounting, a simple set of side-plates into which the gun and cradle fitted together with the 'shell-pit shield', a round steel platform which completely filled the pit. The men actually serving the gun – the breech operator, loaders and gunlayers, were on the platform; the ammunition handling was carried out below it. Two lifts, one for shell, one for cartridges, hoisted ammunition from the underground magazines below the pit and delivered it to hatches in the pit wall. From here the shells were trollied to a hydraulic lift beneath the front of the shield which lifted them up so that they could be clipped into a trolley suspended from an overhead rail running around the shield's under-surface. This trolley was then pushed around until it was over a second hydraulic hoist, beneath and behind the gun

---

The 9.2in Counter-Bombardment Gun Continued

breech. This second hoist now pushed the shell up into it was aligned with a ramming tray behind the breech, from where it was rammed by four men of the gun detachment. The hoist descended, by which time the cartridge trolley had arrived, and the hoist then went up again to allow the bagged cartridge to be pushed into the breech.

All this hydraulic power was generated by a special piston and cylinder on the gun mounting which, as the gun recoiled, pumped up the pressure in the hydraulic system. The pressure for the initial shot was provided by a hand pump and an accumulator, a hydraulic storage device which was essentially a tank of liquid with a heavy weight forming a loose piston on top of the liquid. Pumping, by relays of men, filled the tank and lifted the weight, thus storing energy. When the gun was called into action, opening a valve allowed the liquid, pressurized by the weight, to drive the loading mechanism for two or three rounds, while the recoil-operated piston began generating pressure again. During the course of the war the defects of this system – principally its slowness and reliance on manpower – became apparent and a fresh mounting was planned in which the hydraulic power would be delivered by a constant-pressure system kept up to the mark by a diesel-engined hydraulic pump. This new design also incorporated a power rammer and allowed the gun to elevate to 35 degrees, thus increasing the range. Design was sompleted during the war and erection of some of these Mark VI mountings had begun in 1918, but none were complete when the war ended.

DATA: Ordnance BL 9.2in, Wire, Mk X on Carriage, Garrison, Barbette Mk V

Calibre	9.2in	Total weight	157 tons
Weight of gun	28 tons	Recoil	42in
Length of gun	442.35in	Elevation	−20° to +15°
Length of bore	46.5 calibres	Traverse	Up to 360°
Rifling grooves	37	Shell weight	380lb
Rifling twist	RH, Inc to 1/30	Muzzle velocity	2,643ft/sec
Breech	Screw, electric	Max range	29,200yd

9.2in guns, and the 380lb armour-piercing shell was capable of doing quite sufficient damage to any armoured warship.

The 6in gun Mark VII on mounting, central pivot, Mark II, was the standard close defence gun and was a far simpler piece of equipment. The emplacement was a concrete pit with a circular concrete plinth in the middle, upon which the mounting pedestal was bolted. The gun recoiled in a cradle, controlled by a hydro-spring system, and there was a steel platform on which the gun detachment worked. The gunlayers used the 'autosight', a telescope so designed that when the crosswires were laid on the waterline of the target the gun was automatically laid at the correct range. This served for close actions; but when it was required to fire under central control, range and azimuth were transmitted to dials in the pit beneath the gun, and the gun was laid by two men underneath the platform in the 'sunken way' surrounding the central plinth, leaving only the loaders on the platform and protected by a simple shield.

There were still a number of both 9.2in and 6in guns mounted on disappearing carriages in various forts. These devices had appeared with muzzle-loaders in the 1870s and then, in improved versions, with breech-loaders in the 1890s. The principle was that a revolving base at the bottom of a pit some 10ft deep carried two massive arms hinged to the base at their lower end. Their upper ends were formed so as to carry the trunnions of the gun. Between the arms was a connecting bar to which the piston-rod of a large hydraulic cylinder was coupled. Liquid, usually glycerin and water, was forced under pressure into

The 6in Close Defence Gun

A 6in Mark VII gun ready for action, with shell, powder case containing the bagged charge, spare parts box and sponge bucket. Note the hand-wheels beneath the mounting by which the gun could be laid on information from the fire control room.

A later design of 6in Mark VII mounting, with an over-all shield.

The 6in gun was the first 'modern' breech-loader to go into British service, having been offered by Armstrong's in 1878. It introduced the interrupted screw breech with De Bange pad obturation and bag charges which, with periodic minor improvements, remained the standard until the 1970s. As with most coast defence guns, this one began with the Navy and then moved across to Land Service. The earliest models were largely placed on disappearing carriages (described elsewhere) but when the defects of the disappearing carriage became apparent, and as mountings with hydraulic recoil control began to appear, the 6in was perfected into this 'Mark VII on CP2', as it was universally known, introduced in 1898 and continuously in service until 1959.

The 6in Close Defence Gun Continued

Loading the 6in Mark VII gun; Australian militia at drill.

Its pedestal sat on a concrete plinth in the centre of a shallow pit. A small shield protected the gun detachment. Ammunition was delivered into the pit by two lifts, but shell and cartridge were hand-carried from the lifts to the gun. The gun, being anchored in concrete, recoiled a mere 18in so that the gunners were clustered closely around the breech, and the loading drill was fast and impressive. As the interrupted screw breech was opened, a 'shot guide' swung into place at the base of the opening. The gunner standing to the left of the breech cradled a 100lb shell in his arms, and as soon as the shot guide was in place he dumped the shell on to it; he then swung from the hips, reached back, and the rammer was thrust into his hands. He turned back to his left, and, with two other men already holding the rammer, rammed the shell. He let go of the rammer as it was whisked away and held his arms back to his right side; a cartridge was thrust into them, which he promptly loaded into the chamber. And as he withdrew his hands he shouted 'IN!', whereupon the breech was slammed to and the firing lanyard clipped to the firing lock. The whole business took less time than needed to write this description of it, and allowed the 6in to generate an astonishing rate of fire.

The standard projectile in the coast role was an HE piercing shell capable of penetrating light armour and the upperworks of warships. A common Lyddite shell, pointed and base-fuzed but with little or no piercing capability, was also available for dealing with the less protected parts of ships, and a shrapnel shell was provided for guns in positions where a landing might be attempted, 453 one-ounce bullets travelling at about 1,800 feet per second being a useful deterrent.

DATA: Ordnance BL 6in Gun, Wire, Mk VII, on Carriage, Garrison, Central Pivot, Mark II

Calibre	6in	Total weight	16 tons
Weight of gun	16,875lb	Recoil	18in
Length of gun	279.23in	Elevation	−10° to +20°
Length of bore	45 calibres	Traverse	Up to 360°
Rifling grooves	36	Shell weight	100lb
Rifling twist	RH, 1/30	Muzzle velocity	2,493ft/sec
Breech	Screw, percussion	Max range	12,000yd

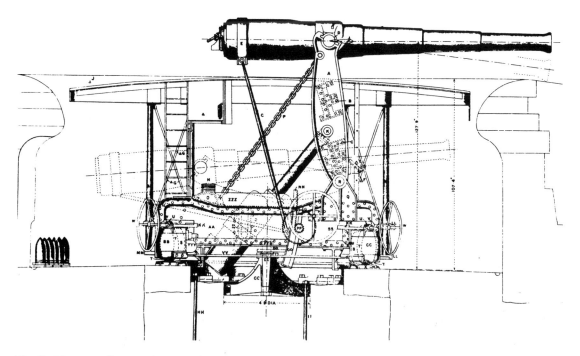

The 6in BL gun on disappearing mounting.

the cylinder and drove out the piston, so forcing the rod to lift the two arms and so lift the gun up until its muzzle was above the edge of the pit. On firing, the force of recoil drove the gun back; this caused the arms to be driven back, pivoting at their lower end and so forcing the piston rod into the cylinder. This forced the liquid out, through a valve, into a tank containing compressed air. The introduction of the liquid further compressed the air and this resistance absorbed the recoil, allowing the gun to descend under control until it settled down on to the base mounting at a height suitable for loading, well down in the pit and out of sight of the enemy at sea, and the liquid valve automatically closed. After loading, the valve was opened and the compressed air forced the liquid back into the cylinder and pushed the gun up into the firing position once more.

The disappearing carriage was a wonderful piece of engineering and it had been developed so that the gun and its detachment would be protected from enemy fire during the process of loading. It also

denied the enemy any target except for the few seconds that the gun was above the parapet before it fired. In the days of slow muzzle-loading, and the early days of breech-loading when operation of the breech was almost as slow as muzzle-loading had been, there was some degree of justification for the complexities of the mounting, but by the middle 1890s the 'axial recoil' principle, in which the gun was mounted into a cradle and connected to hydraulic buffers to damp down the recoil and either springs or compressed air cylinders to return it to the firing position, had taken over. It was faster than the disappearing carriage, since there was no waiting while the gun moved majestically up and down, and practical trials had shown that an axial recoil gun, with shield, offered a target only about 36 square feet in area, almost impossible for a ship-mounted gun to hit at the long engagement ranges which now were to be expected. However, a great deal of money had been poured into disappearing guns, and in several British colonies and coaling

185

A 10in disappearing gun at Landguard Fort, Harwich, in the firing position.

The 10in gun in the loading position.

stations they remained the primary armament until the 1920s; indeed, as late as 1939 it was reported from Australia that there were still two forts in the Port Jackson defences with 9.2in guns on disappearing carriages awaiting replacement.

The 4.7in and 12-pounder guns were mounted on simple pedestals in a shallow pit, the gunners being protected by a shield. Both used separate-loading ammunition, the shell being rammed first and the cased cartridge loaded after it. And both

The 6in Disappearing Gun

A 6in disappearing gun in its emplacement, complete with overhead shield.

In the 1860s the most dangerous part of coast defence gunnery was clustering around the muzzle while reloading the gun, because this presented the enemy warship with a nice target. And so the 'disappearing carriage' came into being, a method of mounting the gun so that its own recoil carried it back and down, into a pit and out of the enemy's sight. In fact the gun normally lived down in the pit, so that casual sailors would never know that a gun was there until it popped up to fire at them. When muzzle-loading gave way to breech loading the disappearing carriage still seemed to be a sensible idea and it was improved and continued, and the idea was taken up in various other countries.

The 6in Mark V shown here was the preferred British equipment for the armament of the many coaling stations set up across the British Empire in order to secure fuel stops for the Navy. It was generally felt that any potential enemy would send only light or medium cruisers to raid these depots, and thus a battery or two of 6in guns would suffice to deter any such insolence.

The design is by Sir William Armstrong's Elswick Ordnance Company and comprises a rotating carriage, two heavy arms supporting the gun, a hydraulic ram forcing the arms and gun upwards, and an overhead shield with a slot in it just large enough to allow the gun to pass through. The ram has a central cylinder full of oil and an outer

The 6in Disappearing Gun Continued

The overhead shield of a 9.2in disappearing gun, Fort Wynyard, Cape Town. The gun rises and falls through the slot.

cylinder full of compressed air. As the gun recoils, so the piston is driven into the central clinder, forcing the oil out, through a valve, into the air cylinder. This further compresses the air, slowing down the movement of the gun until it comes to rest in the pit, nicely positioned for loading. The valve snaps shut, the compressed air and oil are held, and the gun stops moving.

After reloading, the valve is opened so that the compressed air can drive the oil back into the central cylinder and so force out the piston and push the gun back up into the firing position. Aiming was done by dials, setting the angles of elevation and azimuth while the gun lay in the pit. When it rose, therefore, it was pointing in the right direction and as soon as it reached maximum rise it was fired, and promptly recoiled back into the pit. So the enemy warship only saw it for four or five seconds, if he saw it at all.

There had to be a catch in it, of course. And the catch was that, due to the geometry of the gun arms and elevating gear, it was almost impossible to get an elevation greater than 20 degrees, so limiting the maximum range of the gun. And when warship guns got bigger and could outrange disappearing guns, it was time to bite the bullet and put the gun out where the enemy could see it; but only if he could get close enough, and with the gun able to reach its genuine maximum range, he was unlikely to do that unscathed.

DATA: Ordnance BL 6in Wire Mk V on Carriage, Garrison, Disappearing, Mk IV

Calibre	6in	Total weight	20 tons
Weight of gun	5 tons	Recoil	n/a
Length of gun	195.3in	Elevation	−5° to +20°
Length of bore	30 calibres	Traverse	Up to 360°
Rifling grooves	28	Shell weight	100lb
Rifling twist	RH, Inc to 1/30	Muzzle velocity	1,890ft/sec
Breech	Screw, electric	Max range	8,000yd

used a peculiar method of extracting the empty cartridge case. When the earliest QF guns, using brass cases, went into service with the navy, the sailors were still barefooted; and the extraction and ejection of the empty cases on to the deck made them step very lively indeed. When heavier QF guns, such as the 12-pounder, 4.7in and 6in made their appearance the navy was quick to point out the dangers of these much bigger cases falling on to the sailors' feet. The guns were therefore fitted with an extractor which merely loosened the case in the chamber as the breech opened. The case was fitted with a primer which extended about an inch behind the case and ended in a pronounced rim. One member of the gun detachment was provided with a claw-like hook with which he hooked the rim of the primer and jerked the case out of the chamber, then threw it aside into a safe place. Although the army were well-shod, they accepted this naval idiosyncrasy and, indeed, it was not until the 1930s that the 12-pounder gun received a 'proper' extractor which extracted and ejected the spent case when the breech was opened.

That apart, the two guns were conventional enough; the 4.7in fired a 45lb (20kg) piercing shell and the Mks II, III and IV guns had a maximum range of 11,800yd (10,790m). The Mk V gun was five calibres longer and hence had a greater velocity and a range of 16,500yd (15,080m). The 12-pounder gun fired a 12.5lb (5.7kg) common pointed shell to 8,000yd (7,300m).

USA

However much the American field army might have been starved of equipment, the same could not be said of the coast artillery. America had a large coastline, it had some large and important commercial ports, and in the aftermath of the Spanish-American War it found itself with some colonial property, all of which had to be protected. Extensive coast defences were therefore built in the continental United States and then in Cuba, Panama, Hawaii and the Philippine Islands; and having been

built they had to be armed. The range of likely targets was the same as defined by anyone else, so a similar range of armament was developed, from the 'Gun Rapid Fire, 2.24 inch M1900' to the 'Gun, 16 inch, M1919', by way of 3in, 4.7in, 5in, 6in, 8in, 10in, 12in and 14in guns and 12in mortars.

Of these, the 3in and 4.7in were quite conventional; indeed, the 4.7in guns were British, having been bought during the Spanish-American War when the demand for defensive guns outstripped American manufacturing capacity. The 5in introduces a new mounting concept, the 'balanced pillar mounting', occasionally seen in Europe, rarely in Britain (yet, strangely, popular in Australia.) With this system the gun is on a normal pedestal mounting but this is attached to what is, in effect, the piston of a large, vertical, hydraulic cylinder sunk into the middle of the gun emplacement, behind a parapet. When not in use the gun is traversed until the barrel is parallel to the parapet and the pressure is released from the hydraulic cylinder. This allows the piston to sink, taking the gun mounting and gun down behind the parapet and out of sight of the sea. When duty called, the pressure was pumped up, up went the piston and the gun appeared over the parapet ready for action. Apart from concealing the gun from prying eyes in peacetime, there seems little point in the arrangement, which is probably why it was not widely used.

In the USA the disappearing carriage was even more popular than in Britain and was to remain in service well into the Second World War. Six inch, 8, 10, 12 and 14in guns were mounted in this manner all round the USA and in their overseas forts, and during the war years two 16in guns were similarly mounted, one at Panama and one in Long Island Sound. The American pattern of disappearing mounting, called the Buffington-Crozier after its inventors, differed in one major respect from those of other nations in that it used an enormous counterweight suspended in a central pit beneath the mounting. The gun arms were pivoted some distance above their lower end, being attached to the piston rods of two fixed cylinders on the rotating

An American 10in M1900 gun on Carriage, Disappearing, M1901LF. The 'LF' denotes 'Limited Fire' – an arc of fire less than 360 degrees. This gun lacks its breech block, being a preserved gun at Fort Casey, Washington.

A second 10in M1900 at Fort Casey, in the 'down' position.

Rushing in with the shell truck to load a 14in disappearing gun at Fort De Russy, Hawaii.

A 12in gun firing at Fort Wright, New York. The recoil movement has begun, bringing the muzzle back behind the parapet, before it begins to sink into the loading position.

The largest disappearing gun ever made, the 16in M1919 on its mounting M1917 for proof firings before being installed in Fort Michie in Long Island Sound.

mounting. The lower end of the arms held steel rods attached to the counterweight – which, in the biggest guns, weighed over 100 tons. On firing, the gun recoiled backwards, forcing the pistons into their cylinders to brake the initial movement, and then began descending, so causing the lower ends of the arms to lift the counterweight up in its pit. As the counterweight rose, so a rack on its face engaged in a ratchet, so that when the gun stopped moving and was in the loading position, the ratchet snapped in and kept the counterweight up. After loading the ratchet was 'tripped', the counterweight descended into its well, and the gun barrel was lifted over the parapet to fire.

The other major American predilection in coast defence was the use of 'mortars', actually short-barrelled 12in breech-loading guns which fired at elevations between 45 and 70 degrees so as to drop their deck-piercing shells steeply down on to the less well-protected parts of warships. These were generally deployed in batteries of eight or twelve mortars, sited in deep square pits each with four mortars, so that if each pit fired a salvo in succession, on slightly differing data, it was almost inevitable that one salvo would straddle the target, whereupon the other two pits would fire on that data and drench the target in shells. The only defect in this system was the enormous blast caused by firing four short-barrelled guns inside a concrete pit, with their muzzles several feet below the parapet. All the gunners had to leave the pit before the mortars were fired electrically, after which the mêlée caused by four detachments racing in to reload was something to behold. The damage from the blast was also considerable, and eventually it became the practice to fire only two mortars at a time.

(It might be said here that the British also tried using 'high angle guns', as they preferred to call

The 14in Buffington-Crozier

A 14in M1910 gun on Carriage, Disappearing, M1907M1.

Firing the 14in gun of Battery Randolph, Fort De Russy, Hawaii.

The 14in Buffington-Crozier Continued

Aerial view of the single 14in gun of Battery Gillespie, Fort Hughes, Manila Bay.

By 1905 the US government had acquired a good deal of property in the Philippines, Panama, Hawaii and similar places which needed defending, and in that year the 'Taft Board' sat to review the coast defences. At the same time it was found that the existing 12in guns were being worked at the limit of their endurance in order to extract the utmost range and penetrating power from them, and the combination of high velocities and hot-burning powders was wearing them out at an alarming rate. Taking one thing with another the Taft Board decided that the adoption of a 14in gun would solve a lot of problems; it could produce the desired range and terminal velocity without over-strain, and it would have such a range and command of the adjacent sea that single-gun batteries would suffice.

The result was the 14in gun M1907, a 34-calibre weapon, which seems to be a poor way of obtaining a powerful gun until you understand that the gun length was dictated by the fact that the guns had to go into emplacements in Panama which had already been built for 12in guns. After four guns had been built to arm these two batteries in Fort Grant the design was dropped and work began on a 40-calibre model.

This duly appeared as the M1910 gun and, like the M1907, it was mounted on a massive disappearing carriage which managed to achieve a maximum elevation of 20 degrees. It was the first American disappearing carriage to exceed 15 degrees elevation, and it was also a new design of carriage which had a recoil buffer cylinder built into the counterweight, the piston being attached to the floor of the counterweight well. The maximum range of 22,800yd was restricted by the carriage, but was probably more than the fire control system could use anyway, and the shell had a muzzle energy of some 63,000 foot-tons, which seemed to be enough to deal with most warships.

The 14in Buffington-Crozier Continued

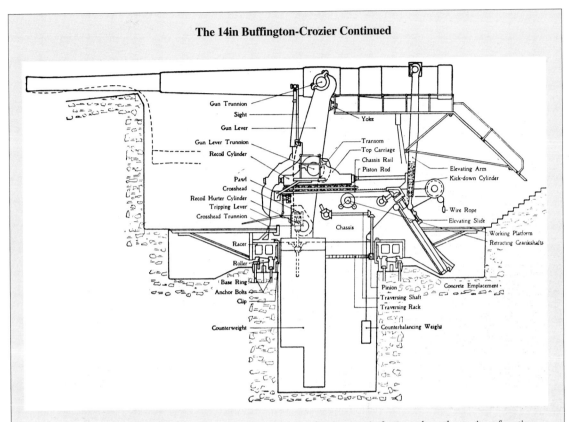

The ultimate disappearing gun: the 16in M1917 mounting in diagrammatic form to show the various functioning parts.

So the 14in M1910 went into the various forts protecting Manila and Subic Bay in the Philippines and into forts at each end of the Panama Canal, always in single-gun batteries. Although installed in time for the First World War, they were not called into action until the Second World War. If the local scrap-dealers haven't got there first, there should be two guns still in existence on Carabao Island in Manila Bay.

DATA: Gun, 14in M1910, on Carriage, Disappearing M1907M1

Calibre	14in	Total weight	305 tons
Weight of gun	61.6 tons	Recoil	73in
Length of gun	590 in	Elevation	–5° to +20°
Length of bore	40 calibres	Traverse	Up to 85° right and left
Rifling grooves	126	Shell weight	1,660lb
Rifling twist	RH, Inc to 1/25	Muzzle velocity	2,350ft/sec
Breech	Screw, electric	Max range	22,800yd

Four 12in mortars in their pit, being laid preparatory to firing.

About to load a 12in mortar.

them, but they were simply the standard 9.2in gun mounted so as to allow elevations up to 45 degrees. The object was more or less the same, but they were mounted in batteries of two guns only and relied more upon highly accurate prediction than upon the swamping effect. But the conclusion is inescapable:

the British were not enchanted by high-angle fire and appear to have had little faith in it. The number of high-angle batteries built throughout the empire could be counted on the fingers, and the standard *History of Coast Artillery in the British Army* doesn't even mention them.)

Firing the 12in mortars; note the shell, caught in mid-air.

FRANCE

At the outbreak of war France had thirty coast defence batteries, plus another eight in their North African colonies. With a fairly shrewd appreciation of the likelihood of naval attack, the responsibility for coast defence was taken over by the Navy shortly after the war began and the army coast gunners were transferred to the field artillery. A considerable number of coast guns and howitzers were removed from the fixed defences, given rudimentary field mountings – or at least, some method of transporting them in the field – and the newly assigned coast/field gunners doubtless had the job of taking them to war.

As with other countries, the range of French guns ran from 57mm anti-torpedo-boat weapons to 34cm counter-bombardment guns. Most were on barbette carriages, though a number of 20cm and 24cm disappearing guns were produced in the 1890s, and 24cm and 28cm howitzers were widely used. The French have never been afraid of technical innovation, and some of their coast mountings, for exaple the high-angle pattern shown on p. 200, are quite unique. However, as another picture on that page shows, once a QF gun reaches 150mm calibre, a fixed round of ammunition becomes too cumbersome and fragile to be of any use.

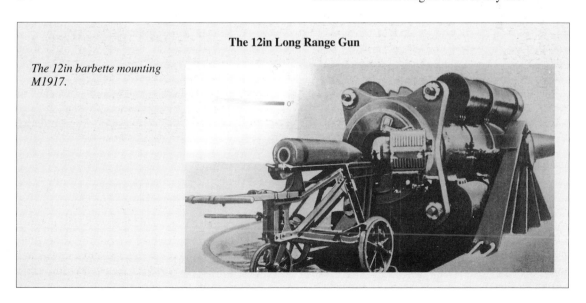

The 12in Long Range Gun

The 12in barbette mounting M1917.

The 12in Long Range Gun Continued

Arrangement drawing of the M1917 long-range mounting, showing how most of the equipment was below ground level.

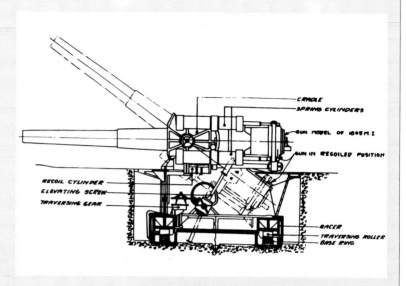

By 1915 it had become obvious that the restricted elevation of the disappearing carriage was imposing an artificial maximum range on the gun, and that the armament of US coast defences had been surpassed by that of the most modern battleships, Some of these were armed with heavy guns capable of ranging to 25,000yd, while the majority of US coast guns could barely manage 15,000yd. After much discussion it was decided to make 16in the standard US heavy gun and howitzer calibre and install these in ten forts. But building such large guns and mountings was going to take time, and so, as an 'interim measure', thirty-six spare 12in guns would be fitted to a barbette carriage capable of 35 degrees elevation, allowing most of the gun's potential power to be used.

The war, of course, ruined all the plans for 16in guns, and the 'Long Range 12in' became a permanent measure rather than an interim one. In the event, thirty of these mountings were built from 1916 to 1922 and installed in various forts to replace disappearing guns. Probably more would have been built, but by 1923 the funds for military equipment were drying up and the soldiers were told to make do with their existing guns. Which is why they went to war in 1941 with a large number of disappearing mountings still in service.

The M1917 mount is a particularly 'clean' design; one reason for this is that the only people to appear around the gun in action were the loaders. Elevation and traverse was done below ground level, underneath the operating platform, relying on information sent by electric dials from the fire direction centre. This let everybody get on with their work in comparative peace and allowed a rate of fire of one shot every thirty seconds. Elevation was done by an electric motor, with hand gear for use in emergency; traverse was by hand only. Loading and ramming was also by hand, though there were vague promises of an electric ramming gear, which never actually materialized.

As with most American coast guns, the 12in (305mm) was provided with a variety of projectiles of different weights. The standard was the 1070lb HE Armour Piercing shell quoted in the data table, which was capable of penetrating almost 18in (457mm) of cemented armour at 1,000yd (914m) range. Using the 900 and 975lb (409 and 443kg) shells, which were also available, increased the maximum range to 30,100yd (27,500m), with a proportionate drop in piercing performance.

The 12in Long Range Gun Continued

DATA: Gun, 12in M1895 and M1895M1 on Carriage, Barbette, M1917

Calibre	12in	Total weight	186 tons
Weight of gun	51.3 tons	Recoil	30in
Length of gun	442.8 in	Elevation	0°to +35°
Length of bore	35 calibres	Traverse	Up to 360°
Rifling grooves	72	Shell weight	1,070lb
Rifling twist	RH, Inc to 1/25	Muzzle velocity	2,250ft/sec
Breech	Screw, electric	Max range	27,600yd

The French 270mm Mortier de Cote Mle 1893.

The St Chamond gun in the loading position.

A 20cm St Chamond coast gun on disappearing mounting, gun up.

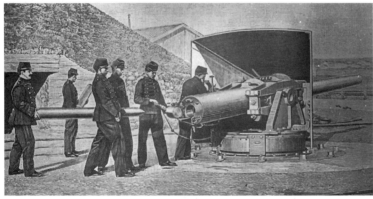

A French 150mm coast gun, showing the problems associated with fixed ammunition in large calibres

An interesting Schneider-Canet design of coast or naval gun without trunnions; the gun and sub-carriage elevate together, the curved sub-carriage riding on a roller race. The design does not appear to have been adopted for service.

7   Ammunition

It is well to remember that the weapon of the artillery is the shell; the gun is merely the last vehicle in the chain of delivery from the munitions factory to the enemy. As a sergeant said to me in my recruit days, 'The only way you can hurt anybody with a gun is to run it over his foot'. So a brief review of the ammunition available to the artillery in the war will complete our survey.

A 'round' of ammunition is defined most simply as 'one of everything necessary to fire the gun with effect'. In other words, one primer, one propelling charge, one shell and one fuze. Primers are classified as either percussion fired or electrically fired. Propelling charges are either cased (ie in a brass cartridge case) or bagged, in a silk cloth bag. If the cased charge is attached to the base of the shell, so that charge and shell are loaded as one unit, then the round of ammunition is said to be 'fixed'. If the case and shell are supplied separately but are fitted together before loading, then the round is 'semi-fixed'. If charge and shell are supplied separately and are loaded as separate items, never meeting until they are inside the gun, then the round is 'separate loading'.

In British service nomenclature there is a further division. Guns, and their ammunition, are classified as being either 'QF' or 'BL'. 'QF' means 'quick firing', but its exact significance in British terminology is that it defines the gun as being one which uses a metallic cartridge case to carry the propelling charge and seal the gun breech. 'BL' means 'breech loading', but to the British gunner it means that the gun breech is sealed by some mechanism in the gun itself and that the charge is contained in a cloth bag. Now, all this may seem

mere pedantry; but in the period we are examining there were, for example, a BL 12-pounder gun used by the field artillery, and a QF 12-pounder gun used by coast artillery. So it was vital that when demanding ammunition the correct terminology was used; a 'Cartridge QF 12pr' would be impossible to load into an 'Ordnance BL 12pr' gun.

Taking the round of ammunition in its logical sequence, we begin with the cartridge. By 1914 this was invariably smokeless powder, usually a nitro-cellulose powder but occasionally, and always in British service, a nitro-cellulose/nitro-glycerin compound which was, bulk for bulk, more powerful than straight NC but also more erosive, wearing the gun barrels out quicker. Although called 'powder' the NC powders were usually in the form of 'grains', short lengths of material rather like chopped macaroni. They could be tied up in bags and loaded into the gun in that form, or the bags dropped into a cartridge case, or the grains simply tipped into the case. The NC/NG powders, exemplified by the British 'Cordite', could be extruded in sticks of varying diameter which were then tied in bundles for bagged charges or, again, simply tipped into the cartridge case. The case mouth was then closed either by putting in a shell or by putting in a cardboard or soft metal cup.

The cartridge case had a primer inserted into its base where, once loaded, it would be in front of the firing pin when the breech was closed. The primer usually contained a simple percussion cap and a 'magazine' of gunpowder. On being struck by the firing pin the cap flashed and fired the gunpowder, which in turn ignited the smokeless powder. The

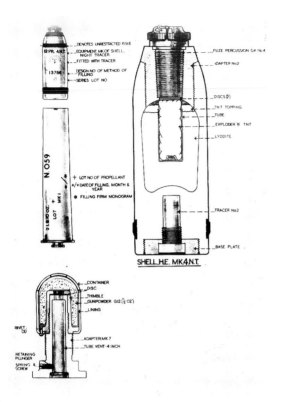

A round of ammunition for a 12-pounder coast gun. The shell is filled with Lyddite with a TNT exploder and impact fuze. The cartridge is fitted with an adapter into which a percussion or electric tube can be inserted to fire the gunpowder magazine, which, in turn, fires the cordite propelling charge in the cartridge case.

A typical firing lock on the breech of a bag charge gun. The tube is inserted into the vent and the lock closed after the shell and cartridge have been loaded.

primer could be press-fitted into the case or screwed in; national preferences guided this as much as anything else.

A bagged charge had to be ignited by a separate primer – known in British service as a 'tube' – which was inserted into the 'vent', a narrow hole running through the breech block. At the rear end of the vent a firing lock was fitted, a sort of miniature breech, into which the tube was inserted and the lock closed behind it. On firing, the tube blew its cargo of blazing gunpowder pellets down the vent and into the gun chamber. Here they struck the 'igniter', a thin bag of gunpowder stitched to the base of the bagged charge. The burning pellets fired this. which then ignited the smokeless powder in the bag.

Coast and siege guns occasionally used electric firing. The primer, whether in a cartridge case or in a bagged charge gun's vent, had a fine wire surrounded by guncotton dust and gunpowder. The 'firing pin' in this case was an electric contact which, when the firing lever was pulled, passed an electric current into the primer. The wire 'bridge' became incandescent, the guncotton dust was fired, the gunpowder was fired, and eventually the smokeless powder was ignited. I say 'eventually' but in fact the entire sequence took about 0.005 of a second.

In the case of guns there were usually two charges available: full and reduced. Full was the charge normally used with the service projectile; reduced was for practice. In the case of howitzers, there would be several charges, so that the gun's elevation and charge could be carefully selected to provide the

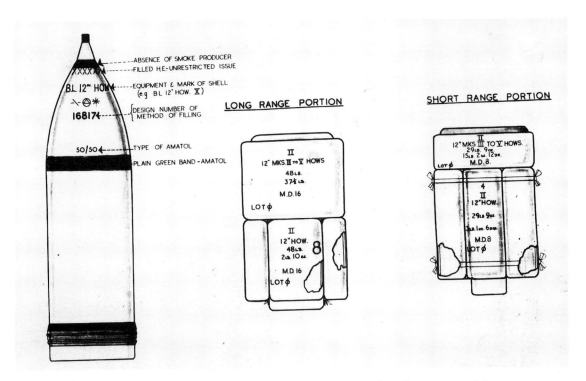

A round of ammunition for the 12in howitzer. The propelling charge is divided into long-range and short-range portions, and each of these breaks down into smaller units so as to give a variety of options to cover all ranges and angles of elevation.

optimum angle of fall of the shell so that the trajectory would pass over intervening ridges or defences and drop down to penetrate cover and disrupt the internal affairs of the defended position.

The primary projectile of the field gun, in 1914, was the shrapnel shell, since this was a prime man-killer against troops in the open and it was perfectly suited to the ballistics of the current guns. The shrapnel shell was basically a steel tubular projectile filled with lead balls and a small ejecting charge of powder, set off at the requisite place by means of a time fuze. The shell would be moving at high speed when the fuze functioned, and it would be on the downward curve of its trajectory and, ideally, about 30ft above the ground. The fuze ignited the charge and the balls were blown forward from the shell like a shotgun charge; their velocity was dependent upon the velocity of the shell, plus a small increment from the expelling charge, and the result was to drive a hail of bullets

down in a cone over the target area. A few rounds of well-aimed and well-timed shrapnel could massacre a marching column.

But for troops protected behind fortifications, shrapnel was of little use. What was needed here was a high explosive shell to blast away the protection and, into the bargain, scatter splinters around to deal with the protected. But the explosive shell was the projectile for howitzers, not for field guns. Howitzers had the ability to drop shells behind cover, and this was obviously the best method of handling the explosive shell, so howitzers it was, and the guns were given only shrapnel. The Germans, though, had an idea that explosive capability might be useful to a gun at some time or other, and in about 1912 they began issuing 'Universal' shells, shrapnel shells in which the bullets were not packed in resin, as was usual, but in TNT. The fuze was also a combination device, capable of being set to a specific time of flight or set to operate only on impact. If set to a time,

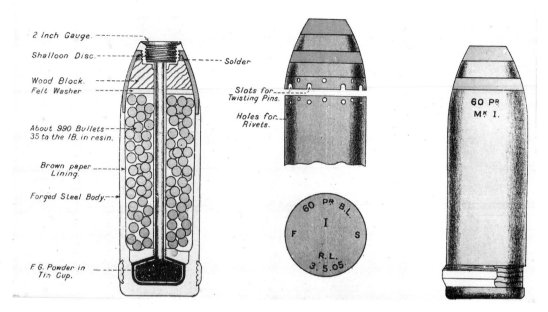

2 Inch Gauge.
Shalloon Disc.
Wood Block.
Felt Washer
About 990 Bullets
35 to the IB. in resin.
Brown paper Lining.
Forged Steel Body.
F.G. Powder in Tin Cup.

Solder
Slots for Twisting Pins.
Holes for Rivets.

60 PR BL
I
F   S
R.L.
3. 5.05

60 PR
MK I.

A 60-pounder shrapnel shell showing the loading of lead bullets, the expelling charge, and the weakened nose unit which blows off to allow the balls to fly out.

then at that time the fuze would ignite the expelling charge and the bullets and powdered TNT would be ejected just like any other shrapnel shell, functioning in the same way, the TNT being ignited and giving a cloud of smoke as it burned. But if the fuze was set for impact, then a detonator fired and detonated the TNT to burst the shell, whereupon the TNT blast dealt with light structures and protective cover and the shrapnel balls became anti-personnel fragments.

The use of TNT by Germany was considered somewhat rash. It was well known that TNT was a satisfactory high explosive, but experiments in Britain and France had also shown that it was difficult to detonate. The usual explosive shell at the turn of the century had been the 'common' shell, so-called because it was a universal design equally efficient for guns or howitzers, naval or land service. It was a steel shell with a cavity in the body into which went a bag of gunpowder, and the nose of the shell was then closed by a simple impact fuze. On striking the target the gunpowder was ignited and the shell exploded. This was considered satisfactory, because, as we have said, the

explosive shell was for use against *matériel* – field fortifications, strongpoints, or, in the case of naval and coast guns, the upperworks of ships.

But gunpowder was not entirely satisfactory; it tended to crack open the shell into large pieces, which were of little use as anti-personnel fragments, and it was not really powerful enough to do much damage in the amounts which could be packed into a field howitzer shell. So, also in the 1890s, most countries had performed experiments to find a high explosive which could be used in the common shell in place of gunpowder.

There were plenty of choices – on paper, that is. In real life it was soon found that the choice was somewhat limited. The drawback lay in the nature of the employment; the explosive was to be packed into a steel tube and then violently ejected from a gun. And this violent ejection was usually far more than the nervous explosives of the 1890s could tolerate, so that they usually detonated inside the gun barrel, destroying the gun. They would also have destroyed the gunners, had they not been conducting trials 'under precaution' – in other words,

An earlier shrapnel shell for the 15-pounder gun; the principles were just the same as those for the later 60-pounder.

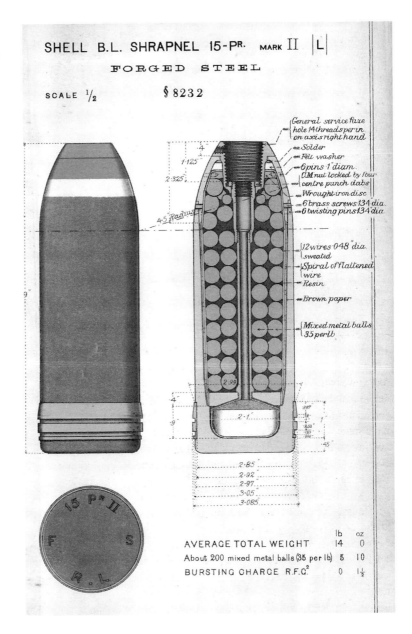

SHELL B.L. SHRAPNEL 15-PR. MARK II |L|

FORGED STEEL

SCALE ½   § 8232

General service fuze hole 14 threads per in on axis right hand
Solder
Felt washer
6 pins 1ʺ diam.
CM nut locked by four centre punch dabs
Wrought-iron disc
6 brass screws 134 dia.
6 twisting pins 134 dia.
12 wires ·048 dia. sweated
Spiral of flattened wire
Resin
Brown paper
Mixed metal balls 35 per lb

	lb	oz
AVERAGE TOTAL WEIGHT	14	0
About 200 mixed metal balls (35 per lb)	5	10
BURSTING CHARGE R.F.G.^{2}	0	1½

hiding behind a thick concrete wall and firing the gun by means of a very long piece of cord.

Eventually one substance stood out: picric acid, or tri-nitro-phenol. This, when melted and poured into a shell and allowed to set, appeared to be impervious to shock and could be fired with impunity. To make it detonate, a hole was bored into the picric acid filling after it had set, and into this went a cotton bag filled with powdered picric acid. This was rather more sensitive to shock but, being in a very small package cushioned inside the main filling, it was well protected and withstood firing. On top of the picric powder went the impact fuze which, on impact, ignited the picric powder. Picric powder has

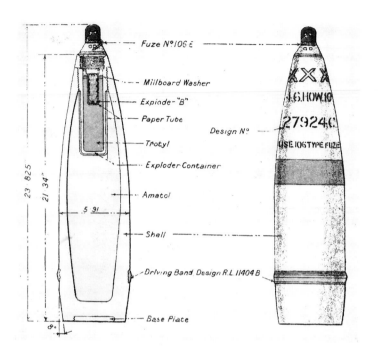

A high explosive shell for the 6in 26-cwt howitzer, filled with Amatol, a mixture of TNT and ammonium nitrate.

the peculiar property of 'burning to detonation'; it can be ignited by a flash and the rate of burning accelerates until it becomes a detonation, so that it is the perfect medium for detonating a high explosive by using a flash. In the normal course of events, application of a flame to high explosive either causes it to burn without detonating or does nothing.

The British called their cast picric acid 'Lyddite' because the trials were performed at the gunnery range near Lydd, in Kent. The French called it 'Melinite', the Japanese 'Shimose', the Germans 'Granatfullung 88', and as time went on they all made the same discovery: it has a fatal affinity for steel. Poured into a shell it would, being an acid, set up a reaction with the steel which, after some time, resulted in the formation of 'picrates', highly sensitive explosive crystals which certainly did not withstand being fired out of a gun and promptly detonated the shell. After a few accidents, the remedy was found – paint the inside of the shell with varnish. Picric acid has a similar affinity for lead, and thus fuzes had to be entirely free of any lead in their construction. As a result, everyone began looking at the second-best, TNT. This was

certainly more powerful than picric acid and a lot easier to work with (picric acid caused a lot of health problems in the filling factories), but it was extremely difficult to detonate inside a shell. The picric powder simply did not generate a powerful enough detonation to guarantee thorough detonation of the TNT.

The solution to this took several years and it was finally achieved by the Germans in the late 1900s and by the British shortly afterwards. The fuze had to generate a detonation; this had to be passed on to a more sensitive high explosive than TNT, which would then detonate at a faster rate, sufficient to produce the thorough detonation of the TNT.

The solution merely generated more problems; there were no fuzes which produced a detonation, so they had to be designed; this meant that some comprehensive safety mechanisms had to be put into the fuzes, because the results of a fuze functioning in the gun barrel were too serious to be risked, and thus the fuze had to be safe until it was some distance outside the muzzle. After that the 'intermediary' explosive had to be discovered and perfected. In British service this turned out to be 'Tetryl' in powder form, filled into cloth bags which were placed on top of, or into a recess in, the TNT filling.

But all this took time, which is why, in 1914, the few explosive shells in British field service were still filled with Lyddite, and TNT was only just becoming a service filling in some of the heavier calibres. Similarly the French were still wedded to Melinite. Only the Germans had begun issuing TNT-filled shells in any quantity for field howitzers.

With the anti-personnel and *anti-matériel* projectiles settled, the new tactics and type of warfare began to make demands for new types of shell to perform new tasks. In some cases this turned out to be a case of reinventing a shell which had been cast aside years ago in the belief that it no longer had any place in war; such as the smoke and star shells. These, known as 'carcasses', had been part of the armament in smooth-bore days, when they were primarily used for incendiary purposes during a siege. They fell into disuse and were ignored when breech-loading came along, but the conditions of trench warfare made smoke (for concealment) and lights (for illumination or signalling) very desirable and breech-loading versions had to be hastily provided. The first smoke designs were little more than the standard HE shell for the weapon, filled instead with white phosphorus. Beneath the impact fuze was sufficient explosive to crack the shell open and liberate the white phosphorus, whereupon spontaneous combustion (on contact with air) took place and generated a thick cloud of phosphorus pentoxide, a relatively harmless smoke with considerable obscuring power. The burning phosphorus was also intended to be a useful incendiary device, and it was soon discovered that it also had a powerful anti-personnel effect, delivering severe burns and being difficult to extinguish.

Star shell were originally developed from shrapnel, filling the body of the shell with pyrotechnic sticks which were ignited by the flash from the fuze and then blown from the head of the shell by an expelling charge. They then fell through the air, burning as they went, making a very visible display when fired at night. By changing the composition of the sticks, various colours could be achieved (though blue was always difficult), and

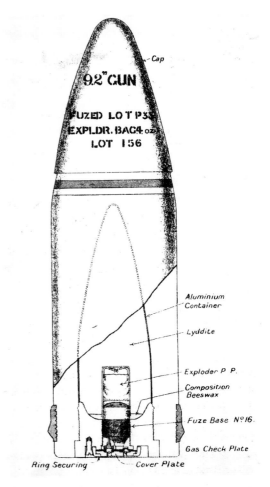

An armour piercing shell for the 9.2in coast defence gun. The shell needs strength to smash through armour, so the explosive cavity is small, and the fuze fits into the base of the shell.

as a signalling device it was a valuable addition. As an illuminating device, white stars were less useful and, again, history was reviewed and provided the answer: Boxer's Parachute Light Ball of the 1860s. This had been a spherical projectile which, by means of a time fuze, split into two hemispheres and released a parachute carrying a canister full of illuminating composition. The idea was now translated into terms of the breech-loading gun projectile and became a shell with the base-plate held in by pins and containing a canister of magnesium

COMPLETE ROUND, PROJECTILE, A.P., 12 INCH, MK. XVI, LOADED IN SEACOAST GUN, M1900

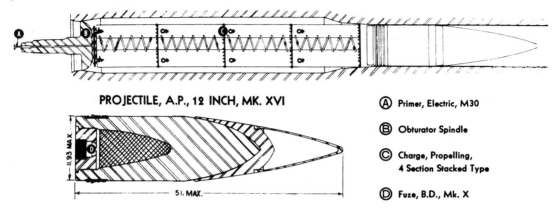

PROJECTILE, A.P., 12 INCH, MK. XVI

Ⓐ Primer, Electric, M30

Ⓑ Obturator Spindle

Ⓒ Charge, Propelling,
  4 Section Stacked Type

Ⓓ Fuze, B.D., Mk. X

A diagram showing the loading of an American 12in coast gun. The armour-piercing shell had a thin ballistic cap, a thicker and hard penetrating cap, a small filling of explosive and a base fuze. The propelling charge is loaded in four separate bags.

composition and a parachute. A time fuze ignited an expelling charge of gunpowder; when this exploded the flash lit the magnesium and the blast blew off the baseplate and allowed the parachute to stream out into the air, dragging the burning canister after it. This then descended moderately slowly to give several thousands of candle-power of light on the battlefield below.

Once these became successful, they ceased to be conversions and became fresh designs in their own right. There was no need, for example, for a smoke shell to be of the same grade or thickness of steel as a high explosive shell, since it was not called upon to produce fragments. So long as it was strong enough to withstand being fired from the gun it was adequate.

Incendiary shells tended to be of two distinct types: those designed for the attack of Zeppelins and those designed as fire-raisers for ground targets. The former, known in British service as 'Incendiary AZ' shells, resembled shrapnel shells but with a pinned-in base. There was a central flashtube running down the axis of the shell from the fuze to a compartment in front of the baseplate which contained an

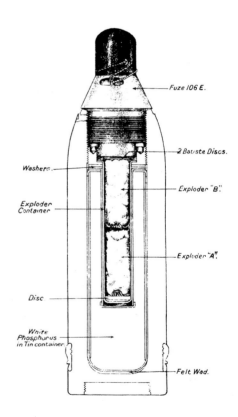

A white phosphorus smoke shell for the 18-pounder gun. The two exploder bags contain powdered TNT and are just sufficient to break open the shell and release the phosphorus, which ignites upon being exposed to the air.

expelling charge of gunpowder. The shell body was taken up by a solid filling of 'Dr Whiteley's Incendiary Composition No. 28', of which no record now appears to exist but which was probably a magnesium/thermite composition. When the time fuze functioned, it sent a flash down the central tube which fired the expelling charge. This ignited the incendiary filling and also blew off the shell's baseplate. The shell continued on its flight but now had a stream of very hot flame coming out of its base, and if the shell now passed through a Zeppelin's gasbag, disaster was inevitable.

The fire-raising incendiary was similar to a shrapnel shell but instead of bullets it held seven layers of incendiary containers, trough-like rings filled with an incendiary composition composed of turpentine, tallow, gunpowder, antimony sulphide and powdered aluminium. These were ignited by the usual central flash tube and then blown through the nose of the shell by an expelling charge in the same manner as shrapnel bullets. On being ejected the containers took up erratic flight paths and so scattered around the target area igniting anything capable of being burned.

But of all the special-purpose shells, the one which became peculiar to the First World War was, of course, the gas shell. These posed special problems in manufacture and assembly, the greatest of which was that the filling of the explosive component and the filling of the gas had to be done in separate establishments, it being considered far too dangerous to try and fill both these items in the same place. Another was the sealing of the shell against leakage, since the 'gas' was actually a liquid in most cases and was invariably what the chemists call 'fugitive', in other words it would find its way through the slightest crack or badly-fitting thread. Moreover the liquids were almost always corrosive or chemically active and the metal of the shell had to be protected against their action.

Various methods were tried in order to solve all these problems. The basic principle was to have a shell containing the chemical substance and, inside it, have an explosive charge sufficient to break open the shell so as to liberate the liquid in gaseous form.

One early idea, adopted by the French, was to place the gas in a glass bottle inside the shell, then fill round it with explosive. Another was to use a shaped lead container to carry the gas, place it inside the shell, and then put a filling of explosive on top of it. The final methods, used by British and French designers, were firstly the 'double diaphragm' shell and secondly the 'container' shell.

In the first design the shell body was in two separate pieces; the body proper, up to the shoulder, where it ended in a screw-thread, and the curved head, also ending in a screw-thread. The body's front end was closed by a steel plate or 'diaphragm' spun into place to make a perfect seal. A tapered hole in the side of the shell body allowed the gas to be filled and, after filling, was closed by a tapered steel plug driven in and filed off smooth. This was filled and sealed in a special gas charging factory and was then shipped to an assembly factory. The head, sealed at its lower end with another diaphragm, was filled with explosive and plugged in an explosives filling factory and then shipped to the assembly factory. Here the two halves of the shell were screwed together so that the two diaphragms were touching, and the fuze was fitted in the nose. On striking the target the explosive would detonate with sufficient force to break open the shell and allow the gas to vaporize and escape.

The 'container' shell was a much simpler design but called for more precise manufacture. The shell body was of the normal shape, with a screw-threaded mouth into which a 'nose adapter and container' was screwed. This was a thick tube, closed at the bottom end and threaded to take the fuze at the front end. This empty shell was now charged with gas through a side hole in the same manner as before, and sent to the filling factory where the container was loaded with explosive and the fuze fitted. The action at the target end was the same. In due course this pattern also became the standard method of filling for British white phosphorus smoke shells.

And finally the fuze. In 1914 there were three kinds of fuze in use: base, nose impact and nose time. Base fuzes fitted into the base of armour-piercing and 'common pointed' shells which were largely the province of coast defence artillery. These shells were intended to smash through armour or other obstructions, after which the base fuze would detonate the shell inside the target.

Nose impact fuzes screwed into the nose of the shell and thus struck the target first and detonated the shell. They were for use against battle-field targets, and therefore what the fuze actually struck was generally the ground, so that the shell burst on, or close to, the surface and spread man-killing fragments in all directions. There were two sub-divisions: the 'direct action' fuze did just that, fired the shell as soon as it was struck. The 'graze' fuze worked differently, having a detonator in a loose pellet which, when the shell's flight was checked, flew forward under its own momentum and drove the detonator against a firing pin. Hence there was a constant delay between impact and detonation which allowed the shell to make some inroads into a lightly protected target or, if fired at a low elevation, it could be bounced up off the ground and the delay would burst it a few feet above the ground to improved its spread of fragments. This was 'ricochet fire', much loved by the French but entirely distrusted by the British.

The time fuze also screwed into the nose and was used with the shrapnel shell, to burst it at the correct height above and distance from the target so as to shower the target with lead bullets. The fuze worked by having one or two metal rings containing

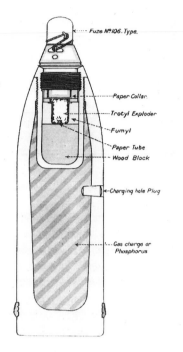

GAS OR SMOKE SHELL CONTAINER TYPE.

Fuze Nº 106. Type.

Paper Collar.

Trotyl Exploder

Fumyl

Paper Tube

Wood Block

Charging hole Plug

Gas charge or Phosphorus

A container-type gas shell for the 18-pounder. The container is screwed and cemented into the shell nose, making a gas-tight joint. The shell is then filled with gas through the side hole, and sealed with a steel plug. The bursting explosive charge goes into the container and an impact fuze completes the assembly.

Stacking ammunition in the field for an 8in howitzer. Surprising to see three people smoking in this concentration of explosives, but compared to the day-to-day hazards of life in France in 1916 ...

gunpowder. At the start of this gunpowder filling was a hole in the metal ring which allowed an ignition flash to light the gunpowder train. In the body of the fuze beneath the ring, and adjacent to the gunpowder filling, was another hole leading to the fuze magazine, a larger charge of gunpowder. On firing, the shock of acceleration drove a firing pin on to a cap, which lit the gunpowder train in the ring. The ring having been rotated to a time marked on a scale, the powder would burn around until it reached the channel leading to the magazine, whereupon it ignited the contents of the magazine and this, exploding into the shell, initiated the shell's action. Where two ring were used, the first was fixed and burned until it came to a vertical channel in the lower ring, leading to the gunpowder filling, which it ignited and which burned according to how it had been set. This allowed longer ranges and had more or less replaced single-ring fuzes by 1914. It was also possible to incorporate an impact mechanism (of the graze type) as a 'clean-up' facility should the time element be set wrongly or fail to work.

The French used an entirely different design, which was simply a lead tube filled with gunpowder and coiled round a conical fuze body in the nose of the shell. It was 'set' by punching a hole through the tube so as to expose the powder to a channel in the centre of the body which led to the fuze magazine. On firing the powder was ignited at the end of the tube and burned along until it came to this hole which it flashed through and fired the magazine.

These types remained standard throughout the war, though some improvements appeared and many varied models were developed to suit the ballistics and performance of specific guns; large howitzers, for example, had to have fuzes capable of arming at much lower acceleration and spin rates than did high-velocity guns.

The principal change came in the almost universal adoption of bore-safe fuzes for use with high explosive shells, a subject already mentioned. Another vital change took place when it was realized that the sturdy impact fuzes of pre-war days, intended to function on 'normal meadowland', failed entirely to function on the grossly abnormal mud of Flanders: the shells simply sailed into the mud without sufficient check to make the fuze work. If they did go off it was not until they were several feet down and struck hard earth or rock, whereupon the effect of the detonation was smothered and quite ineffectual. Much energy was expended in developing super-sensitive impact fuzes which were, nevertheless, safe to transport and fire from the gun, and it was not until 1916 that successful designs were in full production.

A drawback with the powder time fuze was that due to unavoidable fluctuations in the quality of the powder, and to the effects of spin and air density as the burning fuze flew through the air, its accuracy was not good; it was generally taken as being 2 per cent of the time of flight of the shell. Thus, if the shell took 25 seconds to get to the target, the fuze set for 25 seconds might burst anywhere between 24.75 and 25.25 seconds from the gun. And with the shell travelling at 1500 feet per second, this meant it could burst anywhere in a space of 750ft along the trajectory. Shrapnel fire was difficult enough, without adding this imponderable into the equation. And, of course, when shrapnel began to be used on longer-ranging guns, the spread became even more.

Krupp, in Germany, developed a clockwork-driven fuze. The mechanism was wound in the factory; setting the fuze determined the angle through which the clock's single hand had to rotate before it could rise through a slot and release a firing pin. Firing the gun released the hand to tick round to the set time. Its accuracy was in the order of one-half of one per cent of the time of flight – 750 feet came down to 185 feet and longer ranges pro rata. This was introduced in late 1916 for long-range shrapnel fire and, inevitably, one of them failed to function and was found in the mud by a British intelligence officer. It was sent back to England and by November 1917 a working clockwork fuze had been developed. But developing a working model and mass-producing a serviceable fuze are not the same thing, and it was not until the mid-1920s that a mechanical time fuze became a practical proposition in British hands – by which time the Army couldn't afford it.

Appendix: Allied Artillery of World War One

FIELD, INFANTRY AND MOUNTAIN

Britain

	Calibre (in)	Weight in action (lb)	Barrel length (in)	Elevation (degrees)	Traverse (degrees)	Recoil system	Shell weight (lb)	Muzzle velocity (ft/sec)	Max range (yd)	Remarks
10pr Mtn Gun	2.75	762	76.4	25	nil	nil	10	1,290	6,000	The 'Screw-gun'
2.75in Mtn Gun	2.75	1,290	76.4	22	4	HS	12.5	1,290	5,800	Improved screw-gun
2.95in Mtn Gun	2.95	829	35.8	27	nil	HS	12.5	920	4,825	Vickers private design
13pr Gun	3.00	2,236	73.2	15	4	HS	12.5	1,675	5,900	Horse Artillery gun
15pr Gun	3.00	2,168	89.0	16	nil	SS	14.0	1,590	6,000	Obsolescent
18pr GunMk I	3.30	2,821	97.0	16	4	HS	18.5	1,615	6,525	Field Artillery gun
18pr Gun Mk IV	3.30	3,096	97.0	30	4	HP	18.5	1,615	9,300	Improved version
3.7in Mtn How	3.70	1,610	46.8	40	20	HP	20.0	973	5,900	Ultimate screw-gun
4.5in How	4.50	3,010	70.0	45	3	HS	35.0	1,010	7,300	
4.7in Gun	4.72	8,420	194.0	20	nil	HS	46.5	2,150	10,000	
5in How	5.00	2,673	49.0	45	nil	HS	50.0	788	4,800	
60pr Gun Mk I	5.00	9,856	168.0	21.5	4	HS	60.0	2,080	12,300	
60pr Gun Mk II	5.00	12,050	192.2	35	4	HP	60.0	2,130	15,500	Improved version
6in 30cwt How	6.00	7,733	94.0	35	nil	HS	118.5	777	7,000	
6in 26cwt How	6.00	8,144	87.5	45	4	HP	100.0	1,234	9,500	11,400 yd with 86lb shell
6in Gun Mk VII	6.00	25.2t	279.3	22	nil	HS	100.0	2,525	13,700	
6in Gun Mk XIX	6.00	10.15t	219.2	38	4	HP	100.0	2,350	18,750	
6in BLC Siege Gun	6.00	12.05t	172.0	24	15	HS	100.0	2,130	14,200	

France

	Calibre (mm)	Weight in action (kg)	Barrel length (m)	Elevation (degrees)	Traverse (degrees)	Recoil system	Shell weight (kg)	Muzzle velocity (m/sec)	Max range (m)	Remarks
37mm Trench Gun M1916	37	108	0.80	21	40	HS	0.56	363	2,400	Puteaux Arsenal
65mm Mtn Gun M1906	65	400	1.31	35	6	DR	3.81	330	5,500	Schneider-Ducrest
75mm Mle 1897	75	1,160	2.70	18	6	HP	7.25	529	8,500	The 'French 75'
75mm Mle 1912	75	965	2.32	17	6	HP	7.25	500	7,500	Schneider
75mm St Chamond	75	1,090	2.25	17	6	HS	7.25	500	6,200	200 guns only
90mm M1877	90	1,220	2.27	26	nil	nil	8.0	455	7,000	de Bange
95mm M1888	95	1,375	2.26	24	nil	nil	12.3	406	7,800	
100mm M1897 TR	100	6,000	5.89	40	nil	nil	14.5	760	14,500	
105mm Lourde M1913TR	105	2,300	2.98	37	6	HP	16.0	550	12,700	Schneider
120mm M1878/ 1916	120	2,700	3.25	30	nil	nil	18.0	525	12,400	
140mm M1910	138.6	11,000	7.98	30	6	HS	30.5	825	17,400	
145mm M1916	145	12,500	7.36	38	6	HP	33.7	785	18,500	St Chamond
155mm long M1877/1914	155	6,010	4.20	42	5	HP	43.0	562	11,400	Schneider
155mm long M1877/1916	155	5,700	4.20	42	nil	nil	42.0	392	11,000	
155mm long M1917	155	8,956	4.94	40	5	HP	43.2	650	16,000	Schneider
155mm long M1918	155	5,030	4.09	43.6	6	HP	43.0	562	12,000	Schneider
155mm short M1904TR	155	3,200	2.40	41	6	HP	42.9	320	6,000	
155mm short M1915	155	3,040	2.33	42.3	6	HP	43.5	450	11,500	Schneider
155mm short M1917	155	3,300	2.33	42.3	6	HP	43.5	450	11,500	Schneider
145/155mm M1916	155	12,250	7.36	47.5	6	HP	43.1	790	21,300	St Chamond
155mm long GPF	155	10,750	5.92	35	60	HP	43.1	735	16,200	Filloux

Italy

	Calibre (mm)	Weight in action (kg)	Barrel length (m)	Elevation (degrees)	Traverse (degrees)	Recoil system	Shell weight (kg)	Muzzle velocity (m/sec)	Max range (m)	Remarks
65mm Mtn Gun M1913	65	570	1.15	20	8	HS	4.15	355	6,400	
70mm Mtn Gun M1902	70	387	1.148	21	nil	SS	4.84	353	6,630	Turin Arsenal
70mm Mtn Gun M1908	70	508	1.197	20	4.5	HP	5.3	300	5,000	Schneider
75mm Gun M1906	75	1,032	2.25	16	7	HS	6.5	510	6,800	
75mm M1911 Deport	75	1,076	2.02	65	54	HS	6.5	510	7,600	First split trail gun
75mm M1911 Krupp	75	958	2.25	18.5	7	HS	6.5	510	7,600	Krupp
100mm How M1914	100	1,417	1.93	48	5	HS	11.45	430	9,280	Terni-Ansaldo
104/32 M1915	104	3,290	3.64	30	6	HS	17.5	630	12,500	Skoda-Ansaldo
105/28 Ansaldo	105	2,470	2.98	37	14	HS	15.5	570	13,200	Schneider-Ansaldo
149mm M1900	149.1	7,820	5.46	35	nil	nil	43.3	700	10,600	Armstrong
149mm How M1914	149.1	2,344	2.09	43	5	HS	41.5	301	6,900	Skoda-Ansaldo
152mm M1917	152.4	16,670	7.118	45	10	HP	47.0	830	19,400	Ansaldo
155/25 M1908	155	7,180	3.87	28	nil	nil	43.0	523	11,400	Ansaldo

Russia

	Calibre (mm)	Weight in action (kg)	Barrel length (m)	Elevation (degrees)	Traverse (degrees)	Recoil system	Shell weight (kg)	Muzzle velocity (m/sec)	Max range (m)	Remarks
76.2mm M1900	76.2	1,020	2.28	17	4	S	6.5	588	6,400	Putilov Arsenal
76.2mm M1902	76.2	1,040	2.28	17	6	HS	6.6	593	6,600	Putilov Arsenal
76.2mm Gun M1913	76.2	1,003	2.40	16	6	HP	6.5	510	5,800	Horse Artillery
76.2mm Mtn Gun M1904	76.2	426	1.01	35	4.5	S	6.5	295	4,160	Obuchov Arsenal
76.2mm Mtn Gun M1909	76.2	626	1.25	28	4.5	HS	6.4	379	7,100	Schneider
85mm Gun M1902	85	1,930	2.90	16	4.5	HS	10.0	555	6,400	Putilov
105mm Mtn How M1909	105	730	1.10	60	5	HS	12.0	300	6,000	Schneider
107mm M1877	106.7	2,690	3.75	40	nil	nil	15.6	518	9,600	Obuchov Arsenal
107mm Gun M1908	106.7	2,200	3.21	30	6	HS	16.4	560	9,500	Krupp
107mm Gun M1910	106.7	2,180	3.04	37	6	HS	18.1	528	9,800	Schneider

Russia continued

	Calibre (mm)	Weight in action (kg)	Barrel length (m)	Elevation (degrees)	Traverse (degrees)	Recoil system	Shell weight (kg)	Muzzle velocity (m/sec)	Max range (m)	Remarks
122mm How M1904	121.9	1,225	1.46	42	4	HS	21.0	292	6,700	Obuchov Arsenal
122mm How M1909	121.9	1,350	1.71	43	4	HS	23.0	335	7,500	Krupp
122mm How M1910	121.9	1,324	1.56	45	9	HS	23.0	335	7,680	Schneider
127mm Gun M1904	127	4,471	4.26	21.5	8	HS	27.2	634	11,250	British 60pr Mk I
152mm M1877	152.4	4,880	3.35	38	nil	GPC	32.9	463	7,800	Obuchov Arsenal
152mm M1904	152.4	5,437	4.57	40.5	nil	GPC	40.0	623	11,000	Obuchov Arsenal
152mm Gun M1909	152.4	6,700	4.57	40	6	HS	41.0	640	12,600	Krupp
152mm Gun M1910	152.4	5,070	4.26	40	4.5	HS	45.4	610	11,500	Schneider-Putilov
152mm How M1909	152.4	3,790	2.44	60	6	HS	41.0	381	9,000	Krupp
152mm How M1910	152.4	2,175	2.28	45	5	HS	41.0	350	8,200	Krupp
152mm How M1910	152.4	2,130	1.83	43	6	HS	42.0	381	8,700	Schneider

USA

	Calibre (in)	Weight in action (lb)	Barrel length (in)	Elevation (degrees)	Traverse (degrees)	Recoil system	Shell weight (lb)	Muzzle velocity (ft/sec)	Max range (yd)	Remarks
2.95in Mtn How M1911	2.95	1,120	35.8	40	6	HS	15.0	898	5,685	Vickers design
3in M1902	3.0	2,497	87.6	16	4	HS	15.0	1,700	7,500	Erhardt manufacture
75mm M1916	2.95	3,210	90.9	53	45	HP	13.5	1,900	8,865	
75mm M1917	2.95	2,990	88.2	16	4	HS	13.5	1,900	8,865	British 18pr
75mm M1897	2.95	2,657	107.1	19	6	HP	13.5	1,955	9,200	French Mle 1897
4.7in M1906	4.70	8,783	129.2	15	4	HS	45.0	1,700	9,025	
120mm M1917	4.70	8,070	137.2	40	8	HS	45.0	2,335	16,400	
5in Gun M1898	5.0	3,660	135.0	31	?	GPC	45.0	1,830	9,845	
6in How M1908	6.0	8,611	81.6	40	5	HS	120.0	900	6,700	

S = springs only; SS = spring spade; GPC = ground platform control; HG = hydraulic recoil, gravity run-out; DR = differential recoil.

HEAVY ARTILLERY

Britain

	Calibre (in)	Weight in action (tons)	Barrel length (in)	Elevation (degrees)	Traverse (degrees)	Recoil system	Shell weight (lb)	Muzzle velocity (ft/sec)	Max range (yd)	Remarks
8in How Mks 1 -V	8.0	13.75	128	45	nil	HS	200	1,300	10,500	Converted 6in guns
8in How Mk VI	8.0	8.5	128	50	8	HP	200	1,300	10,760	Vickers
8in How Mk VII, VIII	8.0	8.75	148	45	8	HP	200	1,500	12,300	Vickers
9.2in How Mk I	9.2	13.3	134	55	60	HP	290	1,187	10,060	Coventry
9.2in How Mk II	9.2	16.25	170	50	60	HP	290	1,600	13,935	Vickers
12in How Mk II	12.0	36.6	174.5	65	60	HP	750	1,196	11,340	Vickers
12in How Mk IV	12.0	37	222	65	60	HP	750	1,468	14,350	Vickers
15in How	15.0	?	165	45	25	HS	1,400	1,117	10,795	Coventry

France

	Calibre (mm)	Weight in action (tons)	Barrel length (m)	Elevation (degrees)	Traverse (degrees)	Recoil system	Shell weight (kg)	Muzzle velocity (m/sec)	Max range (m)	Remarks
194mm Canon Mle 1917	194	15.6	6.57	35	60	HP	80.0	640	18,300	Filloux
220mm long M1917	220	25.8	7.67	37	20	HP	104.75	766	22,800	Schneider
220mm short M1916	220	10.8	2.28	65	6	HP	100.5	415	10,800	Schneider
220mm Mortar M1880	220	7.20	2.00	60	nil	nil	100.5	300	5,260	
220mm Siege Mortar M1901	220	8.0	2.00	60	40	HG	100.5	300	5,620	
240mm M1884	240	16.25	6.70	43	10	HG	160	614	17,200	St Chamond
240mm Gun Mle 84/17	240	31	7.00			HP	161	575	17,300	St Chamond
270mm Siege Mortar	270	11.5	2.60	70	30	HP	198	326	8,000	
280mm Mortar M14/16	280	16	3.35	60	20	HP	205	418	10,950	Schneider
293mm How	293	16	4.39	60	20	HP	226	466	12,250	Schneider
370mm Mortar	370	19.3	2.95	60	12	HG	400	375	10,500	Filloux

Italy

	Calibre (mm)	Weight in action (tons)	Barrel length (m)	Elevation (degrees)	Traverse (degrees)	Recoil system	Shell weight (kg)	Muzzle velocity (m/sec)	Max range (m)	Remarks
210/8 Mortier DS	210	10.9	2.05	70	360	HS	100.6	370	8,000	
260/9 How M1916	260	11.8	2.73	65	60	HS	219	300	9,100	
305/8 How M11/16	302	20.8	3.05	75	120	HS	380	400	10,975	
305/10 How	305	22.7	3.05	75	360	HP	380	448	12,250	
305/17 DS M1915	305	33.7	5.18	65	360	HP	350	545	17,560	
380/15 How	380	81	5.70	70	360	HS	741		16,300	
420/12 How	420	113	5.04	70	360	HS	1,000		14,650	

RAILWAY ARTILLERY

Britain

	Calibre (in)	Weight in action (tons)	Barrel length (in)	Elevation (degrees)	Traverse (degrees)	Recoil system	Shell weight (lb)	Muzzle velocity (ft/sec)	Max range (yd)	Remarks
9.2in Gun Mk III	9.2	60	310	35	20	C	380	2,100	20,700	Elswick
9.2in Gun Mk X	9.2	90	442	30	360	C	380	2,700	21,000	Elswick
9.2in Gun Mk XIII	9.2	87	335	40	360	C	380	2,100	22,600	Elswick
12in How Mk I	12.0	58	162	65	40	C	750	1,175	11,132	Elswick
12in How Mk III	12.0	61	225	65	40	C	750	1,468	15,000	Elswick
12in How Mk V	12.0	76	225	45	240	C	750	1,468	14,360	Elswick
12in Gun Mk IX	12.0	171	496	30	2	C	850	2,610	32,700	Vickers
12in Gun Mk XI	12.0	221	617	45	2	C	850	2,825	31,550	Vickers
14in Gun Mk III	14.0	248	648	40	4	C	1,586	2,450	34,600	Elswick
18in How Mk I	18.0	250	648	40	4	C	2,500	1,880	22,300	Elswick

France

	Calibre (mm)	Weight in action (tonnes)	Barrel length (m)	Elevation (degrees)	Traverse (degrees)	Recoil system	Shell weight (kg)	Muzzle velocity (m/sec)	Max range (m)	Remarks
160mm Piegne-Canet	164.7	60	7.41	45	360	C	50.0	775	18,000	Schneider
190mm M1870/93	194.4	58	5.89	40	360	C	83.0	640	13,800	Schneider
190mm M75/76	194.4	25		40	nil	C	83.0	470	12,900	Schneider
190mm Mle 1917	194.4	28		40	nil	C	83.0	470	12,900	
200mm How Mle 1915	201	38	3.15	60	360	C	100	428	11,500	Schneider

France continued

	Calibre (mm)	Weight in action (tonnes)	Barrel length (m)	Elevation (degrees)	Traverse (degrees)	Recoil system	Shell weight (kg)	Muzzle velocity (m/sec)	Max range (m)	Remarks
240mm Mle 1876	240	40		40	nil	C	154	460	13,450	Schneider
240mm M1884	240	90	6.84	38	nil	S	140	575	17,300	Batignolles
240mm M1884	240	72	6.70	38	nil	C	140	575	17,300	Schneider
240mm M1893/96M	240	140	10.05	35	360	C	162	840	22,700	St Chamond
240mm Mle 1903TR	240	48	6.47	40	14	C	140	526	17,300	St Chamond
240mm Mle 1917	240	42		40	nil	C	154	460	13,450	
270mm How Mle 1885	270	25	2.60	70	30	C	152	326	8,000	
270mm How Mle 1889	270	32	3.35	60		C	152	420	10,400	
274mm Mle 1870/81	274	78				C	256		16,000	Schneider
274mm Mle 1887/93	274	160	12.33		nil	S	273	785	26,000	
274mm Mle 17 Gl	274	152	12.33	40	nil	S	237	842	29,100	Schneider
293mm How	293	50	4.39	65	14	C	300	322	11,200	Schneider
274/285mm Mle 93/96	274	155	10.96	40	nil	C	273	740	27,100	
305mm M1893/96	305	183	12.78	40	nil	S	348	795	27,500	Schneider
305mm M93/96 a berceau	305	140	12.78	40	10	C	348	795	27,000	Batignolles
305mm Mle 1906	305	208		38	nil	S	348		29,000	Schneider
320mm M70/93 Gl	320	162	10.11	40	nil	S	387	608	20,500	Batignolles
320mm Mle 93/96	320	140	12.75	40	10	C	392	690	27,000	Batignolles
340mm Mle 1884	340	187		40	nil	S	430		19,000	Schneider
340mm Mle 1893	340	183	11.90		nil	S	432		25,000	
340mm M1912 Gl.	340	270	16.15	37	nil	S	430	927	37,600	Batignolles
340mm M1912	340	164	16.15	42	10	D/R	445	970	44,400	St Chamond
370mm 1875/79 Gl	370	250	11.85	40	nil	S	700	745	23,000	Schneider
370mm How Mle 15	370	134	9.85	65	12	D/S	516	535	16,400	Batignolles
400mm How Mle 15 or 16	400	137	10.65	65	12	C	641	530	16,000	St Chamond
520mm How Mle 16	520	260					1,654	450	14,600	

Italy

	Calibre (mm)	Weight in action (tonnes)	Barrel length (m)	Elevation (degrees)	Traverse (degrees)	Recoil system	Shell weight (kg)	Muzzle velocity (m/sec)	Max range (m)	Remarks
381/40 Gun	381	160	15.25	25	nil	C	876	762	23,950	

USA

	Calibre (in)	Weight in action (tons)	Barrel length (in)	Elevation (degrees)	Traverse (degrees)	Recoil system	Shell weight (lb)	Muzzle velocity (ft/sec)	Max range (yd)	Remarks
8in M1918	8.0	70	295	42	360	C	260	2,600	23,900	
10in M1888	10.0	172	340	54	nil	S	510	2,400	28,000	
12in M1895	12.0	143	442	38	5	C	975	2,275	30,000	
12in M1895	12.0	245	442	40	nil	S	700	3,200	45,000	
12in Mortar M1890	12.0	79	145	65	360	C	700	1,500	15,290	
14in Mk IV Mod 1	14.0	256	560	30	nil	C	1,400	2,350	42,500	US Navy

* Note on recoil systems for this section: C = On-carriage, ie a normal recoil system on the gun; S = Sliding, ie the carriage is lowered to the track and slides bodily on recoil; R = Rolling; no on-carriage system, entire unit rolls on its wheels; DS or DR = Dual; on-carriage plus Sliding or Rolling.

ANTI-AIRCRAFT ARTILLERY

Britain

	Calibre (in)	Weight in action (tons)	Barrel length (in)	Elevation (degrees)	Traverse (degrees)	Recoil system	Shell weight (lb)	Muzzle velocity (ft/sec)	Effect. ceiling (ft)	Remarks
1pr QF Mk I	1.457	0.75	43.5	80	50	nil	1	1,800	4,500	Maxim 'Pom-Pom'
12pr QF Mk I*	3.0		120	85	360	HS	12.5	2,200	22,000	Towed
13pr Mk III	3.0	7.0	73.2	70	360	HS	13.0	1,750	17,000	Truck-mounted
13pr 9cwt Mk I	3.0	7.5	97.0	80	360	HS	13.0	2,150	19,000	Truck-mounted
3in 20cwt Mk I	3.0	5.9	140	90	360	HS	16.0	2,500	23,500	Towed, also truck
4in QF Mk V	4.0	6.75	188	80	360	HP	31.0	2,350	28,750	Static mounting

France

	Calibre (mm)	Weight in action (tonnes)	Barrel length (m)	Elevation (degrees)	Traverse (degrees)	Recoil system	Shell weight (kg)	Muzzle velocity (m/sec)	Effect. ceiling (m)	Remarks
75mm Auto-canon	75	4	2.72	85	120	HP	6.25	575	6,500	De Dion chassis
75mm Canon de remorque	75	2.2	2.72	85	360	HP	6.25	575	6,500	Towed

Italy

	Calibre (mm)	Weight in action (tonnes)	Barrel length (m)	Elevation (degrees)	Traverse (degrees)	Recoil system	Shell weight (kg)	Muzzle velocity (m/sec)	Effect. ceiling (m)	Remarks
75mm Gun 75/27 1906/15	75	4.6	2.25	70	360	HS	6.50	510	4,575	Mobile

Russia

	Calibre (mm)	Weight in action (tonnes)	Barrel length (m)	Elevation (degrees)	Traverse (degrees)	Recoil system	Shell weight (kg)	Muzzle velocity (m/sec)	Effect. ceiling (m)	Remarks
76.2mm Gun M1915	76.2	10.2	2.28	75	360	HS	6.50	590	5,500	Mobile

USA

	Calibre (in)	Weight in action (tons)	Barrel length (in)	Elevation (degrees)	Traverse (degrees)	Recoil system	Shell weight (lb)	Muzzle velocity (ft/sec)	Effect. ceiling (ft)	Remarks
3in M1917	3.0	4.5	155	85	360	HS	15	2,600	22,000	Mobile

COAST DEFENCE ARTILLERY

Britain

	Calibre (in)	Weight in action (tons)	Barrel length (in)	Elevation (degrees)	Traverse (degrees)	Recoil system	Shell weight (lb)	Muzzle velocity (ft/sec)	Max range (yd)	Remarks
3pr QF Mk I	1.85	2,464lb	80.63	25	360	HS	3.25	1,873	4,000	Hotchkiss
6pr QF Mk I	2.24	1.9	97.6	20	360	HS	6.0	1,818	7,600	Hotchkiss
12pr QF Mk I	3.0	4.1	123.6	20	360	HS	12.5	2,258	8,000	
4in BL Mk III	4.0	7.4	120	20	240	HG	25	1,900	6,000	Training only
4in QF Mk V	4.0	11.4	188	20	360	HS	31	2,350	9,000	
4.7in QF Mk V	4.7	8.7	212	20	360	HS	45	2,350	16,500	
6in BL Mk V	6.0	20	195	15	360	HP	100	1,890	8,000	Disappearing gun
6in BL Mk VII	6.0	16	279	20	360	HS	100	2,493	12,000	Central Pivot
6in QF Mk II	6.0	14.5	249	20	360	HS	100	2,154	10,900	Pedestal
7.5in BL Mk II	7.5	51.4	387	20	360	HS	200	2,840	14,200	Barbette
9.2in BL Mk VI	9.2	68.3	310	45	360	HP	290	2,048	16,600	High angle gun
9.2in BL Mk X	9.2	157	445	15	360	HP	380	2,643	29,200	Barbette
10in BL Mk III	10.0	130	342	15	360	HP	500	2,040	11,500	Barbette
12in BL Mk VII	12.0	55.2	328	7	45	HG.	714	1,944	8,000	Spithead Forts only

France

	Calibre (mm)	Weight in action (tonnes)	Barrel length (m)	Elevation (degrees)	Traverse (degrees)	Recoil system	Shell weight (kg)	Muzzle velocity (m/sec)	Max range (m)	Remarks
95mm Mle 1893	95	1.8		17	360	HS	12.1	418	8,000	
15cm Mle	150	2.75	3.90	20	360	HP	35	520	8,175	Disappearing gun
270mm Mortier Mle 1889	271	26.5	3.35	60	300	HG	152	420	10,400	
340mm Mle 1912	340	166	15.30	50	360	HP	540	867	30,000	

Italy

	Calibre (mm)	Weight in action (tonnes)	Barrel length (m)	Elevation (degrees)	Traverse (degrees)	Recoil system	Shell weight (kg)	Muzzle velocity (m/sec)	Max range (m)	Remarks
120/50 Mod 1909	120		6.00	20	360	HS	20.0			Vickers-Terni
152mm M1911	152		6.84	20	360	HS	45.5			Ansaldo
280/16 How	280	18.2	4.48	51	360	HS	350	380	11,000	
305/50 Gun	305	74	15.25	35	360	HS	445	620	21,625	
400/30 Gun	400	120	12.00	35	360	HS	916	600	32,000	

USA

	Calibre (in)	Weight in action (tons)	Barrel length (in)	Elevation (degrees)	Traverse (degrees)	Recoil system	Shell weight (lb)	Muzzle velocity (ft/sec)	Max range (yd)	Remarks
3in Gun M1903	3.0	4.14	175	16	360	HS	15	2,800	11,330	Pedestal mount
6in Gun M1900	6.0	50.5	311	15	360	HG	105	2,750	16,500	Disappearing gun
8in Gun M1888	8.0	39.5	278	18	360	HG	323	2,200	16,285	Barbette
10in Gun M1900	10.0	177	420	12	170	HG	617	2,250	16,290	Disappearing
12in Mortar M1912	12.0	74	201	65	360	HS	1,046	1,200	11,755	High angle
12in Gun M1900	12.0	300	504	10	360	HG	1,070	2,250	17,345	Disappearing
12in Gun M1895	12.0	181	443	35	360	HS	1,070	2,250	27,600	Barbette
14in Gun M1907	14.0	284	476	20	360	HG	1,660	2,350	22,800	Disappearing
14in Gun M1909	14.0	1,033	560	15	360	HS	1,660	2,370	22,800	Turret (Fort Drum)
16in Gun M1895	16.0	568	590	20	170	HG	2,400	2,250	27,365	Disappearing

Index